OUR
BIG
ADVENTURE

PART ONE

ADRIAN & JACQUELINE
RIGG

Published by
Jaqade Publishing

Cover Design
Trina Esquivelzeta
SurfaceHug

ISBN 978-0-9574885-1-9

In loving memory of

Frederick Allen Taylor-Rigg
30/10/1923 to 03/08/1995

Marie Veronica Toward
17/11/1935 to 26/12/2011

Contents

Map *7*

Preface – Why? *9*

Appendix

Internet Pictures

www.europetastic.blogspot.com

You can view pictures that accompany this book at the above web address.

MAP

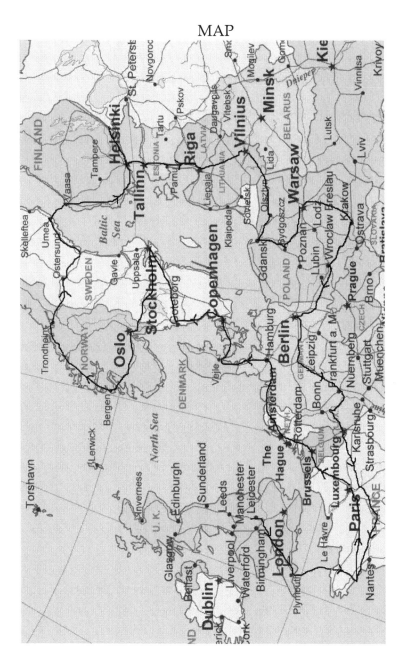

PREFACE

This book is about our experiences, as we take a 'two-year sabbatical' from work, to tour Europe.

This book is not intended to be a tour guide, listing museums and sights to see, there are plenty of other books on the shelves for that. This is basically a travel log, chronicling our journey and experiences along the way. You will find a list of the books we used during our tour in the appendix along with other items which we hope will be of interest to you.

Part one covers the first half of our tour, Northern Europe and Scandinavia, how the whole idea came about and how we put a plan in place.
We hope you enjoy reading about it as much as we enjoyed doing it, and we hope it inspires you to take the plunge in whatever you choose for your life adventure.

...

Most of us are waiting for that 'one day' to arrive when we will do that thing we have always promised ourselves. We tell our-selves 'one day' we will do it, but days go by that turn into weeks and then years and still 'one day' does not arrive. We read about others doing it, we hear about it on the radio and see it on the telly, and yet somehow ours never turns up. But we keep telling ourselves we will do it 'one day'. Then for us, our 'one day' arrived unexpectedly and not quite how we en-visaged it would happen.

Where to begin? What makes you decide to give up everything that you have worked for to go on an adventure? What motivates people to want to get out there and do some-thing out of the ordinary with their lives? Our reasons are deep rooted in our past.

Jackie and I married at the tender ages of 16 and 17 and we soon had a lovely daughter to make up our family. Life was hard going to start with as we watched our friends going out enjoying themselves, while we scraped by on my apprentice wages. That's not to say we were not happy with our lives, because we were.

However, it's at this time we made ourselves a promise that "one day" our time would come and we too would have that quality time to ourselves doing exactly what we wanted to. Time wandered on and we were actually living a lovely life and by then had a son as well. Then before we knew it, the kids had flown the nest and it was just the two of us. But still that 'one day' eluded us, as our life style had its own routine and demands, and we were frightened by the prospect of actually doing something else. Then an event happened that forced us to make a choice and we realised that our "one day" had arrived. Even more of a surprise, it arrived while we are both still alive and well.

This book started out as an internet blog and a journal created by Jackie to which I added my bits and altered as I saw fit. Then Jackie went over it again, added a few more bits that I had missed and gave it a good polish. We quickly realised we were not gifted enough to write the book from a dual perspective. So although it sounds like me writing all the time, some is pure Jackie while other parts are mine, but most is joint. Hopefully you will find this easier to read rather than to keep switching from me to Jackie or vice versa all the time. Finally, we asked some of our friends to read it to see if it made sense, was actually readable and check over for any errors. On that note, we would like to give our very special thanks to Christine Battelle and Alyson Sheehan who have been instrumental in getting the book this far and also to Georgina Coley for her supportive suggestions.

Last but not least to friend and a very talented lady, Trina Esquivelzeta for her input and help in designing and creating the cover artwork.

Chapter One

The Plan

Exchange rate 2011 £1 = 1.1 euro or US $1.55

During another bad day at the office some two years before the event, I found my mind wandering away from the work in hand. I was quietly pondering as to what we would do if the company collapsed, as this was looking more and more likely. So I began to think about what Jackie (my wife and much better half) and I would do if it happened. I knew Jackie had always wanted to travel so that had always been the seed at the back of my mind. I found myself staring at my diary, used only for my business appointments, and turned to the back pages, which contained maps of the world. I flipped to and fro through the maps, considering where we would like to go. I was well aware that Jackie would not like to see real poverty, so that ruled out quite a few places.

The more I went back and forth from page to page, the most obvious place was Europe, after all it was right on our doorstep. I had always been a keen history buff, centred mainly on the wars between mankind through the ages. Touring Europe, I knew there would be lots of historical places for me to visit along the way, as well as fulfilling Jackie's wish to travel. So with a double page spread of Europe in front of me, out came my plastic see-through imperial ruler and a quick consultation with the maps scale, off I went. Being in my mid-fifties, I had been brought up to use both imperial and metric measures, but always found imperial more easy to use having the bigger unit of the inch......... nothing to do with the eyesight.

Firstly, I measured around the coastline of Western Europe, then on into Eastern Europe. As we both like to be beside the sea, I mainly followed the coast. I started in France going down into northern Spain, then through and across to Portugal and the South of Spain. Next the south of France, into Italy across by ferry to Greece, then possibly going across to Istanbul in Turkey.

I then followed the maps northwards up and across to Budapest, Prague, Vienna and into Germany, Berlin then across into Poland, Latvia Lithuania, Estonia and into Russia St Petersburg and back around into Finland. From Finland to Sweden, Norway and down into Denmark and Germany again. Then on into the Netherlands, Belgium and back finally full circle to France. Phew. What a journey by ruler that was.

By my crude calculation, the trip I envisaged was around twelve thousand five hundred miles and I added two thousand five hundred miles on for good measure, as the crow flies via my plastic ruler, so to speak. I was quite impressed with it all. Next, I converted the miles into (yes you've guessed it) the all-important gallons, then the gallons into pounds. By car, usually getting an average of thirty-five miles to the gallon and at a cost of £5 per gallon, it equated to a princely sum of £2142.

Now, that figure sounded "do-able", so the next thing was how long such a journey would take? Thinking along the line of time being no obstacle and that it would be a nice meander through these countries as my base line. On the basis of previous travel in our sports car in Europe, I knew that if we wanted to see the country and get to know the people and culture, three hours travel per day would be the limit, about one hundred miles. Then, allowing time for extended stop overs and city sightseeing of a minimum of two days. All this came out as about one hundred and fifty days to do the tour, taking in around forty cities to visit, at two days each, doubled for a similar amount of sites along the way. By my reckoning, this came out as 310 days or a year thereabouts.

So, a minimum of a year out and £2,142 for the fuel, I was next drawn to the cost of accommodation and sustenance. Drawing again on my previous knowledge of touring France, I hit on a £45 per day average for accommodation, based on £30 minimum and £60 maximum. This was using the budget hotels, Campanile and F1 type accommodation along the way. Hope you are keeping up with all this! So, 365 days at £45 added up to £16,425. I then calculated £125 per week for food and £75 for our spending money, this calculated out at £10,400.

Nearly done. So, for accommodation, food and spending money the grand total was £29,247, rounding it up to £30,000. With that figure in mind I sat back and took a deep breath, it was do-able. After a cup of coffee from the vending machine and some further deep thought I was soon back to reality with people waiting to see me and off back into the real world. I went home that evening and told Jackie of my calculations and the money involved. Far from frightening her she said straight off the cuff, "let's do it, hand our notices in, sell the house and go". "Err let's think about this" says I.

Some days later, after much map reading and looking at things, Jackie said to me that instead of my calculated one year, we would in fact need two, as she wanted to spend more time at our gite in France. We have owned a gite in Brittany for several years and because we love the area where it is so much, have always thought we might like to live there for a while. France has always been our holiday destination of choice and we love the laid back way of life, which sadly is slowly but surely catching up with ours in the UK. This put a whole new perspective on things and a whole new set of more in-depth calculations.

Meanwhile, the situation at the company I worked for was getting worse. More and more my mind would wander back to taking some time out and to what, had now become our two year tour of Europe. At then aged fifty five I still felt too young to take the plunge and retire early, also as I would lose 5% for every year taken before 60 from my company pension. Well, with hindsight, if only I had done it. My company final salary pension would allow me to retire at sixty with a reasonable yearly sum, with which I envisaged topping up my income with non-taxing part time jobs. So my mind was working along this type of time line with some pressure from Jackie to do it earlier.

However, as part of another recovery plan at work and because there was a black hole in the company pension fund, the retirement age was changed to 65. This obviously put a line right through my plan to retire at sixty, suddenly prolonging it to sixty-five. To say I was not pleased is to put it mildly. Compared to what happened next, this was a minor blip. Then the unimaginable happened. I went into work one Friday morning and then to a meeting to be told the company was closing. An announcement was made. Everyone was told to hand in all company equipment, company cars and also that there would be no more pay given out and to leave the premises immediately. What a shock for us all. Some of the sales reps found themselves a few hours later on Derby railway station with their child's car seat in their hands having had their company car taken from them. A few staff, me included, would be kept on to wind things up by the insolvency liquidator. In a nutshell, within five years the company had gone from being a "family run" type employer to being owned by Americans who sadly knew nothing about the business. Bad decision followed bad decision. In the end we were sold to an Investment corporation who put an Investment Banker at the head. They then proceeded to sell off the assets and tried to phoenix the company having taken it under. This all failed miserably and meant most of the employees, including me, were out of work with no redundancy and in most cases no pay. I had worked for the company for over thirty years. Plenty more people had been there longer than that. To be fair I had seen it coming but unlike others, I was not wise enough to get out with a golden handshake while I could.

At this stage, obviously you have to re-assess your future and your finances and what you want to do with your life. As ever, Jackie gave me full support at this time, but also continued with her request to do something with our lives, while we were still relatively young and healthy. However, by now there was also another hurdle to jump. Our daughter had moved to Australia, married and had produced our beautiful granddaughter, Rose. We both wished to see our Aussie family at least every other year, but this takes serious money, which was part of my motivation to get another job.

After coming to terms with the redundancy and many sleepless nights for us both, it was off to the job market and see if I could get myself employed. It was at this time that two parallel plans were taking shape. One was my re-employment, continuing on pretty much as we were with slightly adjusted values, and secondly the plan to go off for two years on a lifetime adventure.

"Where did the Motorhome idea come from instead of the hotels I had started the plan with?" I hear you ask. Well, we realised that if we were going to be away two years, hotel accommodation would work out as a very expensive means of living. We began to look at alternative ways of realising our objective and these involved looking at all options. From Hostels to Camping, Caravanning and a Motorhome, all were considered.

Previously, we had only one experience of camping and that was at Lake Garda in Italy. We drove from the UK, stayed in a pre-erected and fully equipped tent for two weeks and enjoyed every minute of it. It was great fun, as it was a novelty just being under canvas. We had never holidayed in a tent before and the campsite and toilets were immaculately clean. Remembering this great experience put us in the frame of mind that camping could be an option.

We quickly came to the decision that hostels were not for us as we like to sleep together and more importantly not in a dormitory. Also, some of the hostel locations looked a bit dodgy to say the least. So again, camping was do-able, but we still felt this could prove too raw in bad weather and prohibitive in the long term. This left us with the choice of a Caravan or a Motorhome as our realistic options, both of which we thoroughly investigated.

Neither of us had the slightest idea of what Caravanning or Motorhoming really meant as a full time means of achieving our goal. In the past, we had been to a couple of car shows at the Birmingham NEC where there had been a few caravans on display, and which we had taken a passing interest in. We now started to investigate in earnest and began to buy magazines, visit show rooms and speak to Caravan and Motorhome enthusiasts.

Showrooms and Shows proved good venues for gaining first-hand experience from people who owned and used the vehicles for holidays and those who were already doing a similar thing to our plan. We found younger people mainly used them for holidays while the retired generation used them for longer spells often months at a time. It was really in conversations with the retired generation that the whole idea took a step up, when we realised what these people were doing out there. These included visits to Morocco, Turkey, Albania and a whole host of other countries, either singly or as part of a convoy. The lack of fear shown was amazing. More on the fear factor later.

It was while at one show we met a Welsh man named John who was in his eighties. He had just pulled up on an electric bike beside one of the Motorhomes we were looking at. He could see us looking around the vehicle and said, "I've just sold one of these to buy a Cotswold made by Autosleeper". The particular van we were looking at was an Apache 634 by Autotrail. He continued, "Very good these are, and they are a good make, we have had very few problems with ours" It appeared he had had several over the years.

He then gave us a guided tour of the van and we eventually sat down in the rear lounge for a chat as he was waiting for his wife. He then explained where they had been and what they had done over the last few years. Spain, France, convoys to Turkey and they were now contemplating Morocco. I was mesmerised by what he was up to at his age and the lack of fear in tackling countries I had considered being a bit dodgy. His final statement was a corker "Mind you convoys are ok, but the pace is determined by the slowest, which can be a bit frustrating really". My vision of an eighty year old in charge of a speeding van passing a column of younger people made us chuckle.

With that there was a rap on the window with a walking stick, we looked out and there was a little old lady on a four-wheel mobility bike. At first I thought it was Grandma out of the TV series Benidorm. "Is that you John, I have been looking all over for you, I could see your bike but I thought someone had hijacked you" All this in a lovely Welsh accent. I went out and explained that her husband had been kind enough to give us the benefit of his experience. When they had departed we thought what lovely people and more to the point, there was hope for us yet!

Anyway, back to Caravans and Motorhomes. You probably know from seeing them on the roads that these vehicles come in all shapes, sizes and configurations. With that we realised the decision we had to make was both huge and daunting when taking into consideration the need to get it right first time. We would be using whatever we bought for our two year adventure almost continuously. It is fair to say both Jackie and I, on occasion, can be 'impulse buyers' and 'repent at our leisure type' people. Thankfully, we had more time with which to deliberate, we felt we managed to get it right for us. What we would have bought at the beginning was not what we actually bought in the end. Time proved to be of great benefit in making the right choices.

There were a lot of people at the time, who knew what our plans might be, who advised hiring out a Caravan or Motorhome to see if we liked it first. We did not do this, as strangely we felt if we had a bad experience this may end our dream prematurely. We felt part of the adventure was actually doing it first time along with the excitement that this represented and the risk. However, we felt the risk could be minimised by taking plenty of time to get it as right as possible and by talking to people and looking at the options on offer.

We looked at all the different types of Caravans and Motorhomes available. Early in our searches, the caravan started to take second place for two reasons. Firstly, the length of a car and a caravan, posed a bit of a problem, certainly I felt no fear about the UK. But I knew what I had experienced abroad in my little sports cars and felt manoeuvring a Caravan as opposed to a van down some of the roads could prove a risky option for me, although not impossible. The second reason was the loss in value, certainly cars lose big time and the car/caravan combination could prove more costly loss wise than a Motorhome. That's what the sales man said anyway. This still remains to be proved of course and I am sure not all will agree with this assumption. I should also say at this point that we were envisaging buying new or nearly new dependant on availability.

We finally decided it was going to be a Motorhome. Then came the question as to which Motorhome? However, the Caravan option stayed with us to the very end of our search and would also crop up later in conversations while we were touring.

The layout is very similar for both Caravan and Motorhome and this was our next big decision. Really this comes down to preference and the size of vehicle you feel comfortable with. The choice can be from the size of a bus down to the size of a car. In the end we decided on a medium length vehicle (7 metres) which I knew I would feel comfortable driving. This was also based on where we intended to go and what I thought I could easily and successfully manoeuvre in restricted areas.

The next thing to think about was the actual layout. There appeared to be two schools of thought. The continental thought consists of a 'fixed bed', (ready for slumber/siesta's at all times), smaller living area and live outside, al fresco option. Obviously because they have better weather than we do. Whereas, the British thought consists of our preference with the 'make up bed at the end of the day' option, which gives a large rear lounge (put your feet up and watch TV at all times), less dead space and live in/out option, just in case of the usual downpour in the height of summer. Other considerations were the type of toilet and shower facility, level of luxury from cooker to fridge, drop down telly, pull-out furniture and storage space.

Sometimes, we came back from showrooms shell-shocked, not even remembering which van we had seen and which had what to offer as far as essentials. The conversation would go along the lines of................

Jackie, "It had a fridge at the side"
Adrian, "No it did not, it was at the rear"
Jackie, "Is that not where the sink was"?
Jackie, "The bed was pull down from the ceiling",

Adrian, "Are you sure? I thought it had a made up bed with side cupboards"? Jackie, "It had a combined shower and toilet",

Adrian, "Well I thought they were separate with a swivel wall"

...............and on and on and on!

The design of the vans according to our memory was bizarre. If you had drawn a sketch from our recollections you would have ended up with a rear lounge and front living area. Made up bed, pull down bed with mobile cooker and fridge that switched from side to rear and left to right depending on what time of day it was and a shower that you could sit down in. It would have expanding beds that accommodated from one to six people dependant on how many slept on top of one another. Seating could also go from one to ten, dependant on whose lap you sat on.

Now which make would you like? The choice was endless, Peugeot, Mercedes, Fiat, Ford made by Autotrail-Swift-Autosleeper- Dethleffs, then the names, like the Sundown, Broadway, Comanche etc etc. More questions, "Why is this layout not in the brochure then? "Err, yes, but did you see the other one.............?"

It is true to say the choice is bewildering at times. In the end we had to get down to basics of what we thought our day might comprise of and what were we prepared to do, and not to do, as part of our daily routine. We then took videos and photographs and marked the brochure to ensure we knew which vans we had been in. We slowly began to shortlist our preferred layouts and options, with each visit narrowing down what we actually wanted and what we actually needed.

There are some things that we did not consider that would prove important later. Like how much weight the van can take and where you have to store everything. This is very important, as you have to ensure the van is stable whilst moving. Also, the water tank and waste water tank capacity as this will determine how long you can 'wild camp' for free as opposed to camping on site where you can use the facilities to top up. You need to be aware of the wattage of various electrical items that you can safely use together without blowing the fuses if you are connected to only 6 amps on site. More on these items later as this was all part of our learning curve.

Sometime later and with much thought, we did eventually decide on a rear lounge layout with an additional overhead cab bed at the front, which we intended to use as extra storage. The rear lounge, which made up into a bed was for two reasons, we wanted as large a living area as possible so that we could chill-out after our long days sightseeing. Because of my height, 6'2", the make-up bed size is usually much larger than any fixed bed arrangement. Our thoughts were that for ten minutes a day making up/down the bed far outweighed the fixed bed and that this internal layout meant the medium length Motorhome was achievable.

Our next consideration was the age of the Motorhome we could afford versus the level of luxury and the make and size of engine. One advantage of buying new or nearly new was that we would not have to worry about coming back for MOT's as these are covered for the first three years. Also, we intended to rely on any warranties that came with a newish vehicle. Fixtures, fittings and make, it's quite simple, the more you pay the more luxury you get or younger year of vehicle, but not necessarily the perfect layout. We had looked at all those that were within our price range and finally it came down to one we kept looking at again and again, the Autotrail Apache 634U. This fit our bill of requirements having the layout we wanted and the level of comfort we wanted. The engine size was a 2.3 diesel, which according to conversations and reviews gave approximately 25 miles to the gallon.

And so the search began....

As already mentioned, our 'Two Years Out in a Motorhome' was running in parallel with my search for a job. It was a distraction from the reality and the situation we found ourselves in. My days at home were spent full on 8 till 5 writing CV's to fit the job I was applying for, most of which were on line. Some of that time was also getting in touch with Agencies and trying to get them to take an interest in me. Having never been out of work, it was a steep learning curve and the longer you are out of work the more you begin to believe that a job offer may never happen. Still, we did feel lucky in that our families and friends were there for us throughout; I dread to think what it is like for those without this type of support.

In the evenings Jackie would come home from work and we would review where I had got up to on the job search front. Some days I did not want to discuss it at all and Jackie would respect my feelings. Eventually, the conversation would get around to "let's go then" and we would discuss our future plans, again taking our minds off reality for a few minutes.

About this time, we put the house up for sale. In the past we had discussed downsizing to something smaller since the children left the nest, also to release some equity (also because Jackie had grown out of the joys of housework). It wasn't a good time to be doing such a thing as the economy was in downturn and house prices were falling at a pace. Still we weren't in panic mode yet, but felt we should be doing something as we still had a mortgage on the house and it would be nice to get rid of it. We did of course have the value in our gite in Brittany to fall back on to as well.

After about two months I finally started to get some job interviews, albeit lower than the position and salary I had had before and some further afield than practical for me to travel. You have to be a realist in these situations and go with what people are willing to offer and not what they are not. With the house up for sale we were even considering moving to where the work was when it sold.

It was during one evening's conversation that I finally made a commitment, for as you will have gathered, Jackie had already made her mind up. I am also a great believer in fate and that there are times in your life when you should follow the signs and your gut instincts. So out it came "If the house sells for anything like the asking price we will do it". "Really?" said Jackie, "Yes" said I. I thought of adding other caveats like "unless I get a job and or a high paid job or something I really liked doing", but something held me back.

Yes, you've guessed it, within 6 days of this I got my job offer, which I accepted, a six months contract. I did not feel it conflicted with my commitment over the house sale or to

Jackie. Still the house had to sell for a reasonable price didn't it.

Weeks moved on and I was reasonably happy installed in my new job, which is always daunting even if you move within the company you work for. For me with thirty years plus since my last move, it was exciting to say the least. Still I was fortunate enough to have a good young boss who I liked and a good set of work colleagues as I was back in the ranks. We began to get offers on the house, all well below the asking price, which was to be expected as prices were depressed and it was a buyers' market. I almost began to think well this is it then, it looked like my contract would be extended to permanent and the house had not sold.

Wallop! An elderly couple came to look around the house. Such a lovely couple, they even arrived with their slippers to put on so as not to mark our carpets and flooring. They looked the least likely to buy from all the folks who had previously viewed. The reason I say that is because our house had a very modern feel. Decked out in a designer couples minimalistic pad style, I had once told Jackie that if she decked out our house like our mums with one hundred and one knick knacks and ornaments, I would get my air rifle out and shoot them off the shelves…she never doubted me.

Sadly, the gentleman had been diagnosed with cancer and was terminally ill. Despite this they had a good look around and we had a good chat over their and our lives. There was a book in this alone. They went away and we heard no more for a few days, then the estate agents contacted us to advise that they were very interested and wanted a second viewing, also that they were cash buyers. Well, you could have knocked us down with a feather. They came again with slippers in hand. A further full inspection was carried out where they did not miss a thing and away they went stating, "We are definitely interested". The following day we got an offer which was well below the asking price, but because we liked them we made a counter offer. We haggled a bit on the price but soon came to an agreement and so they were ready to go through with the sale immediately.

Where did this leave us? Well, I can tell you, with a big decision. Even though I had made a promise, it still stunned both of us that we had sold the house. Suddenly we were faced with reality and not just glib conversation, however well meant. We went through the whole process again, agonising over every aspect of our lives and where we were going. I had a job, we could now downsize, we could see our daughter each year in Australia, and we could live our lives pretty much as before. We were both well away from retiring and would have to go back to work even if we took the two years out we were dreaming about. What sort of people are we? We had always thought ourselves as doer's not if's, but's and maybe's. Our glasses were always half full, not half empty. We both saw it as a failure to follow our principles if we did not do it, but still should we risk everything we now had?

We come back to fate and whoever you feel looks after you. If you read the signs there is always an answer and if this is truly what you believe, you must follow those instincts, mustn't you? The reality was, if I honoured my contract I had to work till May 2011. The buyers of our house wanted to move in as soon as possible, or latest by the end of January 2011. The decision was put in abeyance until we could sort out the house move and where we would stay. The issue had to be resolved quickly as we had to either buy a new house or rent until we embarked on our tour. It was then early December 2010.

The final piece of the fate jigsaw took place a few days after the agreement over the house sale. As previously mentioned, we had settled on the Autotrail Apache 634U as our preferred Motorhome if the plan went ahead and had been to view several, both new and used. We had planned to buy a year old model as the specification had not changed much over the past few years and this would mean we would not lose as much money when we came to sell it. On the other hand we did know that there was a brand new model for 2011 with a revised specification that was 100mm wider. Now, this does not sound much, but if you stood in the two vehicles side by side you would quickly understand how significant it was. We had only seen it once at the NEC show, as this was the only one in existence at that time made especially for the show.

While making our minds up on the "big decision" we decided to store some of our worldly goods at my mother's house, and to do this we needed to erect a garage. We viewed a few garage retailers, one being right next door to one of our local Motorhome dealers, Leisure Kingdom in Derbyshire. Whilst there, we took the opportunity to look at the Motorhomes again, as Leisure Kingdom is an authorised Autotrail dealer. We had visited them several times in our search for our ideal Motorhome. How lucky were we? We couldn't believe it when Simon the salesman said "you're lucky", we have got the one and only extended rear width Apache in the compound and its here till Monday. 'Of all the places and all the towns', it had to be in ours! Was that fate telling us something?

We had a good look around it and talked over the options and price and because it would be a new vehicle, enquired as to the availability. If we ordered in the next few days, it would be April 2011 delivery. Now how's that for a plan coming together. If I finished my job, it would be May anyway before I would want one. Fate!

That night Jackie and I discussed the options in a whole new light. It was as if we were being pushed to make a decision whether to buy new or not, because of the delivery date for a new vehicle.

We arranged to visit the following day, so that we could have a test drive. Actually, it was Simon who suggested the test drive, we had been concentrating that much on the specification we had forgotten about the driving. I had not driven a Motorhome before, but I had previously driven a five tonne lorry and a long wheel base van when moving furniture for our families and ourselves.

So, that Sunday, a very, very excited couple set off for Leisure Kingdom to commit to their immediate future and hopefully order their first Motorhome. The whole thing went like clockwork, we were looked after by Simon. A price was agreed, based on negotiations we had previously had with other dealers during our time viewing various Motorhomes. Next, everything about the Motorhome was demonstrated and explained and off we went for a test drive. It was better than expected power wise. Simon then left us alone to make our final decision. Looking back it was a forgone conclusion after months of dreaming and planning. We decided that our tour of Europe was no longer a dream and that we were going to do it. Scary, but so exciting. Not only that, but blow the extra expense, this was going to be a once in a lifetime experience, we agreed, it was to be new. A deal was done. Well, just as we thought all the decisions had been made there were more. Simon advised that we could change the seat cushion fabric if we wanted to. Yes, of course we did, and yes of course it cost us a bit more. Could there be more decisions? Yes.................. "Would you like another cup of coffee" Our answer was, "No thanks, we need something a lot stronger than that.

Wow! It was time to face reality now as our dream began to take shape and the realization of what we had done suddenly began to hit us. We started by making the actual plan fit to the time scales involved. We then had to tell our respective employers and organise a short stay somewhere until we departed. Finally, we came to the "actual plan" as we envisaged it before we started out.

We decided we needed to leave at the end of April in order to give us chance to visit the countries for "part one" of our tour of Europe. We chose to tour Northern Europe in 2011 and Southern Europe in 2012. For 2011, May was going to be the latest departure because of making the most of the summer months in Scandinavia. We had worked out that for 2012 March to October was about the limit of what we could realistically do in the Motorhome, taking in more countries on the second leg of the tour.

There was also the insurance cost to consider, the price goes up dramatically if you stay out of the UK for longer than 9 months. As well as that, we did want to come back and see our friends and families at some point. For 2011 we had also made a commitment to go to my brother's stepdaughters wedding in Poland in August, which was another reason for touring Scandinavia first. This was the complete opposite of my original plastic ruler route, which I had mapped out all that time ago. We then drew up a revised spreadsheet of the costs with some contingencies built in for eventualities and the unknown.

Year one
To commence in April and visit: Northern France, Belgium, The Netherlands, Germany, Denmark, Sweden, Norway, Sweden, Finland, Russia (St Petersburg), Estonia, Latvia. Lithuania, Poland, Germany and Central France.

Year two
To commence in March and visit: Western France, Northern Spain, Portugal, Southern Spain, South of France, Eastern Italy, Croatia, Albania, Greece, Turkey, Bulgaria, Serbia, Hungary, Austria, Czech Republic, Southern Germany, Switzerland, Central France.

Basically, we planned to use the capital cities as our aiming points and work around from there with other points of interest added in as we go along. This was another change to the costal route I had planned using the plastic ruler. We also decided we wanted to meet people from each country and get an insight into their culture, learn about their current economic situation and how this was affecting them.

The new plan for the two years was roughly as follows:

- £150 per week for food
- £75 per week spending money
- £150 a week for campsites
- 15,000 miles worth of petrol (which subsequently got revised to 20000 miles)
- £1,000 van insurance
- £1,000 contingency plus some other ancillary costs

This all worked out at a cost to live of around £50,000 for the two years.

On top of this was the cost of the Motorhome, which, with all the extras, stood at around £50,000.

We anticipated selling the Motorhome at the end of our adventure for around £30,000, thus giving us a net £20,000 cost. This gave us an all up cost of around £70,000, which was a considerable part of our accumulated wealth.

Due to the nine months insurance rule for the van being out of the country, our son kindly offered to put us up for the three months each time we returned to the UK.

The additional costs on the Motorhome which were:

- £2,000 for satellite TV
- £600 Bike rack (tow bar)
- £800 alarm system
- £3,500 for two electric bikes

Why electric bikes? Well, we realised we had to have some means of transport when we had parked the Motorhome up. Originally, I preferred a 'twist and go' motor scooter, but Jackie was having none of that. So the next option was electric bikes, which we had tried out at one of the shows we had visited. Whilst we are not totally unfit, neither of us fancied riding bikes up huge hills as a pleasurable pass time, so the electric assisted option was very attractive to us. It also meant we had another pass time, cycling, as well as our love of walking.

This proved to be one of the big wins of our adventure as we now both enjoy riding our electric bikes. As soon as we get to a hill or get tired, we switch on the electric assist and we get up to 50% assistance. The Kalkoff bikes we chose have batteries which offer up to 140km assistance in them, so we have never run out yet while out and about. The other bonus is you can take bikes down cycle paths and along coastal and woodland tracks, which you could not do with a motor scooter. Why are women always right?

For us £70,000 was still quite a frightening sum and considerably more than we had started with, although we had added a touch of luxury by buying a new Motorhome. We had only ever been used to accumulating wealth or at least remaining cash neutral. We had certainly never lost large sums of money, although some of my cars had proved expensive outings. Ultimately, it comes down to what you want out of life and 'what is money for anyway?' The old saying 'you can't take it with you' kept springing to mind. The truth of the matter was that as long as our financial plan held water, we would still have enough to come back to and buy a house at the end of it all. Still it's far easier said than done and even after the fact, we still asked ourselves if we were doing the right thing.

We were both determined that this was "our time" to take advantage of our situation and there was no going back, for better or worse, the wheels were in motion. More than anything the thought of having our life adventure took on a whole new meaning for us, so yes, we were doing the right thing.

We would subsequently meet people doing near enough the same type of journey as us, but obviously for far less money. So do not be put off by our figure. With a second hand Motorhome, reducing the food/spend budget and more wild camping, I think you could half this figure.

Jackie was the first to hand in her notice, which was quite daunting for her, as she liked working for her boss and had a very good set of work colleagues. She had been at the company for 11 years and had built up some strong relationships and also felt people relied on her for certain aspects of her work. It came as quite a shock to most, but they had realised that my being out of work had unsettled her. It was a mark of their respect for Jackie that some went out of their way to help me get re-employed, even setting up job interviews and giving me verbal support, which was very much appreciated.

For me, it was slightly different, I only had to give a months' notice and had a six months contract in place, which still had three months to run. I was in a situation where I had to wait for the right time to let people know as I did not want to finish prematurely as there was a 'one month get out' on their part. Then the company made an announcement that due to acquisitions there was going to be a restructuring with possible redundancies. I used this as my opportunity to tell my boss that I wished to leave at the end of April, a month earlier than contracted. I explained it was for personal reasons and not that I intended to take another job. I was asked to keep this quiet for two months due to the circumstances within the company.

It was quite bizarre having conversations with people who were close to retirement age saying, "if they offer me the opportunity I'm going to take the money and run", from past experience knowing full well they would not. My re-joiner would be "Do it then, what are you waiting for, would you if you could?" It was a funny feeling knowing I had already made the leap from dreaming to reality.

Anyway, the die was now well and truly cast with the house sold, notices in and only the little (huge actually) matter of moving house and finalising the plan. We started to accumulate travel and campsite books on each of the countries we wanted to visit and used these to determine the areas we might like to visit in each country.

We were also avid readers of MMM (Motorcaravan and Motorhome Monthly) Magazine and it's on-line forum pages. It was here I posed a few questions about the countries we were proposing to visit and travel insurance. All were answered enthusiastically. A list of the books we used can be found in the Appendix at the back of this book. Also notes on how helpful we found them.

We had a notional route we would take, along with the places we would like to see, this of course, could be overtaken by what we gleaned from the people we met along the way or on a whim on the day. We had decided quite early on there would be no time pressure or miles per day, rather a nominal time in each country that could be varied according to how interesting we found it, or in the case of Norway how expensive it was to be there, The only date fixed in the calendar was the wedding in Poland on August 20th, which was months away.

The next milestone was moving out of our house and into temporary accommodation with our family. Then our departure date started to creep up on us. Jackie finished work at the beginning of February, as she wanted to spend time with our family and friends before we left. Also, there was heaps of organising and finalising of all things in the UK.

Around this time we made the important decisions about how we would conduct some of our other needs whilst traveling. We decided to do our banking on-line via a secure network and chose Vodafone Data Passport. This appeared to be the most secure, convenient and cheapest method for us to conduct our business as well as keep in touch via the phone. We had a lap-top and intended to take it along for keeping our costs on a spreadsheet. I had also been bought an Amazon Kindle for Christmas, so that I could upload and read books. Jackie had an iPad for the same purpose. Having electronic books had two benefits, firstly the weight-saving of not having to carry any books and secondly the ability to buy and download on-line. The latter, was a big plus as we both like to read and do get through a fair amount of books.

We also paid a pleasurable visit to the Autotrail factory in Grimsby to see how motorhomes are built. They conduct about one tour a month so we booked ours around the time we had ordered the Motorhome. It was a very interesting experience for both of us to see how everything was put together. Not only that, we also got to see the level of craftsmanship and dedication that was being put into their products. At one stage we thought one of the Motorhomes being built might have been ours. Unfortunately, the number didn't match up with the build number which was on our confirmation invoice. It's a very interesting experience and one we would recommend whether you plan to buy or not.

April 22nd, I finished work.

April 23rd. The big day finally arrived and the Motorhome was waiting at Leisure Kingdom, ready for collection......

Chapter Two

First Encounter

The Traveller
(A Rigg)
He looks around once more, his mind is set
He ties his lace and looks to the door
The path leads him to the gate
He takes a hug, a kiss and is on his way
The road stretches out before him
He looks back, waves and is gone

We were told to be at Leisure Kingdom for 1.00pm to collect the Motorhome as they had a few other handover's to do. Needless to say, we were both awake early talking about our exciting day ahead. We planned to pick the Motorhome up and then show it off to our families and friends so they could all see what we had been talking about for so long. We would also say goodbye to some, as we would be off on our journey within days. Others had opted to come and see us at a local campsite we had pre booked. It was important for us to have a few days to familiarise ourselves with the Motorhome and also to check it over thoroughly for any serious snags before setting off.

Up and dressed at the crack of dawn, our first port of call was my mother's house where we had stored the accumulated items for the Motorhome. We needed to check them over once again to ensure that we had everything laid out and ready to put into the Motorhome when we arrived later that day. These items included: reclining chairs, ramps, gas barbecue, extension wire for the electric, converter for two pin electric supply, crockery and cutlery to name but a few. Luckily for us the kitchen sink was built in. We had also set out the clothes we were taking and these were all neatly ironed ready to hang in the wardrobe. We had been quite thorough in our research as to what purchases and clothes we would require, so after the final check, we called our son Howard and asked him to pick us up at 12 noon to take us to collect the Motorhome.

So the appointed time arrived and we set out for Leisure Kingdom. We were so excited by the prospect of receiving our Motorhome, but also a little bit nervous about the fact that the moment of truth was arriving. Would we like Motorhoming?

We entered the site and there she was. She looked gorgeous. Our hearts were racing. It may sound a bit over the top emotionally, but don't forget this vehicle was our home for the next two years, give or take a few weeks. It was lined up, in amongst a few other Motorhomes, which were all waiting to be collected.

We pulled up in the car park and went over to look around our Motorhome. Would everything be as we had requested and anticipated? The first thing we did was to peep in the windows to check they had put the right fabric on the cushioned seating areas. We hoped they had remembered as we had asked for a different fabric than the standard one. It was the first time we had seen it and we were concerned in case we had made a mistake having never seen it with this particular layout.

We had had first-hand experience of having chosen the wrong fabric a few years ago. We decided to buy a new three-piece suite and chose a different colour from the pattern book in the furniture shop. It looked really nice on the 6-inch square swatch, but when the three-piece suite arrived and was placed in our lounge, we almost needed sunglasses on to look at it. We quickly chose to decorate the walls in darker shades, just to tone the whole thing down. It was really quite bright and took us a long time to adjust to it. We eventually had it recovered. Never to be repeated.

Anyway, much to our relief all was well, it looked great. Our salesman, Simon duly arrived and introduced us to Danny who was going to give us our introductory tour of the Motorhome. If you have never had a Motorhome before the numerous instructions amongst other things to remember can be quite daunting. The driving cab was relatively straightforward and very similar to a car, but the house on the back was totally new to us. We had been warned to take a notebook with us, as we would never remember it all.

Jackie poised herself, pen and paper in hand. Danny began. "We'll start with the inside. This is the control panel and it does all of this" Switches began to flip, different coloured lights began to flash. Jackie scribbled down as quickly as she could. "This is the cooker, it has two modes... This is the fridge and it has three modes..... This is the heating and it has two modes plus blown or fan.....".

It was a loaded question, but I had to ask "Jackie have you got all that down? No answer, too busy scribbling.

Danny continued "This is the fuse box and electrics, you need this button on and these lights too............. I then very bravely said "err got that all down Jackie?" The look said it all. Oops! "Danny" I said, I think you are going too fast, can we go over that last piece again just for Jackie?" (I of course had remembered it all).

Danny went on... "No problem". The red light and the three green lights should be on, oh and that blue light as well, and the fuses are in here with a nice diagram for you to fol-low". "Yes, all straight forward... err.... I think, Jackie have you got it all down? "So have I explained that to your satisfaction, is there anything you want me to go over again about the in-side?". What a silly question Danny, the answer was ....."Well yes...the whole lot actually".

We then moved outside and he was off again.......
"Now this cover is for the electric, this for the fresh water and this for the waste water, oh, there are two then "and here is the rear stowage locker and this is the toilet locker and here's how you remove and empty the cassette".

I just thought I'd better ask......"Are you listening Jack-ie? What do you mean that's my job".

On and on he went......... "Here is the gas locker and this is how you switch it on and off, you remember about what we said in the interior about the gas and electric modes?"

Of course we do (does he think we're thick?).
"Look at the notes Jackie". "What do you mean you can't read your notes on that bit".....

Not much more to go now....... "This is how you roll the awning out, oh dear, something wrong here".........Just then a piece of plastic catapults to the floor. "Don't worry we'll have that fixed before you go". Thanks Danny, I should hope so too. Well after hours of introduction and information, we were as ready as we were ever going to be, without getting our feet wet. Danny asked if we would like to go over anything else. Not wishing to look stupid (having asked for everything to be repeated three times already) we say no. The look of relief on Danny's face is a picture, at this stage I got the distinct impression he wanted to go home and rest, rather than have to do the other two Motorhome introductions awaiting him. He was dribbling at the mouth and mumbling incoherently as he handed us back over to Simon. He did manage to say, as we shook hands and said our farewells.... "Everything will be switched off and ready to roll when you leave". Little did we know he had a cunning plan to get his own back.

We followed Simon into his office and he asked if all is well. We both agreed all looked fine, except for the awning, which Danny promised to have fixed. We then went through all the paperwork and documents. We made a bit of a boob, here. We didn't realise at the time that the registration document was missing from the pack. This will come back to haunt us in Russia.

Simon confirmed we are booked in their secure paddock, situated just behind Leisure Kingdom showrooms, for our first night alone in the Motorhome. This is the norm for new owners like us, so that if there are any initial problems, we would be close to them for a next morning debrief. At this stage we couldn't contain our excitement, as we were that close to getting our hands on our beautiful first new Motorhome. Simon handed over the keys. We quickly walked across to where we had left her. After a quick discussion and demonstration, it was revealed that the awning was now all in good working order. "There you are, it's all yours", says Simon "Happy Motorhoming".

Wow, what a feeling! Howard (our son) had been with us all this time, and was just as excited as we were. We had our first photo shoot, before he headed off back to Derby, leaving us to enjoy our first journey through the countryside. There were two last purchases we needed to make before we set off. We dashed over to the onsite shop, which sells just about everything you need for the Motorhome, Caravan or Tent way of life and quickly bought a clothes line (too big to get in our car) and an extra piece of gas pipe for the barbecue. It was a great feeling when we sat in the cab for that first time, contemplating the first step in our "big life adventure". We sat for a good few minutes drinking in the experience and savouring the moment. I turned the ignition key and we were off. As simple as that!

As this was only the second time I have driven a Motorhome, the other being a test drive, I took it steady. The experience was so enjoyable as we both sat there, I driving, Jackie twiddling with every knob and opening every compartment on the dashboard.

Where to first? It had to be the petrol station as there was not a full tank of fuel. Ah well, it's all part of the learning curve. Which side is the filler cap on then?

A short distance down the road we passed a Motorhome coming the other way. We looked at each other. Did they just wave at us? This we were to find out would be a major feature of our Motorhome life. "To wave or not to wave", that is the question. Occasionally, when we had our open top sports cars, people would wave as they passed by if they had the same car. This was something new and how nice it was too. We were buddies with all other Motorhomers.

We drove to Jackie's mum and dad's house first as the family had assembled in the local car park for their first viewing. It was quite an emotional experience as this was part of our "send-off" and we would not be seeing them again for the best part of a year. We could tell from the looks on some of the faces as we showed them around that they are both happy but apprehensive for us. We knew they were thinking that it was a bit small to live in for a year and how would we get away without murdering one another. Little did they know that these were also our main concerns. Having completed all the guided tours, it was handshakes, hugs and kisses all round as we bid farewell. We could both see them in the wing mirrors waving and shouting "bon voyage" as we depart.

Now, as with all beautiful ladies, it is apt to give them a beautiful name. Our Motorhome was no exception. Prior to us becoming the proud owners of such a vehicle, someone had asked what we planned to call her. This started the big debate, in the end we settled on "Bluebell" as she became ours in the springtime and there were so many Bluebells in bloom, we thought this was very appropriate. Like most names, we shortened it to "Belle".

Next stop along the way was my mums. Unfortunately, my brother and his family were on holiday, so it's just my mum and Howard. Mum thought it was great, couldn't believe how lovely Belle was. We began the loading process. This was where reality started to kick in. Will everything go on board? It took us the best part of two hours to stow everything on board, amazingly it all went in. We left the electric bikes in the garage as we still had the rack to be fitted the following week. We didn't need to use them anyway as we had our car. We were looking forward to staying in Leisure Kingdoms Paddock overnight, then on to a local campsite for four days to compile a snagging list (if any) and say goodbye to our friends.

Fully loaded off we set to Leisure Kingdoms Paddock with the anticipation for our first experience of a campsite, albeit just a small field. We arrived safe and sound but I had noticed already that Belle handled differently being nearly fully loaded. Now came our first Krypton factor test. Number one: How to hook up a Motorhome to the electricity supply. Simple, I hear you say. Surely Jackie has made a note on that one. Well no. We were shown where the connection was but not how to connect it. It can't be difficult.... can it? I first proceed to the electric box on the site and tried to open the locked door (having been given a key by Simon) to open it. Well, can I get the door open? No! "Jackieeee...... help". In the end, we resorted to a kitchen knife to try and prise the door open, cursing the dud key. Luckily, before we vandalised the door, Jackie spotted a small sign stencilled on the door saying "Electric Door this side". Yes, you've guessed it. The key fitted the door on the side of the box. We were soon in and one end of my electric cable was duly fitted. Easy. Now for the other end.

I lifted the cover and attempted to fit the connector, would it go in? No. The cable protector lid would not allow it to slip in; 30 minutes later we gave up. We moaned......"Can you believe Leisure Kingdom gave us the incorrect cable connector?" By this time of course, they were closed for the day.

Fortunately, we had arranged to go out for a curry (favourite food) that night and celebrate with some of our best friends. So not having electricity did not pose a problem.

Krypton Factor test number two: I open the gas locker to turn on the gas for the cooker and to power the fridge. I had been told everything would be turned off so found it odd that I was turning the control ant-clockwise. Jackie reports no ignition. "That's strange", says I. We soon realise that I have turned the gas off and that the Motorhome was not exactly 'ready to roll' as Danny had promised. Still, we expected to have some teething problems so had a "good old cuppa" and began to take it all in. We checked out the Motorhome as much as we could that day and soon forgave Danny remembering how tired he looked when we left him.

A short time later our friends Freddie and Alyson arrived with a bottle of Champers to celebrate and take us out for a curry. Now Freddie knows something about electrical hook ups, having had a river boat and worked on roadside dig ups. Even he couldn't get the lead plug in the Motorhome socket. The cap on the lead was still stopping it going into the socket.

For non-motorhome people, let me explain. There are two ways to power a Motorhome. First you can use a cable to hook up to a mains socket provided at nearly all campsites. This allows you to use all the sockets in the Motorhome to power electrical items. The second option is that you run off the internal batteries and gas bottles in the Motorhome. In our case, the batteries get topped up by a solar panel fitted on top of the roof, or recharged when the Motorhome engine is running. We also chose to install refillable gas bottles, so that we can refill as we go. Gas can then be used as an alternative method of running the fridge, heating, water and cooker.

We had a great evening with our friends. Plenty to eat and drink. To end a perfect day, we now wanted a perfect night's sleep. As previously mentioned we have chosen a Motorhome where the bed is made from the cushions from the seating area at the rear of vehicle. We also have an over the cab bed, but this was already being used, as we had planned, for storage. We made up the bed for the first time and were surprised how easy and quickly this is achieved. We were also pleased with the size of the bed when it was made up, it being bigger than a king size we had at home, good news for me being over 6 foot tall. A short time later we are tucked up in bed and the lights go out. After a short chat and a giggle we soon fell to sleep.

The next I know I get a nudge in the back "what was that" says Jackie, I listened. Sure enough there was a sound of movement from outside, obviously I had to investigate. So, having made a lot of noise getting dressed, in the hope whoever/whatever was lurking about will have left. Out I go with my Police Intensity Torch, guaranteed to initially blind anybody who looks directly into it.

My exploration of the outside reveals the dreaded eyes of the "Killer Sheep" cunningly disguised as normal sheep in the field next to the van. These ninjas of the night can creep up on unsuspecting Motorhomes, having blacked up their faces and have hooves that can kill, with one blow. Fortunately for me and Jackie they are still trying to work out how to cross the fence and are now blinded by my torch and more interested in trying to find grass that was there a second ago. Phew! What an escape.

Off to sleep we go again and fortunately the rest of the night passes by without incident, well those that we care to mention. We woke up having had a good night's sleep. Believe it or not, this is one of the most important things, for without a good night's sleep, the whole thing would become a frustrating nightmare. It was not just a good night's sleep, but a comfortable one as well, with both of us having enough room to spread out. So, our first night had gone relatively smoothly and the bed was re-made into our lounge area in no time. Breakfast was also achieved with ease, the table erected easily and we had more than enough room as it would accommodate four settings.

By this time we were used to the workings of the toilet and found this to be fully functional (a number one), having decided we would not use our toilet for any other bodily function (a number two), unless in an emergency. I have no idea why we made this decision other than the wish to keep Belle clean, the debate over this would rumble right the way throughout the tour. This part of the lifestyle is so important and needs to be taken seriously and discussed. We had made the decision to use the campsite facilities wherever possible to start with, or failing that, a café, restaurant, public or supermarket facility.

We then moved on for a shower, which we both agreed was excellent, but used up our fresh water rather quickly. We only have 90 litres in our on-board tank.

We then had the last one of Danny's strike backs. As we prepared to go back to Leisure Kingdom, I discovered a big pool of water at the rear side of the Motorhome. Yes, the waste water tap had not been closed. This allowed all the washing up and shower water to run straight out. Waste water should be emptied out at designated drains. We were to discover this practice is not universal with a lot of Motorhome owners who dispose of their grey water when they think no one is looking. I would like to make the point for non-Caravan or Motorhome owners, this is not toilet waste water which is a separate system altogether.

The following day we made a quick trip back to Leisure Kingdom to complain about our electrical hook up lead and ended up with egg on my face. Enter Ken who as I explained what had happened, lifts the lid on the Motorhome, lifts the cap on the lead and inserts the electrical lead with a smug look. Yes, it was not the electrical lead that was wrong, but a faulty user, the offending cap that prevented me from plugging it in, had a special slot that it slid into. Easy when you know how. Well we all have to learn. I was sure there would be more for us before we had finished.

Next stop and for the next four nights, was over to our local campsite in Castle Donnington, Derbyshire. For the following four days it was to be a thorough acclimatisation of the vehicle, reporting back to Leisure Kingdom if we found any further snags. Jackie and I had also organised for a steady stream of friends to visit. The weather was glorious and it was in fact Easter weekend. Fortunately, the getting to know the Motorhome and snagging went smoothly with no major incidents to report. We continued to enjoy a good night's sleep and begin to understand the workings of the Motorhome. By this time we realised we needed an electric kettle and toaster. Rather than wait an eternity for the gas to boil our little whistler and the grill to warm up. I made the mistake of buying ordinary domestic items and not low wattage travel items. More on this later.

We do like socialising and are very lucky to have a larger than normal set of friends, which was destined to get us into trouble. If you have never been on a campsite before you cannot be expected to know the etiquette or rules. To be fair to us, when booking the site, Jackie had explained our future plans to the lady owner and that we were expecting a large number of friends to visit us over the weekend to view our new home and say our goodbyes. All of which was ok for the lady. However, it turned out to be a case of 'the left hand not telling the right hand', as seems to be the norm these days. The lady had not informed her son, who co-owned the campsite, that there would be visitors arriving to see us, at various times, over the next four days.

Enter our first visitors, who drive their car right up and park next to the Motorhome on the grass. Then a second set who do exactly the same. No problem, thinks us, as there is plenty of room. By now, some of the other campers are looking and starting to take an interest in us. Our friends proceed to stay for the best part of the day and into the evening. When they depart we walked down the drive to wave goodbye to them and it's at the point of walking back that I spotted a sign advising "Visitors Car Park" and "No Non-residents Cars beyond this point" also another sign saying "Visitors may only stay for 2 hours or a charge of £4 is applicable". On our return to Belle, Jackie and I discuss the situation. Jackie says that none of this was brought to her attention when she booked or when she came to see the site. Certainly the sign or the charge had not been pointed out or mentioned.

In the morning I walked down to the owners lodge to have a chat with the son and explain about what had been agreed with his mother and why we had chosen his site. He was quite amicable about the situation and we come to an arrangement that visitors would park in the visitor's car park with a notice in their windows to say they are visiting the Rigg's in the Autotrail. Also, I agreed to pay a nominal fee. He explained the reason for the new rule. As usual it turned out that a few bad apples caused a problem. Apparently, the previous year a party of tent campers arrived and thought they were being clever by not paying for everyone who was stopping, slipping them in a few at a time, and also had had visitors who were very rowdy, parking their vehicles anywhere they pleased. There were two concerns with this. Site security was an issue, as they did not know who was wandering about the campsite, therefore putting the safety of people and their belongings at risk. The other issue, being the noise factor. Campers who had come to the site for peace and quiet, found it not to be.

Over the next few days we quietly entertained more of our friends, ensuring that we did not disturb anyone else. We did have a few more incidents when our friends weren't aware that they couldn't park close to us. We quickly moved them back into the visitor parking area. I must say it still made us feel uneasy when we had quite a few people around all at once. In some ways it took a bit of the shine off things, as we were always conscious of how long our friends were on site and what other campers may be thinking. Having said that, we were pleasantly surprised how friendly all our fellow campers were. Our closest and our first campsite neighbours were really nice and offered all sorts of useful advice. We needed it.

Still, the acclimatisation to our new campsite life with Belle continued and we began to get a better understanding of the restrictions and capabilities of the water system. 90 litres of water equals four days brief wash or two days showers. The wastewater normally requires emptying every two days. I find out how far the fresh water pipe will stretch to the site water tap and what connections I need. All this forms the early part of our learning curve and the continued excitement at what we were doing. Suddenly, it's our last day on site. Having said goodbye to all our friends, we depart on good terms with the owners and our fellow campers who by now fully understand why there has been so much activity in our part of the site.

Next stop is back to my mums to collect the bikes, which we managed to get in Belle. We covered them with lots of cardboard, making sure if they moved, they wouldn't damage any of the interior. We say a tearful goodbye to my mum. God bless her, she is in her mid-eighties and would sooner we stayed close by, still, she puts on a brave face and wishes us well. She hands over two St Christopher's to keep us safe as we finally set off on our journey of a lifetime.

It's early morning as we travel along on the A50 over to TowSure at Stoke on Trent to have the bike rack/tow bar fitted. We arrived for our appointed fitting at 10.00am. We knew the process would take two hours so we decided to go into Hanley, on the outskirts of Stoke, just to pass the time. It was quite a nice experience. We arrived back slightly late, having had a good look around the place and trying out the McDonalds free Wi-Fi service. This service was to be one of the ways we communicate for free whilst on our travels. I am quite partial to a MacDonald Cheeseburger by the way. Their tea is also consistently good and hot which is what Jackie likes, but not so the Cheeseburger's.

Back at TowSure we discover a problem, our Motorhome hasn't even been started, as there has been a major problem with a Motorhome chassis that was being fitted before ours. We hung around the premises, drinking coffee by the gallon. Finally, it was completed and we were very pleased with the design and the workmanship. We chose to have a tow bar type bike rack rather than the harness type rack which fits on the back wall of the vehicle, as we didn't want to obscure the view from the large rear picture window. It looked great.

We had planned to travel down to Taunton in the afternoon at an easy pace, as the following day we were having the alarm system fitted to Belle for extra security. As we didn't set off for Taunton until 5.00pm, we called ahead to the campsite to let them know we would be arriving later than expected and thankfully, they were very understanding. Part of the deal with VanBitz Alarms, included one overnight stay at their campsite. Jackie booked an extra night so that whilst it was being fitted we could visit some more friends who conveniently for us, lived locally.

Now, the drama started as another part of our learning curve progressed. We headed onto the motorway and I proceeded to accelerate up to 70mph. It was at this point we both noticed that the Motorhome felt a little unstable. Every time a high-sided vehicle went by we began to sway from the buffeting. At times, it felt like the back axle had become lose. We began to wonder if TowSure had done something or forgotten to tighten something. We slowed down to 50mph and the problem eased considerably. I decided to stay in the inside lane which caused a travelling chicane for HGV lorries. Our situation was not good and we both started to panic, although I didn't let Jackie know just how concerned I was.

We pulled into a service station and I checked Belle over as far as possible, not finding any visible problems. We also rang TowSure who could only suggest that we checked the tyre pressure. We duly carried out the procedure, again, no problem. Suffice to say it was a long and somewhat nervous drive to Taunton. I managed to do about 60mph to avoid being overtaken by the HGV lorries. We noticed at times the swaying at the rear worsened, even at a constant 60mph. What on earth could be wrong?

We eventually pulled into the campsite about 10.30. We were both fit for nothing, as the nervous tension of the drive had taken its toll. There on the notice board in large writing was 'LATE ARRIVALS – THE RIGG'S'! Had our friends been talking to the owners (we are always fashionably late).....? We hoped this was not an omen for the future.

Time for a quick cuppa and off to bed. We both had a rather disturbed night's sleep as we were worried as to what could be wrong with Belle. We had another early start as Belle had been booked in for 8.30am. In the daylight we could see what a fabulous campsite it was. The facilities were superb and each pitch was large and well kept. It was another hot and sunny day and we looked forward to catching up with our friends who had kindly offered to collect us mid-morning.

Luckily, the fitting station was adjacent to the campsite. I handed over the keys to Belle and we discussed the options on the alarm to be fitted. We had chosen the VanBitz Strike Back alarm because it was designed especially for Motorhomes. Passing vehicles cannot activate the alarm. It can be alarmed whilst occupied, includes a bike rack security system and also a panic button to set off the alarm immediately if required. All this of course comes at a price. One of the first decisions we made was that there would be no compromise on our safety.

While we are on the subject of security its worth discussing our main concerns at this stage. We had read about criminals dressed up as police particularly in Spain and Italy, stopping Motorhomes and robbing them. Other horror stories of sleeping gas being dropped through skylights, robberies at petrol stations and many more different scenarios. We read and listened to our friends warning us about all these incidents. We took all this on board and decided on the level of security we would be comfortable with, but also we knew that we would not let these threats stop us doing what we wanted to do and go where we wanted to go. To be truthful an attack on the Motorhome while we were not in it would be heart breaking. But a successful attack on the Motorhome and us, while we were in it, would probably prove a showstopper. So prevention and deterrent were the bywords whilst being alert to situations, which could pose a threat. We had bought a gas detector before having the alarm fitted. The device can be hard wired or plugged in to the cigarette lighter in the cab, which we had yet to do.

In the end it all boils down to the person you are, and if you are the sort who will let fear rule your life. We have always felt it is a balance between doing what you want to do and accepting the risks involved. We are both very positive thinkers (our cups are always half full, not half empty) and we are the sort who will do, not won't do, occasionally we are a don't want to......!

As a matter of interest the VanBitz engineer said he believed that the threat posed by sleeping gas was minimal as the amount of gas needed to knock us out would probably require a lorry to carry it. He had had discussions with chemists and had carried out a lot of research on the subject. They do offer it as an option on their kit. Anyway, we agreed on the options for ours and left them to do their bit.

As arranged, our lovely friends Trina and Carlos arrived to collect us. We went back to their house for a catch up with them and to have some fun with their three adorable children. At around 16.00 we took the call to say that the alarm was fitted and Belle was ready for collection. Carlos and I drove back (30 minutes) to the site.

We then had a very interesting conversation with the owner. He explained they had a wealth of knowledge concerning Motorhomes and all things fitted to them. Eventually, our discussions got around to my experience on the previous day's drive from Stoke to Taunton.

Well, what a relief the conversation proved to be. It turned out that we had got our weight distribution all wrong, coupled with a phenomenon called tram lining. First the tram lining, this is caused by HGV lorries wearing grooves into the road as they continuously drive on the same piece of tarmac. In a car you would not notice this so much, due to possibly the width of the wheelbase and also most of the time being in the middle or outside lane. Also, a car is more stable having no major load on board other than the passengers and luggage.

Now, what had happened to Belle was that the wheels were aligning with the grooves in the road caused by the HGV's, causing them to follow these grooves. This meant they were heading in a different direction to the way I was steering, causing us to snake and wobble as we went in and out of the grooves. In addition, the front wheels on Belle are slightly narrower set, than the back, this was why it seemed there was a problem with the rear end resulting in me thinking the back axle was loose.

Next the balance. When we had set off from Derby with our bikes centrally secured inside Belle, we had been completely stable as the weight was distributed evenly. However, once the bike rack had been fitted to the back and then the bikes loaded up on the rack, the sum total was an all up weight approaching 90kg. Consequently, we had shifted the balance to the back. Our stowage area also runs right across the rear and as we had put everything we could in there, to free up space inside, the net result was we were almost popping wheelies. The front almost lifted, causing the steering to become very unresponsive.

This brought visions to my mind of a new craze for young dudes in their immaculately suped up cars, to proclaim, "I want one of them Motorhomes man, that can pop wheelies" and "just imagine the size of speakers and boom box woofer we could get in that". "Yeah and we'd have a cool place to take the chicks back to as well". Wild dude, we could then go drag racing at Santa Pod"... Cool baby.....You see, I *was* young once upon a time!

In any event, over the next few days we would redistribute our weight and get the Motorhome back to stable. What a relief. However, even with our weight re-distributed we still couldn't get away from the dreaded tram lining in the roads. Little did we know that we would meet this phenomenon many more times before we finished our tour.

It was also pointed out to me whilst at VanBitz that the satellite receiver should have been capable of running from 12v and not just the 240v I had bought. He explained this would only work when I was connected to mains electric via my cable. 12v would then have allowed me to watch TV while 'wild camping'. Wild Camping is when you choose not to camp on a recognised site, the general rule is there are no facilities provided or available. Anyway, it was a big thanks to the very helpful guy at VanBitz for steering me in the right direction, so to speak, on many things and for which we were very grateful.

Once Belle was safely returned to her pitch, Carlos drove us back to the house to spend the remainder of the day with the family and Jackie. The ladies had prepared a tasty bbq for tea and after a short rest to aid our digestion, we all went down to the village pub for a few drinks. What a great day.

What excitement! Friday 29th April 2011, not only for us, but for many more people throughout the UK and beyond. It was the day of the much anticipated "Royal Wedding" Prince William and Kate were to be married.

We, on the other hand, were off to France. We set off for Plymouth early in the morning to get the midday Ferry over to Brittany. The drive down to Plymouth proves a relief, as Belle is now handling a lot better, although I still drive at just above 60mph. There is a silver lining to the story and the dilemma we had with the weight distribution. Firstly, I soon realised that you cannot drive a Motorhome like a car. If I am honest, I like many others do drive above the speed limit on motorways. Secondly, fuel economy. At around 60mph I am returning 25mpg, while at 65+mph more like 22.3mpg. As we are not in a 'one or two week holiday rush', we have the time to meander at our own pace. Last but not least, we were well aware that it would take us some time to adjust and get out of the quick pace of modern day UK life.

Upon our safe arrival at Plymouth, we drove directly to the Hoe, luckily finding a perfect space for Belle to sit nicely overlooking the bay. We had a quick cuppa and a sandwich all made freshly in Belles galley and then drove a short distance to the port to board the ferry to Roscoff. Jackie couldn't wait to get on the ferry to ensure a front row seat to watch the Royal Wedding. We missed the actual ceremony but saw the highlights along with hundreds of other passengers.

On board there were life-size cardboard cut-outs of Prince William and Kate with red, white and blue bunting hung all around. There were flags and balloons also decorating the ferry, it appeared the French were celebrating with us too. As it was a very special occasion, even Champagne was on sale at the bar at a reduced rate. I couldn't resist the temptation, so we not only raised our glasses to William and Kate, but also to ourselves, and the adventure that lay before us.

Chapter Three

France

29 April - 12 May

Roscoff – Moelan Sur Mer – Mayennes – Paris – Valenciennes

We docked in Rosscoff at 21.00. We had a two hour drive ahead to reach Moelan sur Mer. We were to stay at our gite in a little hamlet called Kerambellec, just a short drive from the centre of Moelan sur Mer, a very popular tourist area. Roscoff is a beautiful ferry port and well worth a visit in its own right. We have stayed overnight many times before and eaten out at the Ports many restaurants. On this occasion it's straight off the ferry and hit the road, the only deviation we make this time, is sticking to the main roads. Normally we drive down in a car so we take the very narrow back route through La Fouay down to Quimperle on the way to Moelan, but we thought it would be too risky in Belle.

Where to begin with France? It's fair to say we are in love with the country. We could spend a lifetime touring France, there is always something different and often magical around each corner. Since we first visited, some twenty years back now, we have noticed a quickening to the pace of life, even in the remote areas. Even so, it still has a laid-back life style that we envy and want a piece of. One other thing we have noticed over this time are the cars, at one time they were predominately of French origin, being Renault or Citroen. These days, there is a fair proportion of foreign makes with perhaps German and Japanese manufacturers forming the main imports. But this is a good representation of how the French way of life is altering with the "no it is not French, I will not buy" changing to "it's a bargain" or "it's a better brand".

The French are a big Camping Car (Motorhome) nation and most towns and cities provide cheap forms of overnight stays called Aires. In many cases these are free for overnight parking. Some of the ones on the motorways or at petrol stations have had a bit of bad publicity for being places where Camping Cars have been attacked when on their own. As we were just starting out, we made a conscious decision to only stay on proper campsites, even though this proved to be more expensive. It was a comfort factor for us being new to the game, as we progressed we hoped we would become more confident and start to try free camping or even go 'wild'.... Steady on now!

Brittany is very much like Cornwall with its rugged coastlines except in one very distinct way, the beaches are empty most of the time, except for August, when the majority of the French take their main holidays. Our arrival in the hamlet caused a lot of interest due to our very British version of a Camping Car (that is what the French call the vehicles). We spent an enjoyable week with our friends while getting further accustomed to our van in a more relaxed atmosphere.

The weather had been so kind to us up to now, with the odd cloud, but mainly blue skies, no rain and warm enough to wear shorts and short sleeve shirts. It was also time to get out the 'de rigeur' (sandals) footwear for campers, (flip flops are also acceptable). There is a very good reason for this habit....no socks to wash. Also, in a never-ending quest to keep the van clean and tidy, they are easily dispensed with as you enter the van. We feel like the real deal now.

We had plenty of time to try out our electric bikes in anger, doing things such as getting groceries from the supermarket and visiting bars and restaurants. No laws regarding intoxicated cyclists, not that we know of anyway. The electric bikes will prove to be a big win over the course of our adventure. We will be asked many times "what are they like?" the answer is always the same "excellent". Now this is all relative to how young and fit you are and how used you are to riding a bike. Jackie only ever rode a bike when she was very young and certainly before her teens, so was very nervous at first. While I had ridden bikes on and off throughout my life, but not regularly. There are two different types of electric bikes. Those that require a twist to engage an accelerator enabling the motor to take over completely and those that assist with you're peddling by up to 50% depending on which setting you choose on the control unit. All kinds require the battery to be charged which can take from 4 hours to 8 and cover from 20 to 80 miles, dependent on what you buy and how intensively you use the battery assist. We decided to opt for the pedal assist, as we felt this would be more in line with our quest for some fitness as well as the enjoyment of the ride. We can sum it up as simply as this, on the flat and downhill you do not need assistance, but up hill, believe me, it certainly takes some of the strain out of it. Basically, you find yourself wanting to go on the bike as you are no longer "put off " by the thought of the uphill struggles ahead, it puts the enjoyment back in there. The down side is, the really fit bikers who do not need any assistance whatsoever, look at you as if you are an 'old knackered goat' grinning as they pass you by in a flash.

As we depart Moelan we feel this is the true start of our adventure. We left our well-loved and familiar haunts to visit new territory. We head off toward Paris, having arranged to meet some more friends on the way at a campsite near Mayenne. By chance they were crossing our path on their way to Spain in a car. The rendezvous was set for midday at the campsite in Ambrieres les Vallee.

The good weather continued as we travelled east, and we met up with our friends as planned and on time. They had arrived first and so had already reconnoitred and booked themselves into a charming well-equipped chalet at the campsite, 'Les Bryeres' for two nights. We found a nice spot for Belle, a short walk from their place, alongside the river, very picturesque too. It was a hearty welcome from Clive, Keith and Eddie (Keith's wife). We agreed to move most of our cooking items and drinks up to the chalet where we planned to spend most of our time. We also took some time to check out the toilet and shower block, which prove to be both modern and clean. A bonus for us was that there was free Wi-Fi in the reception area. Over the coming months we will learn to inspect the toilets and shower block first, before booking in as standards vary considerably.

Clive, Keith and Eddie were on their way to visit Clive's sister in Calpe, Spain, for a few weeks. Clive had just bought a new car, the Vauxhall Insignia. So after having joint inspections of our respective vehicles, we soon settled down for a few drinks out on their veranda. Before too long we began to think of what we were going to have to eat. The only ingredients we had were potatoes and leeks, which we had bought to make a soup, me being the soup chef! It was decided Keith and Clive would go to the supermarket to get breakfast provisions for the next two days (we planned to go into Mayenne for lunch the following day) while I made the soup. Jackie and Eddie chose to stay on the veranda, as ladies do, looking cool calm and elegant while having a good chat. They also decided to befriend a black and white kitten, which Eddie fell in love with. It must have been very hungry as it ate everything we put before it over the next two days. The poor little thing even attempted to eat the plastic rind on the garlic sausage. It took the two ladies to fight him to retrieve it before it was swallowed up. Clive found this highly amusing saying it was like watching two kids fighting a lion...........meow! Meanwhile, I wondered if its poop would come out pre-packaged ready for disposal.

Anyway back to the plot. Clive and Keith soon returned bringing 24 eggs, a kilo of bacon fit for an army, two massive cartons of mushrooms, two huge tins of tomatoes, 2 huge tins of beans, 4 baguettes and of course plenty of alcohol. We were soon all tucking into my leek & potato soup with fresh crusty baguette, which only the French can produce to this quality. It all went down a treat as we were all starving by this time. I think I made two gallons of soup and it all disappeared in no time. I was now designated "Soup Chef". By this time it had started to rain so we moved inside for the rest of the evening where we broke out the dominoes and played a few games, whilst listening and singing along to our sixties collection of music which I had on my iPhone. It played a treat through Clive's portable speakers. It's amazing how we all knew the words to sing along to and recounted old memories that went with some of the songs. We had great difficulty remembering some of the artists or proper titles though, but never the words. We had a great evening and the alcohol flowed freely until it was time for bed. It was pitch black and very quiet on the site as we made our way back to Belle.

The next morning we went up to the chalet to find Keith cooking the breakfast. He looked very professional. Tea towel draped over the shoulder, shorts and 'fit flops'. He had been nominated 'Breakfast Chef'. There it was, all the usual for a 'full English' except there were no beans or tomatoes? Keith couldn't find a tin opener. We must have been hung-over, as we never thought of using the one from our van until after breakfast was cooked. After a relaxing mornings banter we headed into Mayenne at midday, where we spent an hour walking around the very pleasant centre. Mayenne wasn't too big and really didn't have enough of interest to keep us there longer than an hour. We decided we were still full from our breakfast so did not take lunch and all had coffees instead. Think we were all still feeling a little delicate too.

On our return to the chalet Keith suddenly shrieked with delight. He found that the tin of beans and the tomatoes could be opened easily without a can opener. "How"? We enquired. Much to our amusement, Keith turned the can over to reveal a ring pull! We fell about laughing. It must have been fate, saving them for another meal. Keith decided to rustle us up a snack of beans on toast. I volunteered to make another soup for our evening meal, there were so many mushrooms left. I suggested to Keith he put cheese into the beans, as this was one my favourites, yummy 'cheesy beans'. Another alternative is 'garlicky beans' where you crush a garlic clove and add to the beans, a very tasty little dish. Of course Keith had to go one better and so decided that the beans must be French, so added a good glug of red wine. Jamie Oliver, eat your heart out. As you can imagine it turned out to be another memorable day, rounded off with a good helping of my mushroom soup. I must say it tasted great but was a strange muddy colour. Well, you don't always have to eat with your eyes.

I had to mention the soup escapades because I had, against Jackie's wishes, bought our food blender along in the van. My theory being that, we could each week use the food leftovers to make a soup, thus saving us money against our budget. Suffice to say this was the last time it was to see the light of day on our journey. We even went as far as buying packet soups on our return through Germany. Still, I am sure the blender had a lovely time relaxing in the cupboard along with all the other unused items.

After another hearty breakfast it was time to say our fond farewells to Clive, Keith and Eddie. It was nice to know that we would see them all again when we were in Poland, as they were also to attend the "Big Posh Polish Wedding" in August. This occasion was to be the marriage of my brother's stepdaughter. More on the big day later.

As our friends headed south to Spain, we continued northeast to Paris. The roads in France in the main are a pleasure to drive, having far less traffic than the UK. Sometimes you can travel an entire road without seeing another car. This cannot, however, be said for Paris. I once drove five times around the Arc De Triumph, before being able to exit, and even then I took the wrong turning. The countryside in this area is similar to England, with well-kept fence and hedge fields, and a lovely greenness to it.

In the early planning stages of our tour and whilst preparing ourselves for our campsite stays, we purchased membership of Camping Card ACSI, which included two campsite books along with location maps detailing campsites all over Europe. I also purchased the software version, which provided additional campsites and countries which are not included in the books. I uploaded the programme onto our laptop to use along the way. ACSI have an arrangement for members, where at some of the sites, you only pay 11-15 euros out of peak season. The campsite at Mayenne was the first one of these that we used. Our Camping & Caravan Club site book covered all Europe except France, Spain and Portugal. We planned to visit these countries in depth next year, so would not be buying the directory with these countries until we needed it.

We were also using a Garmin satellite navigation system with European maps to guide us down the roads which were not always covered on maps. In the campsite guides you usually get both addresses and coordinates to enable you to find the campsites. A good Sat-Nav is essential, but even then they should not be completely trusted. Ours is called Sheila as

I have it switched to the lady speaking the directions in Australian. This is because the English speaking lady makes the speakers on the unit vibrate. Having Sheila as our guide will often prove very amusing as she tries to get her Australian vocabulary around some of the foreign street and place names. Anyway, we head to a campsite called 'Bois de Boulogne" situated on the river Seine close to the centre of Paris. We arrived about 17.00, having stopped en route for food shopping, traffic and a bridge. Bridges can be extremely hazardous to Motorhomes as the height can be a problem. Belle is 3.2 metres high. As we drove through Paris our lovely Australian lass (Sheila) in the Sat-Nav decides to lose the signal, causing us to make a wrong turn. When Sheila picked it up again she tried to take us down some side streets, one of which lead us to a bridge/tunnel. I could see it looming in the distance and so my first instinct was to alert Jackie. "Bridge Jackie", no response. Again I said, "Bridge Jackie", still no response. Finally, it was a somewhat higher pitched "BRIDGE! That got her attention. Only for her to say, "What do you mean BRIDGE?"!! By this time we had to make an emergency stop.

Fortunately, there were no cars following. It was obvious we could not go under the bridge. The sign warned that the height was only 2.8m. We had been advised early on to beware of bridges and tunnel heights and I had agreed with Jackie that we must *both* look out for them. We had to reverse carefully out of the narrow approach and find a different way out of the offending area.

It was a large and very busy campsite and we are lucky enough to get a pitch next to the river Seine. Through a linked fence we had a great view of some very beautiful houseboats, complete with their own small river boats. A quick reconnoitre of the facilities reveals fairly modern toilets and showers, which are obviously well used due to the volume of people and its convenient location, a walk away from the centre of Paris. We planned to stay for two nights as we only intended to visit the Sacre Coeur and Monmartre areas this time, having taken in the other main attractions on previous visits.

The next morning we are up and away for a 3km walk into the centre, though a beautiful park and the woods of the

Bois de Boulogne, which allegedly was full of transvestites. This proved to be erroneous information, as we did not see one, only very chic ladies riding bicycles and fitness fanatics jogging and punching into thin air. One hour later, we reached the Arc de Triomphe. Ready for a snack, we sat under the fabulous monument and ate half of our packed lunch. I had the usual, spread cheese and onion, Jackie had ham and Dijon mustard (how very French.). Everyone around us was also munching away happily in the hot sunshine.

We bought a day metro ticket from nearby and travelled to Montmartre. By the time we arrived the sun was high in the sky and so very hot. We were extremely thirsty, so sat down at one of the many gorgeous roadside café bars for a drink before climbing up the steep streets of Montmatre. I had a 33cl glass of beer, Jackie had two small bottles of Perrier water and a slice of fresh lemon. L'addition came to 15 euros! Still it was well needed and it was a lovely spot.

We ascended the steps to the magnificent Sacre Coeur to take in the breath-taking view of Paris. The rooftops and chimney pots were a sight to see along with the Eiffel tower in the distance. As we walked around we could just imagine old Paris, with the street markets of Montmartre. People were having their portraits sketched and there were artists painting all along the pavements. It was picture book stuff. Montmartre was heaving with people, the hustle and bustle, the restaurants were alive with chatter whilst their customers dined on delicious food and wine. We went into the church, which was beautiful and very peaceful compared to outside. The area directly in front of the church was crowded and sadly covered in litter, particularly beer bottle tops. The surrounding fences were covered with the latest travel fad, padlocks with people's initials or messages painted on. We would see these again and again in many other cities or tourist spots. It seems to be the modern day equivalent of writing on your school desk 'I was ere'.

We sat ourselves down on the grass in front of the Sacre Coeur, along with many others and finished off the remainder of our packed lunch, accompanied by a nice bottle of red wine. The sun seemed even hotter so we sat for a long while talking and taking in the views and atmosphere. We both thought, 'this is what our tour was about'.

We caught the metro back into Paris and had a stroll through the Tuileries for old time's sake along with a refreshing drink of juice. The Tuileries is an open space in front of the Louvre, with tree lined walkways, flower borders, and places to sit and reflect, whilst resting aching feet. We caught the metro back as near to the campsite as we could (half an hour walk), by this time our feet felt as if they were on fire.

Back at the campsite, we ate our evening meal, coffee and liqueur (our stocks were dwindling fast) then lights out for another blissful night. We have to say, our bed is so comfy, you would not believe it. Also, it was so quiet on the campsite once our heads touch the pillow, we are out like lights.

After another 'al fresco' breakfast by the river Seine, we packed Belle ready for our next campsite, Les Armand des Eaux, north east of Valenciennes.

We had a good journey north east, making our way across France. The roads were long, tree lined, straight and traffic free, which made for easy driving (says the lady of the van who hasn't had a go yet!). The reason for the roads being tree lined was so that in the olden times the armies could march in the shade. For us it is a pleasurable sight and adds to that French feel. Again, it was sunshine all the way (felt sure it must change soon though). Sorry…. our cups must always be half full………

We arrived at the campsite, Les Armand des Eaux, just outside Valenciennes and close to the Belgian border. The campsite was so nice. We were soon hooked up and settled in for the next few days. There were cycle paths and walking routes all around and the site was situated in a lovely wooded area. The facilities were good and very clean. Another fine choice from the ACSI book.

Restful, peaceful slumber, did we speak too soon? Somewhere lurking in the vicinity was a very vocal Cockerel whose 'cock a doodle do' woke us every hour on the hour from 4 o'clock in the morning. Obviously he didn't know just one wakeup call was all that was required, and only at daybreak. It was a good job we didn't have a gun with us, feathers would have been flying.

It really doesn't take long to get used to the camping way of life, especially eating breakfast in your 'pj's' in the warm sunshine. Apart from being the map-reader, laundry maid and a whole host of other things, Jackie is also chief pot washer. Now this isn't exactly a chore (her words not mine) for her, in fact it can be a great social event in itself. There is usually someone else in the kitchen area washing their dishes and chatting away to the person at the next sink. Before the bubbles have risen to the top of the bowl, she's been included in the conversation and comes back and tells me all the local gossip. We can speak enough French to get by in quite a few situations, but I am afraid to say we are a little ashamed too, that we don't speak any other languages. Fortunately, for us, most Europeans can speak some English and we think that is why most British folk are a lazy lot as regards learning other languages. This is something we are guilty of and admit it.

We decided to stay put, chill out and stay with Belle for a change. Jackie did some clothes washing and cleaning (definitely chores, not all fun you know!). I tried to get the TV working again, but to no avail. After a call to the manufacturer of the satellite system, still no joy, they could only assume that because we were surrounded by woodland, the dish wasn't able to pick up a signal. Very frustrating. Not that we watch the TV much at all, we prefer to read, but we had paid for an 'All singing, All dancing' system and it just wasn't functioning as it should.

We had a great day relaxing. As the surrounding area was so lovely and ideal for cycling, we decided to get the bikes off the rack and go for a ride and work up an appetite for our evening meal. It was so peaceful and the woods seemed endless. We were riding around for an hour and a half, stopping occasionally for a photo shoot. The experience was just as we had imagined it would be, perfect. All good things come to an end. As we approached the campsite, in fact we were right outside the main entrance, for all to see, Jackie for some reason, lost control of the bike, wobbled all over the road, just missing me by a gnat's whisker (do they have them?), and proceeded to fall off her bike. One hell of a crash, bang, wallop. Oh dear! Luckily, we always wear our helmets. In this case, Jackie's did it's job and had taken most of the impact. She got away with a bruised cheek (face, not rear!) and a few grazes on her hands and knees. Not much damage to the bike either, a broken bell and a few scuffs on the handlebar. We had a good laugh when we got back and looked at the photos we had taken. There was one of Jackie pointing in the direction of the campsite below a signpost with the name on. Little did we know when we took it, it was showing us where Jackie was going to throw herself off her bike.

After a couple of painkillers, Jackie prepared the evening meal, 'omelette complet', which translated by the Rigg's means, 'omelette complete with leftovers'. Another tasty delight, which I cooked on the bbq. That got rid of 6 eggs, we were still going at the 24 Clive and Co. had bought a week ago.

Later in the evening, Jackie composed her blog and of course had plenty to report from the day's events. Whilst we were on our travels we posted a blog as often as we could so our friends and family could read what we were up to and keep a check on our whereabouts. We included lots of photos and when it was ready to upload onto the web, we would try and get Wi-Fi at a reasonable cost or better still, free. We were a little naive to think that all the campsites would provide free Wi-Fi. It was available at most but nearly all charged for the use of. We paid 3.5 euros for 1 hour on the web at this one. The hour soon went and we had only created a list of email addresses. We are obviously still at the beginning of that very long learning curve.

Next day we are up and off to Belgium……….

Chapter Four

Belgium

May 13th – 15th

Wezembeek - Brussels

Waking to blue skies, our daily routine in Belle was beginning to take shape. Normally, we get up around 9.00am. Whilst Jackie makes breakfast of tea and cereal, I take down the bed. Next, if we have not already decided the day before, we discuss our plan for the day ahead. This usually consists of consulting our laptop and the ACSI program, travel guides, maps and Sat Nav. Once we agree on the day's schedule, we give Belle a quick tidy (I remove and empty the chemical toilet cassette at the designated disposal area) then we're off to get a refreshing shower (depending on how fresh the facilities are!). More often than not we make up a packed lunch and take a couple of bottles of water with us. This is because we are on a budget. We only treat ourselves to a good meal in a nice restaurant once a week.

During the major planning process we created spreadsheets on the laptop to keep up with both dates and budget. We update these as we go, either the night before or the morning of departure from the campsite. We monitor our spending on one spreadsheet against the budgeted total spend. To date we are pretty much on target. Early days yet though, we could soon scupper the budget if we have a sudden spending frenzy, which has been known to happen from time to time in the Rigg household.

We hoped to be fairly consistent on our weekly spend. The biggest variable we estimated would be the fuel costs based on the miles that we travel. What came as a bit of a shock were the mobile phone bills. They were over the top by a long way, Jackie's £33 and mine £94. Double what we normally pay in one month. I would point out that we both used my iPhone as it has the data service on it. We did check with the service provider and there were a couple of errors their end, otherwise it was correct. We agreed to curb the calls, watch the word count on texts and our data usage.

We find it easier to visit a supermarket as close to our destination campsite as possible whilst en route. We aim to get four days' worth of food, as this normally fills the fridge and prevents having to make more frequent visits. The supermarkets and food shops we visited were another great way of judging the standard of living in each of the countries we visit. The standard of food stores in the UK is very high and so sets the benchmark. We found France and Belgium are of a similar high standard/quality, with regional variances based on taste.

Our visits to the main cities are also taking on the same pattern. We choose to stay on a campsite closest the city we plan to visit. It makes it much easier to get public transport into the centre. Most campsites offer some information on how to get into the city using various transport options. If the information isn't available, then we consult our travel guides (Belle is full of them) of the city and take a few minutes to study and work out a route and also locate the nearest Tourist Information. The Tourist Information is usually our first port of call, with our first request being the free street map and ask them to mark and recommend any attractions that shouldn't be missed.

We are not ones for spending our time in museums or art galleries, although if there is something we really are interested in, then we would. Our aim is to get a feel for the city, admire the architecture, absorb their particular way of life, especially the street life and people which is a pastime in itself.

We also try to buy the cheapest travel into the city to suit our needs, be it ordinary day return tickets or 24 hour all inclusive (train, tram or bus) tickets. We get a lot of joy and entertainment from using the public transport. Back in the UK we very rarely used any form of public transport, being car owners and using the occasional taxi here and there. Trains, buses and stations prove a great place to people watch and gain first-hand experience of how the transport services deal with 'Joe Public' and us tourists, of course. As you will know, in the UK we are not too tolerant when waiting around for the bus. Yes, up to now, we've not seen many orderly queues.

As we leave the rolling countryside of France and cross over the border into Belgium there is a marked change in the state of the roads and a big difference in the volume of traffic. The roads are in much need of repair and the traffic is as heavy as ours in the UK. The roads also prove a true test of our storage capabilities and of how we have securely packed each item. This is so important. If an item has not been securely stowed, the slightest bump will cause movement, resulting in a lot of noise, rattle and bang. The unit doors and fridge door need to be closed and secured properly. We've already had a tin of beans and the odd onion fly out and roll down to greet us in the cab. We'll get it down to a fine art in the end.

I know that Belgium is just across the channel, as is France, but Belgium seems to have more of a similar feel to the place. Some of the streets and the houses are very much the same as in the UK. Actually, Jackie and I have driven through Belgium several times and we have visited Bruges, Ostend, Waterloo and Gent. I visited Brussels many years ago as a Young Master Printer. I recall what a great place it was, so thought it would be nice to go with Jackie for another look at the beautiful city.

We arrived later that day at the two star campsite "Royal Camping" in Wezembeek. A metro ride from the centre of Brussels. The lady on reception spoke perfect English, was extremely nice and very welcoming. She gave us a good pitch, and before you could say 'Jack Robinson' we were set up and hooked up to the electricity. We're not long into our tour but are really getting into the swing of it now, everything seems so easy. Low and behold, we even managed to get a signal for the Satellite TV. The toilets and showers were duly inspected and while quite basic, are very clean. We now check there's loo roll too, having been previously caught out.

The weather was still being kind to us and so again we ate outside with food freshly cooked on the bbq. Jackie decided this was the best way of cooking. We have to sleep next to the kitchen area and the thought of breathing in garlic and onion smells all night put us off. With the weather as it was, who would want to eat inside anyway? We have an outside gas point on the side of Belle and have bought a Carrie Chef bbq, which cooks the food perfectly. It is a joy to use and easy to assemble/pack away. Today we are having one of our favourites:-

King Prawn Pil Pil (one of our own concoctions)
Heat a little olive oil and a generous knob of butter in the bbq pan
Add some chopped garlic (to your taste) and dried chillies (to your taste)
Add the de-headed washed prawns (keep the shells on as this retains moisture and flavour) and flash cook for just 1 to 2 minutes until hot and sizzling.
Serve with fresh bread, pour over the pan juices, a squeeze of lemon. Wash down with a nice bottle of Chablis............mmm, delicious.

Tip - It can be a messy business when removing the shells, so don't forget a napkin and a bowl of water for each person.

We took off after tea for a little walk up through the village of Wezembeek. Our very nice campsite receptionist gave us a photocopied map of the area, which directed us to the nearest Metro station. We needed to check out how far it was for us for the following days visit to Brussels.

It took us a 45 minute steady walk to the Metro Station. It was a very pleasant walk. We passed lots of houses, so many different styles. Nearly all had well tendered gardens and they must all love roses, nearly everyone had a rose bush of some kind in the border. There were so many different varieties, fabulous scent and colours. Jackie just couldn't resist smelling some of them..........honestly, she does embarrass me sometimes. It was getting late in the evening and so nobody in attendance at the Metro Station kiosk, but there were machines for the tickets. So no problem then, or so we thought, all to be revealed the next morning.

Up and out a little earlier than usual. We made our way to the Metro Station, no time for rose sniffing today. The day was bright and fresh, but a bit on the breezy side, so thought we'd better wear our jackets. When we reached the station, the kiosk was still closed and so we realised the only option was to buy the tickets from the automated machine. Fine, with us. Oh dear, we only had notes and the machine wanted coins. The cost of each day ticket was 7.5 Euros. Now hands up those of you who would carry 15 Euros in coins. Most purses would bulge and well belted trousers would barely remain up. The lowest denominations we had were two 10-euro notes. Some thirty minutes later, having worked our way from 10's to 5's and 5' to 1,s and having asked what appears to be everyone in the village. We finally purchased our tickets. Everyone was very obliging, well, as soon as they realised we weren't begging! Another lesson learnt and not to be repeated.

The metro system is very swish and clean and we are soon deposited in the heart of Brussels. There were bands and discos blaring, balloons, street marquees and the streets were heaving with people. All of sudden we saw huge banners advertising the event. It was the 'Pink Party', a day for gays and Lesbians to celebrate their sexuality and pride. We were a bit hesitant at first not knowing what to expect, but everyone was enjoying themselves and what a fabulous atmosphere.

We pushed and weaved our way to the Grand Place, which is the heart of Brussels. It is a magnificent square surrounded by wonderfully ornate buildings, flower sellers, bars and restaurants. We then proceeded to find a MacDonald's to post Jackie's blog. Luckily, we found one just across from the city hall, which is the epicentre of the Pink Party. We were treated to a street parade, with bands, floats carrying a spectrum of Gays from the Village People to Drag Queens that made Danny La Rue look respectable. The noise was enough to burst your eardrums with streamers and fliers littering the pavements. What was nice was that the 'straights', like us, embraced the occasion and everyone was having a good time.

With the blog posted successfully and a few emails answered, we head off in search of the "Mannequin de Pis" This is the very famous little boy statue and fountain. He stands proudly pissing in the street! We walk through beautiful streets lined with very nice buildings. We found some seats and ate our packed lunch in the sunshine, still watching the flamboyantly dressed party goers pass by. We eventually find the 'Mannequin de Pis', and took some photos having jostled our way to stand in front of him. The area was thronging with people and then we got waffled.

We are meandering down a narrow cobbled street when we were greeted by what must be the "waffle centre" of Belgium. Every other shop sold them, and every other person on the street was hungrily devouring one. Queues radiated from each counter. The typical square sweet waffle base had every sort of dessert topping imaginable. The temptation was too much. We chose fresh strawberries, vanilla cream and Belgian chocolate topping. Yummy, just the one between us, but I didn't realise how competitive we were……..

"And now live from Belgium"

The main fantasy bout of the day
For the undisputed Waffle Crown of the World

In the blue corner, weighing in at 160lbs (in his dreams): Adrianicus Wafflehammer of the North, with 10 wins and two knock outs.

In the pink corner, weighing in at an undisclosed figure due to European ladyship laws: Jacquelinicus Titanicus Woffalumpus of the Midriff, with 20 wins and 8 disqualifications for overzealous pummelling of the pork pies.

Here at ring side the tension is now reaching fever pitch. The referee is just reminding them he wants a fair fight and that the plastic tray is to be grasped equally with no thumbs on the waffle.
No gouging, pinching or treading on toes (and that goes for the audience as well).
Plastic forks at the ready
The crowd fall silent.
On my count……

It became a plastic fork frenzy, but it ensured we both got our equal share. Needless to say, it was gone in seconds.

We wandered back through the Grand Place as we tried to find the Hotel Metropole. You see, I was on a pilgrimage. This was the hotel I had stayed at all those years ago on my trip with the 'Young Master Printers' at the tender age of 26.

It was supposedly a trip to educate young printers on what our brethren in Belgium were doing in the "print trade". I went with a work colleague (and friend) of mine called Paul West and it was all expenses paid for by our employees. We had one of the most fun packed trips I have ever been on. Most of the young master printers were between thirty and fifty, I look back now and they were right, at the time I thought it was a 'miss print'. One guy was asleep all of the days on all of the trips and disappeared at night. Suspiciously, he knew where to find the red light district, when we decided to pay a sight-seeing visit….as one does.

The Hotel was very grand and very luxurious, fabulous sweeping staircase, huge crystal chandeliers, burgundy leather and velvet upholstery and gold leaf architrave. Well worthy of its 5 star rating and certainly well worth a visit, if only to have the black with white aproned waiters serve your drink whilst you take in the atmosphere, either inside or out. During our stay Paul and I saw the famous and beautiful actress, Ingrid Bergman having cocktails with her friends in the bar. Also, Ray Bucton and Moss Evans (who were big railway union magnets at that time) were at the bar, who according to the newspapers were at one another's throats, looking very friendly and pleasantly tipsy at the bar. Who believes newspapers anyway?

Another memorable moment of the trip was when I had my Inspector Clousseau incident. We were due to set off early one morning to visit 'Casterman the Printers' who at that time printed the 'Herges Adventures of Tin Tin' books. Because we needed to be up and out before the usual breakfast service time, I decided to arrange room service by hanging a tick box tag on the door handle as requested for room service. I had chosen boiled eggs and toast to be brought to the room for 6.30am. I was fast asleep one minute, then suddenly woken up by a loud and continuous banging, that I could hear even through the double door entrance to my room. It was only 5.30am? After about 5 minutes I thought I'd better get up and see who was creating all the noise in the corridor. What's this? I am greeted by the waiter, at "MY DOOR", who entered with boiled eggs and toast. I sheepishly look out into the corridor. Sure enough, there are several other sleepy guests at their doors, all giving me the evil eye. I went back inside, had a little chuckle and reset my travel alarm clock to European time (I had already done my watch).

One evening Paul and I went out looking for somewhere to eat. We came upon a restaurant that unbeknown to us, had an entrance on two streets (it was L shaped). We spent quite a while debating whether to go in one side but didn't bother as we both didn't really like the look of the menu, only to walk around the corner and decide, "yes we like the look of this one". It's only later when Paul went to the toilet and came back, killing himself laughing and said "You know that restaurant we didn't like the look of? Well we are in it! There's a door in this street as well".

It's also hard not to giggle and take photos of shops with names like "Fanny" and "Tits".................when you're in your twenties anyway! Apologies. I didn't mean to digress, but these memories came flooding back as we entered the Hotel Metropole.

Jackie was as impressed as I had been with the Hotel and could easily imagine why it was one of *the* places to be seen in. We didn't blow the budget. We just had a nice drink in the bar, still a sumptuous setting, then we set off for the metro and our next stop the 'Royal Palace'. We were getting quite tired by now and so debated whether or not to go. What a mistake that would have been. The Palace was a stunning building. A little along the lines of Buckingham Palace, but without the guards and the gates. Opposite was a beautiful park which we took the time to stroll through. There were many statues, fountains and shaded tree lined walkways, just what we needed and lots of places to sit and relax. By this time, we were not only exhausted due to wandering around all day but the temperature had risen somewhat and we were sweltering in the heat. We caught the metro back to Wesembeek and reflected on our day in Brussels. Our feet were aching but we managed to enjoy the walk back to the campsite. We passed several restaurants, which we were very tempted to go into, not only for food but for another sit down. It was a busy area in places, people coming and going about their business. We do love to people watch. We notice that Belgian men have a slightly different take on colour when dressed up. They wear predominantly lighter coloured jackets and trousers than we in the UK do. Jackie observes the ladies, of course.

Back to the campsite, I rustled up another meal on the bbq. Unfortunately, we didn't chat to anyone here as all the motorhomes and caravans were closed. We assumed that like us, their owners were all out visiting the capital.

We did see quite a spectacle whilst at the campsite. We could hear a low rumble in the sky and looked up to see a huge aircraft. We had never seen anything quite like it before, being of a very light weight construction. It had gigantic long multi-engine wings and was obviously some type of experimental design to achieve some sort of record. Typically, the camera battery was flat, so we couldn't take a photo of it. We never did find out what it was, or where it came from.

So, that was Belgium, and very nice it was too. For anyone who hasn't visited the country, we would recommend visiting Brussels, Bruges and Ghent. Bruges is our personal favourite. It is a beautiful place, quaint buildings, cobbled streets criss-crossed with canals and bridges. We would have liked to have stopped by again but have to keep telling ourselves that we just we can't do everything.

Next stop Holland, or is that 'The Netherlands' inhabited by the Dutch?

Chapter Five

The Netherlands

May 15th to 24th

Middleburg – Rockanje – Delft – Edam – Volendam – Amsterdam –Zaan Chaars – Dokkum

As we head into The Netherlands our Australian lady "Sheila" in the Sat-Nav decided to take us on an alternative route. "This looks a bit odd" declared Jackie, who was co-navigating, "this isn't the way I would take us". We ended up looking at a river and a ferry crossing. Sheila obviously had a spanner in her works again. We had already noticed that on occasion, she had taken us on some obscure routes. Jackie managed to get us back onto the beaten track and we let Sheila take over again, with the famous words "recalculating".

Several detours and river crossings later, we realised something was fundamentally wrong. We pulled over and I had a look at the Sat-Nav settings. My fault, I still had the ferry crossings option ticked. Sorry Sheila. Well, there aren't that many ferry crossings in the middle of the UK or France are there and I had not thought about the rest of the tour. Sheila was now back in our good books and so we travelled on letting her guide us along the way. We had such a laugh as she tried to pronounce the street names, which are hard at the best of times, but with an Australian accent were absolutely hilarious.

I'm sure most people know that The Netherlands is a very flat country, most of it below sea level, but it still came as bit of a surprise, "it's *very* flat isn't it" declared Jackie. It certainly was, as far as the eye could see, not one little hump in the landscape. We were also expecting a rush of windmills, but none we could see, there were hundreds of wind-turbines instead. Where had all the windmills gone?

Our first destination for that day was to be Middleburg (Zeeland) and then to the campsite at Rockanje. The roads were relatively quiet, in good condition and so a joy to drive on. Oh, by the way, did I mention it's *very* flat?

We arrived mid-afternoon in the small town of Middleburg which has a circular layout to its street system. We parked right next to a Frittery (Dutch chip shop) but managed to resist, still being very aware of our budget and our waistlines. Middleburg is a lovely little town intersected with waterways, bridges and some wonderful streets and houses. Outside nearly every house is a bicycle of some colour, size and shape. This was our first taste of Holland and we were very impressed. Wide cycle paths run alongside all of the roads. It is the centre of "bike culture", with the majority being those 'sit up' old style bicycles. It was just how we imagined it. We were also very impressed with how clean and tidy everywhere was, even the back streets. Yes, we do tend to see a few of these as we weave our way round looking for appropriate parking places.

We just had a quick snack and the bikes were soon off the back of Belle and away we went to join the rest of Middleburg's residents on their bikes. It was coats on too, as the weather had turned a bit cold and cloudy. We meandered around Middleburg taking in all the views and its very "different" feel. We took lots of pictures of the houses, which in the centre of town are of a very Dutch design, small, typically terraced with triangle brick faced roof fronts, which are stepped down to the main body of the house. There appears to be one main living room which runs from the front to the back, with lovely picture windows overlooking the gardens. Some are totally open plan with well-designed ultra-modern kitchens. Most canals are tree-lined and backed by these pretty little houses. Picture book stuff.

The Dutch will prove to be one of the most open and friendly people we will meet, not just in the Netherlands, but on our journey throughout Europe. We spent a very pleasant couple of hours exploring Middleburg.

We took the route southwest to Rockanje, hoping to find our chosen campsite for the night. We travelled along the coast and encountered our first Dyke, which was a very impressive structure that we drive along the top of. At times there were sea views on both sides of the dykes, along with gates running for a kilometre or so to control the flow of water. But there was still a surprising lack of windmills. When we eventually saw one, we were like excited children. Unfortunately at this time, they were far from our path and few and far between. Our first intended Dutch campsite was closed for the evening. We had arrived just after 6pm. This was quite normal procedure as it was only mid-May and so classed as low season for camping and holidaymakers. Back to the campsite guidebooks, we found another site a few minute's drive away, still coastal. We just managed to get there as they were about to close. We tried to practice our Dutch but he wanted to speak English. Always so much easier for them. Our Dutch language expertise will get no further than "dag" and "dank u" as they all appear to speak perfect English. The campsite proves to be very pleasant and the young guy was very welcoming to us, even though we are a late arrival. In fact he pointed out our pitch, let us through the security barrier and said, "That will be 11 euro's, you can settle up with me in the morning, have a nice evening". For 11 euro's we had the most perfect pitch. The facilities were excellent and we were a few minute's walk to the beach. As it was getting late Jackie quickly prepared one of my favourite meals.

'Derbyshire' Hotpot
This is our adaptation of 'Lancashire' Hotpot

½ kilo of minced beef
Peel and slice 3 large potatoes
Peel and slice 1 large onion
Peel and slice 1 large carrot
4 tbsps frozen peas
2 Oxo beef stock cubes
Freshly milled black pepper
Dried chillies – optional.

Put the minced beef, onions, carrots and peas in a deep oven/roasting dish. Add some dried chillies and grind some fresh black pepper on to the meat.
Dissolve the Oxo cubes in enough boiling water to completely cover the meat mixture, pour over.

Place the sliced potatoes on the top, slightly overlapping each slice until all the meat etc. is covered.

Put the dish on the middle shelf in the oven and cook on high for about an hour, or until the potatoes are golden brown and crispy. Serve with additional vegetables of your choice. Enjoy.

Whilst the dish was cooking, we decided to take a walk to the beach. We had to walk through the campsite. There were lots of static caravans/mobile homes on the site. These were extremely well kept. They had patios, decking, well tendered plant pots and blooming garden areas. The facilities were excellent too.

The wind was now blowing and there was quite a chill to it. We had to wend our way through some huge sand dunes to the beach, but the sandy pathways were well trodden by the bucket and spade brigade. It had also started to drizzle by the time we reached the beach which swept its way around a large bay. We could imagine how busy it would be on a hot summer's day. Sadly, it was too cold for us, so we stayed all of three seconds and headed back to Belle. As we opened the door we were greeted by the lovely smell of the Derbyshire Hotpot. It wasn't far off cooked, so we had time for a pre-dinner drink to warm us up. One thing that is good about having the oven on is that it makes it cosy and warm, especially on a chilly night. It soon heats up the vehicle and uses very little gas. Not that we would encourage anyone to use the oven rather than the proper heating system.

The following day we pay our dues and set off for the journey northwards to Delft. Weather wise, it was a bit of dreary day again but we were in good spirits enjoying listening and singing along to the playlists we had created. Sheila was doing well until we got near to Rotterdam. Jackie and I discussed going into the centre, just to have a quick look as we were passing so closely to the city. We could see from the map it was a huge sprawling place. The traffic was naturally very heavy, the norm with any big city these days, especially a large and important port as Rotterdam. We were doing well, following the signs to the centre. All of a sudden, there were only signs directing us North or South, but none for the Centre.

Of course, we had to make a very quick decision. Oh dear! This was our first proper barny! Jackie and I often bicker, which usually ends in a witty comment that makes us both laugh. This one did not. Jackie had no idea where we were on the map as it wasn't detailed enough and I was trying to get into the right lane on a four-lane ring road. The air was *light* blue, Jackie blamed me? I blamed Jackie? Needless to say we ended up missing the exit for the centre and so drove on in stony silence, until we arrived in Delft. We decided to go straight into the shopping centre to buy a detailed map of The Netherlands. Another lesson had been learnt. Actually, we did have a good map that we had bought back in the UK, but even I have admit it's very hard to read in places and missing some finer points of detail. By the way, did I mention it's *very* flat and still no windmills to speak of? Just thought I'd better change the subject.

We parked up in Delft and had a pleasant walk around. The centre is picturesque in parts and to our surprise, not that nice in others. It felt a little run down in places. The main square was beautiful. Surrounded by small gift shops and as expected, numerous shops selling the famous 'Delft Blue' pottery. We resisted the temptation to buy. There were some lovely pieces of pottery but of course they were pricey. When we were first married I told Jackie if she ever cluttered our house with ornaments, I would shoot them off the shelves with my air rifle! Bless her, she took my words to heart and we have always been minimalistic ever since, only having a few ornaments around our house.

We did, however, manage to buy some cheese. We love all kinds of cheese, particularly French cheeses. We went into a little old fashioned cheese emporium, which defied temptation; we could have had a cheese fest there and then. We enquired if there was a local variety. A very official looking young lady took us to one counter and pointed out some 'Delft Cheese', blue of course. She said it wasn't actually produced in Delft, but made in a small village close by. There was a medium sized piece already wrapped so Jackie asked politely if she would cut it in half for us, as the price was ten euros. The young lady looked at us aghast and quite indignantly declared, "I have only just wrapped that and cannot cut it in half" we were quite taken aback. Due to the tone of her voice she had attracted an audience, so not wishing to look cheapskates, or was that 'cheeseskates' I declared with panache "we'll take it". Outside Jackie said "I can't believe we have just paid ten euros for a piece of cheese and you would not buy me a piece of pottery". Nor could I!

We left Delft to journey north to the bulb fields and the famous Kuckenhoff gardens. We arrived only to discover the fabulous displays had been and gone. It was only mid-May, so we thought we would see at least a few late blooms. March and April are the best months to visit. What a shame. Jackie was so looking forward to seeing them. As we headed out of the area we did spy two rather bedraggled rows of tulips and some very nice dandelions….. in full bloom.

We stopped en route to take in the view. As flat as it was, and even without the flowers, it was still very pretty, the fields had been neatly ploughed which made for interesting patterns as far as the eye could see. We sat by one of the many canals and ate some very expensive, but indeed tasty cheese on toast. It was a bit blustery, so we were soon back inside Belle and off on the road toward Edam. More cheese!

We followed the signs for our chosen campsite in Edam, which for the next four nights was to be our base for visits to Amsterdam, Edam and Vollendam. As we approached the site, we had an eventful half hour trying to cross the canal, the only way we could see was over a couple of mini-wooden Bailey Bridges, which were way too narrow for us. Obviously Sheila thought we would be riding bikes by this time. After further consultation of our newly purchased detailed map, we could see that there was in fact another route to the campsite.

The campsite was very nicely laid out. The staff were very welcoming, it had excellent facilities and was in a perfect location overlooking the sea. The next day dawned grey and drizzly. We lounged in bed all morning, reading our books. When we did eventually open the door, we were greeted by two families of ducks who had the art of begging, off to a tee. We soon had the bread ripped up into bite size pieces and dispensed out of the door to a round of "quack, quack quack

quack" which we took as a thank you. It was such a lovely sight to see. Now in true Dutch style the ducks appeared to be inter-racial, with white mixing with light brown, mixing with dark brown. We couldn't work out which chicks belonged with which brood, as each set appeared to be mixed. Perhaps Dutch ducks take several partners in Dutch liberal style. Once the bread had gone, they quickly separated off into family groups and waddled off to the next camper.

We had a relaxing day, looking out to sea and watching the old style Dutch sailboats come in and out of the canal at the side of the campsite. The weather had picked up by this time so we decided to take a teatime stroll into nearby Edam. We walked along the canal and into centre. There were some fabulous houses, very trendy, with terraces overlooking the canal, most with moorings, some with very expensive river-boats.

We stopped to buy some more bread and have a people watch at a bar. We liked Edam very much. It is an absolutely beautiful little place with many quaint shops. There was the most colourful cheese shop we had ever seen, all varieties of Edam cheese, but each round of cheese, was a different bright colour, not just the usual red. Also, to our delight, Edam had its very own Windmill!

As we wound our way through the pretty cobbled streets we took the opportunity to have a good nosey through the windows. The houses here were amongst the most delightful we had seen. Again, they were ultra-modern inside, tastefully and expensively decorated. The terraced houses we passed were predominantly small, had two large windows with a front door and a single window above. What stood out the most and what we found most peculiar, was that they all, and I mean each and everyone, without exception, had two identical ornaments or vases in the two front windows. We pondered as to why. Jackie thought perhaps it was tradition, or superstition maybe, to bring some sort of balance in the home. To put our minds at rest we asked a lady in the supermarket. Apparently, there is no reason whatsoever. She said it was just the modern style and they like it. Talk about 'keeping up with the Jones's'.

We bought a very informative cycle path map of the local area, from the tourist information centre. The Dutch have an amazing system of paths and way marked signs that should be idiot proof once you get used to how they work. There are names of the village/town/tourist attraction and the distance on each sign, so it should prove straight forward, shouldn't it?

Next day, after another feeding time with our adopted family of ducks, we are off to Vollendam on our bikes. The weather had changed yet again and it was back to grey skies. It's about a 5km ride, except we, as we do, took the wrong turn out of Edam. 5km turned it into 10km. We did literally go around all the houses with our idiot proof cycle path map.

Vollendam is a small port and very touristy. It has a harbour and a pretty promenade to walk along. There are some interesting sailboats in the harbour too. We took some time to do a bit of window-shopping. There are many little shops selling all sorts of locally crafted items. There was one shop which only sold cuckoo clocks. We both quite like these timepieces, particularly the very ornate ones. We feel we might be tempted to buy one at some time in the future.

On the way back to Belle, we stocked up with groceries at the local supermarket. It's amazing how much we can cram into the panniers on the bikes. The Dutch ladies not only have all sorts of brightly coloured flowery panniers, they also have brightly coloured baskets on the handlebars, they must be able to get a whole weekly shop on one bike. Some have garlands of flowers draped all over their bikes, they look colourful and fun. It is just such a different culture. Mind you, they ride their bikes so confidently, no hands when answering mobile phones. No helmets. Speed.... well, watch out for your life, they go so fast, thankfully they are experts in manoeuvring out of the way at the very last minute, as unsuspecting tourists suddenly step out in front of them.

As we relaxed by the van that evening we had a spectacular view of a Heron, fishing for his dinner, not four yards from where we sat. Jackie quickly grabbed the camera to capture the beautiful creature. We decided to have a Heron photo contest; mine were somewhat blurred, having taken them through my special wine lens. Jackie won, that was one for the blog.

Later that night the wind picked up and it started to rain heavily. At some unearthly hour of the night, about 2.30am to be precise, Jackie woke me up. Was my luck in I thought? No of course not! Jackie was worried, "I don't like the sound of the sea". It was crashing against the bank as the wind whipped it up. Jackie had visions of Belle being swept out to sea by a freak wave, or even a Tsunami!

Despite my efforts to re-assure her that she was just being silly and that we would be fine, I had to unhook the van in the pitch black, howling gale. We moved twenty feet further back from the waterside and closer to the toilet block, which of course made us totally safe........

After surviving the previous night's elements, we were up and off into Edam to catch the bus to Amsterdam. We had no trouble getting a return ticket (9 euros) and explaining our destination as the bus driver spoke perfect English.

Amsterdam. We had both wanted to visit this place for so long, it had been built up over the years, by our friends and holiday programmes to a 'must see' place. It was everything people said it was, with its water-lined streets, its bridges with bikes parked on them, smoking dens, bohemian bars, red light district, restaurants and the hustle and bustle. The weather had improved somewhat, certainly a lot brighter and a little warmer, so we were able to wander about and take in the ambience of it all. There is a buzz about the place, but somehow it just does not grab us. I can't explain it; perhaps too many people had built it up in our minds to be something out of the ordinary. When it does not quite match up to those expectations, and, our opinion only, we found that it was a bit 'shabby chic' and quite grubby in places. Don't get me wrong, we did like it and would definitely go back again, it's a fun place, but just not in a rush.

Let's also face up to the 'bloke thing' and red light districts. If the truth be known, I could have window shopped all day. There were some beauties on show. We did see one chap in a raincoat and dark glasses actually enter one of these dens of iniquity. Jackie said "I bet you would have liked to be him" I said "Not really, I don't suit rain coats"! But I found myself thinking that even if I had wanted to, the thought of catching something would prove too much for me. Anyway, we nonchalantly saunter through the area and I throw in an "it does not interest me at all" for good measure, Jackie didn't look impressed. We also chose not to try the 'happy cake'. We know some folk who did and it made them so ill it spoilt their weekend. We didn't even loiter too long outside any of the Hashish joints (joints – get it? ha ha!), you could inhale the smoke from the pavement.

While wandering down/up/around one of the delightful side streets, we came across one of those shops that take you back in time. This one was a bike shop. There were hundreds of bikes hanging from the ceiling, walls, in fact everywhere, not all new and some were very interesting in their art deco design. There were all sorts of accoutrements for sale, from pedals to locks to pumps to lights to bells. Now, if you remember some time back Jackie had thrown herself off her bike which had resulted in the bell getting broken. We thought it would be a good idea to buy a new one here, as a memento from Amsterdam. With a ting-a-ling here and a ting-a-ling there, in fact a ting-a-ling everywhere. Passers-by could have been forgiven for thinking they were passing a campanologist shop. It was a major decision-making time. Should she have the black? Or the harlequin? Or the pink? Which ring sound was the best? We can be pretty indecisive at times, especially if we are spending 6 eruos! An hour later, which seemed like three, Jackie finally chose a neat black and silver chequered one with a proper ding-ding, ding-ding.

As we had been very good and felt that we had held onto our purse strings far too long, we decided to have a meal in Amsterdam. So, later in the day, after a few drinks at some very trendy bars, we chose to have a meal at an Argentinian restaurant. It was tucked down one of the busy side streets and looked as if it had some atmosphere. We were rather hungry and as our eyes are usually 'bigger than our bellies', we both chose 'all you can eat spareribs'. We thought 'let's go for it'! We could have a couple of sets at least as we hadn't eaten anything since breakfast and it was now early evening.

Wow, when the racks of ribs arrived, they looked like giant panpipes. We weren't sure whether to play them or eat them. After the initial meat orgy, (passers-by getting splattered and wondering if they were walking down 'Piggy Strasse') we couldn't even manage to eat the first plateful. By the time we left, our stomachs were fit to burst and felt like we were about to give birth. We take a bow and leave to a round of applause from the other diners. Bravo, Encore!

That was Amsterdam. A good day out but the biggest disappointment was......... we never saw any mice with clogs on.

Next day we are up and on the move again. Great, the weather had taken a turn for the better, with blue skies, sunny and warm. Our search for authentic Dutch Windmills continues. Although we had seen one or two, they had been nothing like we had envisaged. Looking through the guidebooks, I found somewhere called 'Zaan Chaars' which had windmills. We decided to take a look. It took about forty minutes to drive to the area, south west of Edam. What a beautiful sight. Dutch Windmills, at last we have them. The whole area was very picturesque and just how we had imagined all of Holland to be. The place was full of tourists and there were gift and craft shops and a museum, all very nicely set beside a winding river. We stayed only for a short time but took plenty of photographs. There were six windmills in all, all of which were still working. There were huge ones and a couple of small very old ones, all so colourful. A truly splendid sight, a 'must see' if you are ever in this part of Holland.

The reason why we didn't tarry too long at Zaan Chaars, was that we were heading for a place called Dokkum, in the Freesland region in north east, not too far from the German border. This would be our last stop in The Netherlands. We had an enjoyable journey and stopped for lunch on one of the many dykes along the coast. These things are great feats of engineering, with roads running along the top of them. There are lay-bys all along the way too, with seats and benches provided, so you can take in the views. We had a nice chat with a Dutchman who had also pulled over for a rest while his car cooled down. He said he had a problem with the air conditioning. That day he needed it too. We offered him a cold drink but he declined. He was on his way home after finishing his morning shift at work. What a lovely chap. As he waved us goodbye, it reminded us both how lucky we were, to be doing what we were doing and not have to go work.

We arrived at Dokkum. Another beautiful little Dutch town. The campsite was right in the centre, just behind the river. Luckily, the bridge was just wide enough for Belle. Once again, the staff were very welcoming and it was a friendly site with good clean facilities. The pitches here were very nice with hedged screens so we were soon pitched up and ready to settle down for the evening. It was still gloriously hot so the loungers were out ready in no time. Being typically English, the kettle is usually one of the first things that goes on. Oops! Here we go again, we managed to trip the pitch fuse. Of course, this also caused the chap next doors electric to go off as well. I had to go back to the reception, tail between my legs, and tell them what I had done (stupid English). I couldn't gain access to the trip switches, as they were behind a locked door just by the connection box. The site man came back with me and re-set the switches next to Belle. For some reason our electric didn't come on, but the chaps next door did? The three of us set about trying to find the cause in our van, Jackie consulted her notes. We eventually located where the vans trip switches were (hadn't needed to before) and so we were soon up and running again. The site man went back to his office and we started to chat with our next-door neighbour.

We soon got to know our neighbour who was a very nice Dutch gentleman called Kees, pronounced Case. He was holidaying alone in a Motorhome, a little smaller than Belle. Sadly, his wife had died three years before. Kees came to Dokkum for his holidays because it used to be one of their favourite places and so he felt close to her here. He even declined to eat with us saying he preferred to keep his own company now he has adjusted to his solitary way of life. I am sure he can't have heard about our cooking! Kees proved to be a great source of information on Motorhomes and camping in general, and took on the role of mentoring us on all things 'Motorhome'. By the time he has finished with us over the next few days we had our awning up at a slant so the rain could drain off properly, guide ropes to keep it down in the wind, a piston jack as well as the scissor type which had been provided with the van, (as they should never be trusted on their own with the weight involved). We also had some self-inflating spray for the wheels, just in case we get caught out in some dodgy place, (we should spend as little time by the road as possible). We had an electric pump and pressure gauge for the tyres (it's easier to keep an eye this way, than having to relying on garages). We now owned a breathable floor cover for outside the van (to reduce ingress of dirt off our shoes into the van and to keep us clean underfoot in the rain). He even provided the stakes and retainers for the ground sheet, which he produced new out of a packet and refused to take any money for. All the advice was greatly received. All the money would prove to be well spent.

During one afternoon chat, Kees revealed that he and his family had been held in a Japanese prisoner of war camp during WW2. His father had been a policeman working in Indonesia when the war broke out. Kees, his mother and two brothers spent three and a half very hard years as prisoners. He said he was pleased when the USA dropped the A-bombs to end the war. We were quite shocked by this but as he explained, by that time, they were all starving to death. It had saved their lives.

He also told us about the Dokkum town clock called the 'Maiden Clock' which chimes at ten minutes to ten each evening as well as on the hour at ten o'clock. This was to warn the maidens (and the workers), that the village gates were about to close and they needed to get back into the village before being discovered missing. This tradition is carried on to this day, although I am sure the maidens now totally ignore it, more likely now reminding them it's time to go out!

He was a really nice chap, but unfortunately we forgot to take his contact details. It would have been difficult anyway as he admitted he didn't bother with computers as he was not of the electronic age.

Along the way, we often talked about him with much affection. One thing he did say was that he was a Dutchman and that he came from The Netherlands and that Holland was a term more often used by outsiders. So from now on we know the country as The Netherlands.

Back to Dokkum. We walked out of the campsite, along the road by the river and within a few minutes were in the centre of Dokkum. There are riverside bars and restaurants, two windmills, the central shopping area and surrounding streets are very nice too. We found the Tourist Information Centre and went in to find out what there is to do and see locally. We also picked up a cycle map of the area. We were very impressed with, and liked the feel of the place, so much so, we decided to stay for a few days.

The next day we were off on the first of our cycle tours having chosen to head for the coast. It had rained during the night and dawned a bit overcast but warm, we decided to take a packed lunch with us, spread cheese and onion sandwiches, a banana and a bottle of red wine. Did I tell you I like spread cheese and onion? I know I did, boring isn't it? Our route took us out to and along the coast, about 10km. The Netherlands is *very* flat, and as we keep bleating on about, which makes for easy riding, or so we thought. On the way back we found ourselves riding into a fierce wind that had blown up, nearly sweeping Jackie off her bike, even though the battery power was set up to full assist. The routes are clearly marked so we managed not to get lost. We passed a church with a life size figure of a 'worm' lady. These ladies used to go to the beaches each day and dig up worms to take back to their fishermen husbands to use as bait, out on the boats. It must have been a very hard life. There were also some war graves from world war two, in the churchyard. Some British and Commonwealth airmen had been buried there. Kees also told us that there were many such war graves dotted about The Netherlands.

We enjoyed another few days relaxing, eating and cycling. Finally we said our fond farewell to Kees. We really had enjoyed our time in this beautiful and interesting country. Our memory of The Netherlands will be the friendliness of the people and the amazing landscapes. Jackie and I will definitely be going back one day. There is certainly plenty more we want to see and do there. Oh, and did I mention it's *very* flat!

Chapter Six

Northern Germany

May 24th to 30th

Bremen – Hamburg

Crossing the border into Germany the countryside remained much the same, flat with cultivated fields, still very pleasant to the eye though. What was immediately brought to our notice was the increase in the traffic, which also moved at much faster speeds.

We headed southeast to our next campsite, which was at a place called Oyten, not too far from Bremen. Lady luck was with us again, it was blue skies and the campsite was on the edge of a small lake, all very picturesque. The guy at reception spoke good English so we had no problems checking in. We set up camp and had a relaxing day lounging in the sun and chatting to our fellow campers, mostly Germans. This being our first encounter with the German campers, we found that they were very interested in what we were doing, and very happy to chat to us in English. We took our usual after dinner stroll up to the village to find out where the bus stop was for the following day's journey into Bremen.

The next day we were up and away by eleven, making a nice early start for us. The bus ride took half an hour, taking us through the busy suburbs. We are always amazed, wherever we go to see so many people going about their business, here it seemed in as much a rush as we are in the UK. We arrived at the bus terminal, directly in front of the central railway station, the "Hauptbahnhof". The station had a very impressive façade with several modern art statues in front. There were lots of food stalls at the bus station that offered every variety of German 'Bratwurst' imaginable, huge great things. People stood and ate them at small counters whilst waiting for the next bus, others opted for a take away and ate on the run.

Bremen is a really nice city, well worth a visit. Its claim to fame is the fairy-tale by the Brothers Grimm called 'The Musicians of Bremen'.

A donkey, a dog, a cat and a cockerel (the musicians) became friends after each leaving home to find their fortune. They foiled a robbery, which was taking place at a little cottage in Bremen. By making fierce noises with their instruments, the robbers fled. The four animals became known as 'The Musicians of Bremen' and all lived together in the little cottage, happily ever after.

There were many gift shops selling the book and also little souvenirs of the animals, which stand on top of one another. There is also a statue of them in the main square, allegedly if you touch the donkey's hoof and make a wish, it will come true. "Why did I get a kick in the teeth?" I ask Jackie.

After a visit to the tourist information we made our way to the city square and the 'Rathaus' or town hall to you and me. The town square is very pretty so we decided to eat our packed lunch sitting on the church steps, along with the locals and tourists alike. The architecture here is magnificent and the tourists walk around craning their necks to see the intricate stone work on the tall buildings. Fed and watered again, we made our way to an area called 'the Schnoor' which is very old and has narrow cobbled streets full of cafes and small craft shops. We spent a pleasant time wandering up and down window-shopping. We visited an old house in the Schnoor, called 'Die Ole Schnoorhuus'. Jackie was quick to point out that is where I should sleep ....Cheeky!

The following day dawned, bright and sunny, perfect for a 10km bike ride around the lake and over the fields to a large shopping centre. We rode about half way, and were out in the open fields, when we noticed that the sky ahead had turned very dark. The wind suddenly blew up and in minutes there was a thick curtain of red dust directly in front of us and it was heading our way. It was quite a phenomenon to see, blowing across the countryside, it was as if someone had drawn a straight curtain wall of dust as it approached. We thought we were in for a real storm. As it was such a nice day, we had left the awning up on Belle. We quickly turned our bikes around and beat a hasty retreat, the dust wall following us. However, by the time we got back to the campsite it had somehow blown itself away. I think we only got the tail end of it. Within half an hour of our return, the sun had come out again. We wondered if it was the ash from the Icelandic volcano that Scotland had experienced around the same time.

The great thing about being on a campsite is that everyone is so nice and always ready to offer help, advice or just pass the time of day with a friendly smile. It really does make you feel good and very welcome. It's such a small thing to smile, but it makes all the difference. Our evening was spent discussing the dust cloud with Olga, our neighbour for that night, a lovely German lady who had also travelled all over Europe including England. What is nice to know is how much they enjoyed visiting the UK. We also chatted to some people from The Netherlands who had just been to Norway. They told us how beautiful the Fjords are and advised us to take the ferry from Denmark to Sweden. At this stage we were thinking of driving over the bridge, but the advice was greatly appreciated. The same evening we managed to watch three episodes of "Phoenix Nights" on DVD, as the satellite TV again did not pick up a signal. "Who planted that tree there"? I ask!

It was whilst we were here that I first had to upload some more books onto my Kindle e-book reader, having read all those I had loaded prior to our departure. I had worried that it might not work whilst abroad, but I didn't need to, it was just as easy to do and so I was soon in possession of another few months' worth of reading matter. Because I had the time, I read some fairly heavy going history books whilst also reading some light fantasy novels to break it up. I usually have a quick read while Jackie does a crossword, then its lights out between 11.00 and 11.30. All part of our daily routine.

We left the campsite at Oyten and headed northeast towards Hamburg. This time the campsite we had chosen was in a place called Drage and named Stover Strand, some 30km east of Hamburg on the banks of the river Elbe. As previously mentioned we are using the ACSI camping program and the book for locating campsites that offer discounted rates in low season at hundreds of campsites throughout Europe. The cost ranges from between 11 to 15 euros a night. Some are inclusive of electricity while others charge extra. All are of a high standard, but some are a little further out of the cities than we would like, this is one of them. What we save on the campsite costs against our budget, we sometimes will have to pay in travel costs into the cities. We can't have it all ways.

This was the first campsite where very little English is spoken and we had to resort to our phrase book. It caught us somewhat by surprise, having been lulled into a false sense of security. This also had its repercussions as we tried to catch the bus the following day, we had totally misunderstood the instructions we had been given at reception. Also, this was the first site that had an electric meter for the hook up. We had to feed the meter with coins, so different to what we had been used to up to now. We had always paid a flat fee at reception.

We had fun and games finding a suitable pitch. The reason for this was because I wanted to get good TV reception to watch Manchester United play Barcelona in the Champions League Final, being shown on TV the following day. Anybody watching us must have found it very amusing. "The crazy Englishman is on the move again with his swirling satellite dish, what can he be up to?" We moved from pitch to pitch, each time with Satellite up (one, two, three), Satellite swirling (one, two, three), Satellite dish down (one, two, three) It reminded us of the TV series 'Dads Army'. So we moved on, until we eventually parked up on the edge of the campsite, miles away from anyone else. At last we were clear of trees and had an open aspect south to the Astra 2 Satellite. The down side was that we no longer had a beautiful view of the river Elbe and also that the shower/toilet block was a ten minute walk away. I would like to point out that I love football and I am, of course, a Derby County fan, but like to support all UK clubs when they play abroad.

It was fun and games again the following day as we tried to get the bus to Winsen (10km), from where we then had to catch the train into Hamburg. We were backwards and forwards from the bus stop, first to take our coats off, as it was really quite warm, then to realise that the next bus wasn't for over an hour. As time was passing, we decided to get a taxi into Winsen. We had to go back, yet again, to the campsite, as this was where the local firms picked up from. We had a pleasant conversation with the taxi driver who we booked for our return. We only just made it to the station as the train pulled in. This was another stroke of luck as they were only every hour. It was a packed double-decker train, but we managed to get a seat on the top deck so we could take in the views. One tip to make at this point. Make sure you note down the train number and platform for the return trip. This will save you time and frustration on the way back. That too was part of the learning curve for us.

Hamburg is a big city with a huge port. It has mostly modern buildings, as it was re-built after being heavily bombed during the Second World War. The train station is also a huge building (but not picturesque) having lots of shops and cafes within. We both enjoyed looking around the centre. It has a typical central shopping area, some impressive old buildings, including the Rathaus in the market square. There was a great atmosphere as there was a musical festival in progress. No packed lunch today, so we each tucked into a giant Bratwurst sausage, yum, yum, and a beer from one of the many stalls on the square. We ate our tasty morsels while being entertained by a school choir on the stage. All very pleasant.

We wandered across the city to the harbour, where there was a jazz festival in full swing. Mmmm, nice! Jazz, what can I say, we both like some of it, but we aren't really lovers of this type of music. We find it too, Mmmm, nice! There was a group playing on the quayside when we arrived but we couldn't work out if they were playing, or warming up. Jazz. Mmmm nice.

The dock area was lined with very big, old and impressive storage houses, some of which have been converted into shops and museums, even a Vampire nightmare house. Others had been converted into trendy apartments, overlooking the river and harbour. There was also a variety of old ships on the harbour wharf, steam and sail types.

We went back to the centre and crossed to the other side of the main square. We looked around to find somewhere nice to eat, but just couldn't make our minds up. We wandered around some very nice cloistered restaurants and eateries with views of the harbour but they were all so busy, hardly any vacant seats. Eventually, we went back into the busy shopping area and ate at one of the buzzing street restaurants. We had 'Steak mit frits' accompanied by a nice bottle of wine. With that meal and the bratwurst and beer earlier in the day, it wasn't quite healthy eating. Never mind, plenty of cycling and walking for us to look forward to.

We had a good journey back home, chatting to a young couple on the train. They were from Leiden, in The Netherlands and were visiting relatives who lived in Winsen. Stefan was a professional golfer, hoping one day to be one of the best. He was so nice, so we hope his dream comes true. We told him that we would go and see him when he is famous and that he must remember us.

As arranged, our taxi driver was waiting at the station, ready to take us back to the campsite. Back at Belle, just in time for the match. Oh dear, not a good match for United (Barcelona 3, Manchester United 1). The thing was, the best team on the day won.

We needed to rest up the following day as we were 'citied out', which was just as well. The weather in the morning was appalling, heavy rain and overcast. By the afternoon it had picked up somewhat so we went for a walk along the banks of the Elbe. Very pretty area, lovely views along the very wide river. It was a very relaxing experience, watching working barges plying their trade up and down.

Whilst at this campsite we met a very nice retired couple from England, who were travelling through Germany to Denmark. Sheila and Robert had noticed our GB sticker, so walked over to introduce themselves and to have a chat. We were the only other Brits on site. By this time the upper half of our beloved Belle was splattered with dead flies and all other sorts of flying insects. It was difficult for me to reach the top and front of the vehicle above the windscreen. Robert had the perfect solution. He had just bought an extending arm cleaning brush, for this very purpose. He very kindly lent it to me to try out. Belle was soon looking clean and shining again. He should have been on commission. I would buy one as soon as possible.

We invited them round for a drink on our last evening. They were such a laugh and again we picked up some good tips for our future travels. They come from the Gatwick area south of London. Robert had been a submariner and they had met whilst in the navy. Sheila was an administrator. They brought their own drinks and glasses with them, saying this was the norm while motor homing. They had travelled extensively in their van. Their tours included organised convoys to Greece and Turkey, which they said were really nice, safe and hot. The lovely Sheila (not our Sat-Nav), like most ladies, was very weight conscious and so refused to eat any of our nibbles. We couldn't even entice her with our Bounty bars and Digestive biscuits. Sheila told us that she had been a very weighty lady at one time but had persevered with a healthy diet and now looked amazing. I couldn't help but tell her that I once went out with a very, very big girl and it was not till I went around her other side that I realised she was two timing me! I went on. Sometime later this same girlfriend fell ill and had to go into hospital so I went to visit her. I asked the nurse which ward she was in and she told me that she was in Ward 3, beds 5, 6 and 7! Sheila and Bob laughed at my jokes. Jackie didn't, she had heard them all before.

After breakfast, all safe and securely packed, we set off on the road again. It's all go you know this relaxing! We drove north and excitedly head for Denmark. We planned to stop just before the border for a big food shop, to stock up with supplies, as prices in the Scandinavian countries were supposed to be expensive. My spread sheet showed we were slightly better than budget at the time, so we still had a feel good factor. We filled our trolley with food and drink, as much as we dare pack Belle with and then filled up with diesel. We found the shops and supermarkets in Germany were very much like the UK, except for one very important difference the sausage aisles. The range and choice of sausages and processed meats is never ending and bewildering, if only we could read German.

Also, by this time we had also ran out of instant coffee. We found that the instant coffee we like was quite expensive and it wasn't any dearer to buy all the things to make the filter coffee. The Germans prefer to drink filtered coffee. We decided that we would buy ground coffee and filter our own, just for a change, it does taste better anyway. For this we needed to buy a plastic funnel that sits on top of the cup in which you place the paper filter and the ground coffee, then pour over the boiling water. We also decided to buy a German style hot water flask too, similar to a coffee pot with a press button water dispenser.

We left Germany having had a lovely time and looked forward to returning later in the year on the second leg of this, the first part of our European adventure.

Chapter Seven

Denmark

May 31st to June12th

Tonder - Asperup - Odense - Copenhagen

Again a similar theme to the surrounding countryside, reasonably flat with the fields well cultivated. We arrived at our next chosen campsite at Tonder, just over the Danish border. Very welcoming staff. Another well laid out campsite, all with hedged pitches, giving some privacy. We chose to stay at Tonder as it is supposed to be the oldest town in Denmark. The campsite was perfectly located, 10 minutes from the centre.

The next morning it was drizzling with rain when we went into Tonder, a small and pretty market town with just one main shopping street. Besides being the oldest town, it is also famous for its ornate entrance doors and their surrounds, all very intricate and very different. We went into the information centre to pick up the local cycle path maps as usual. It had started to rain heavily by this time, so to drown our sorrows, we bought our first real Danish Pastries and ran all the way back to Belle so that they wouldn't get wet.

When we arrived back at the campsite, who should be there, but our friends from the last campsite, Sheila and Bob. They were en route to Copenhagen so had also decided to stay at Tonder, just for one night. Needless to say we had another good evening of fun and laughter.

The following day dawned bright and beautiful, so we decided to cycle to a small village called Mogeltonder, a couple of miles away. This is where one of the Princes of Denmark lives. The Prince had apparently built the track from the town to the village so that the children could visit in safety on their bikes rather than by road.

Wow, what a little beauty it proved to be. We were delighted with our find. There were thatched cottages that were 'chocolate box' pretty and the most beautiful church, where the

Prince had married, it was all absolutely gorgeous. The large white house was of course the Prince's. Jackie pretended to be a damsel in distress at the gates in the hope that she might be asked in! It was one of those perfect days. Just how we imagined we would spend our time. I can only explain it as the feelings you get when you look in magazines and see pictures and wish that was me, well it was just like that. Blue skies, idyllic bike ride, beautiful scenery and good company.

After visiting Mogeltonder we rode to a village on the coast, famous for its 'sluice', also for seeing the visiting seals. Surprisingly too, it had a windmill! It was a working one of sorts, it housed a café. The seals, according to our guidebook, do come close to shore to fish, as this is where the salt water meets the fresh water. Sadly, the only one we could see, was made of stone sitting outside the gift shop.

Back to Belle and ready for our evening meal. With regard to sampling the local food, we had been eating (by the carton load), Kartoffel salat (potato salad, which tastes exactly the same as it does in the UK), Bratwurst sausages and the Danish Pastries. We hadn't really sampled much else that was different, so far. We tended to stick to bbq'd chicken curry, pork steaks, omelettes, and pasta dishes. I hadn't made any more soup. The supermarkets seem to sell much of the same produce as ours. They have lots of processed meats and sausages as in Germany. Surprisingly, not much fresh fish, we see more in France. What we can tell you is that in Denmark food is expensive. We were glad we had bought all the kit to make our filter coffee. The smallest jar of coffee (that we like) here worked out to £6.50 compared to £3.50 in the UK.

Whilst at this campsite we made friends with a lovely Danish couple called Rita and Bent who were parked opposite to us. They told us that it was a bank holiday on 2nd June and that many people would take at least 4 days leave from work, extending the bank holiday to the following week. As that was the day we had planned to leave Tonder and head over to Odense, they recommended a few campsites to us, so that we could pre book and reserve a pitch. Unfortunately, when we rang the campsites they were all fully booked. We had a great evening with them. It turned into a bit of a tasting session.

They gave us some of their favourite Schnapps, which they buy just over the border in Germany, as it is half the price of that in Denmark. It was very nice too. We liked the flavour. 'Taffel Akvavit' tastes of herbs, quite strong but with a nice warming feel. They sampled Amaretto and Frangelico, our favourite liqueurs. Imagine the scene, by 11.30pm we were all 'happy campers'.

We had a very memorable stay in Tonder and left there to travel north, then east through Denmark, eventually taking us to Copenhagen. We travelled through beautiful rolling green countryside and the weather was perfect, cloudless blue skies. We crossed our first big bridge which gave spectacular views all around. This bridge was toll free and took us over to the island of Funen. We managed to find a campsite with availability at a place called Asperup. The campsite was perfectly located, overlooking the sea and long narrow beach. We arrived mid-afternoon. On first impressions, the campsite did not appear to be quite as up to date as the others, however, as was the norm, the staff were more than helpful and welcoming and we were given the most perfect pitch. We had wonderful views of the sea and it was very quiet, despite being right in front of the on-site restaurant.

Shortly after our arrival we felt a little intimidated as we witnessed what we thought was the aftermath of a Viking celebration, just after a successful raid. The scene was of several drunken Vikings littering the area around the bar, close to the site office. Well, not actual Vikings, but with their flaxen hair and stocky build, you could just imagine them in Viking dress. Amazingly, by teatime, they had all disappeared and the campsite went back to quiet normality.

That evening we were given a guided tour around the campsite by one of our neighbours, a very nice Danish gentleman called Hans. He and his wife, Aase, (pronounced Oosa) spent a lot of time at the campsite with their family, mostly their little grandchildren. They had many friends there, who were also regular visitors to the campsite. Their caravans were large and had huge enclosed awnings, which added extra living/outdoor space. Hans spoke excellent English so we had many interesting conversations with him. He had worked as a butcher, but had an accident which had forced his early retirement. He sliced off part of his anatomy on the bacon slicer. Calm down ladies, just the top of one of his fingers!

During the course of one of our many lounging sessions in the hot sunshine, we thought we saw a dolphin in the sea, then it disappeared. Had we imagined it? Hans confirmed there are many 'bull nosed dolphins' around the island of Funen and this was probably what we had seen. The sunsets here were magnificent. Surprise, surprise, we never saw the sunrise, as we are not known for being up and about at dawn, even though we all know it is the best time of the day. Hans was always up with the lark. He took some lovely photos of the sunrise for us. I bet he could hear the dawn chorus, Jackie and I snoring our heads off in Belle!

Another of our neighbours introduced themselves, again a lovely Danish couple Jan and Merete, from Odense (our next port of call). Next day Merete came to us and said she would make some traditional Danish bread for us. We thought she had a bread maker with her, so thanked her for thinking of us, and looked forward to tasting the bread. A short while later we were called over to sit with them. The table was set and Merete had prepared lunch for us. We had traditional open sandwiches, which consisted of rye bread with various toppings. They were delicious. How kind and thoughtful. It was great to sample traditional Danish food, especially the smoked cheese, Rogoest – made and sold only in Funen, Also, Remoulade, very much like mayonnaise with sweet piccalilli which Merete served with cod fish dumplings, very tasty too.

Merete told us how she loved to cook and bake. After a discussion about local foods, Jan said there was a really good fishmonger's close by, who smoked and sold their own freshly caught fish. The next thing Jan and I were in his car and off to buy some smoked salmon. We had to be quick, as he was sure it was near to closing time. We were soon there and luckily they were still open. The selection of fish was extensive, and the aroma was wonderful. I bought two different types of Salmon, smoked and plain, and also one of the fish dumplings. Jackie liked them as they were something quite different.

That night I cooked the smoked Salmon on the bbq. Hans came over to advise how best to cook it. He also gave us his own recipe for Remoulade with a secret ingredient (never to be told) to accompany it. The meal was delicious.

Merete had also cooked some fish that evening. She told us that it was a delicacy and their particular favourite. She brought a couple of pieces over for us to try. It was called Ale Kvabber and had a bright green bone running through it. It looked almost like a small eel. She had prepared it by coating the fish in flour, salt and pepper and frying it in olive oil and butter on the bbq. After a deep breath (we can be a bit squeamish when tasting different fish) we took the plunge and tried it, its looks belied its taste. It was absolutely delicious.

We were by then sitting out until 10.00pm, in what could easily pass for daylight. The darkness only lasted for around six hours, lovely long sunny days. Little did we realize it would decrease to just two hours of darkness the further north we travel.

The following day, the weather remained perfect, so again we made the most of the hot sunshine. Jackie and I covered ourselves in suntan lotion, put on our swimwear (luckily, for the other campers, we were in a secluded spot) and that was it for the day, bliss. We really needed to just lie in the sun, all that sight-seeing is tiring – ha! ha!

On days such as it was, I am quite happy to just sit in the shade and read my book. However, Hans had other plans and sauntered over armed with a cold beer for us. We had a few drinks and chatted the afternoon hours away. Their son had visited them on the campsite and we saw that he drove an old American Mustang. Hans explained to me that the Danes have quite a passion for old American cars, and for that matter the rest of Scandinavia too. He told us we would likely see many stunning examples during our visit.

We decided to stay one more night as the forecast was for another hot and sunny day. Sadly, Jan and Merete had to go home as Jan was at work on Monday. What a small world, we discovered Jan is a Printer which had been my trade and works for a small company where he has a key part in the running of it. During the course of the day Hans and Aase also say goodbye, as they had to go and check up on things back home before returning to the site for the rest of the summer season. What a memorable time we had had there. Thanks go to all those kind, warm hearted and generous people.

It was only a fifty minute drive to Odense City camping – next stop on the tour. Excellent facilities here. We had again chosen a campsite based on its close proximity to the centre. Hans Christian Anderson came from Odense and there is a possibility Odin did too. We are fans of Hans Christian Anderson's wonderful fairy-tales and as children remember being told the stories by our mothers. Jackie always sang the 'Ugly Duckling' song to our children.

It was a 15 minute bus ride into the centre, 2 euros each for a return ticket, so good value. We made our way to HC Anderson's house, which is now a museum. What a quaint little cottage it is. There were a few streets with very old houses, some empty and run down. Although it was very pleasant, we were rather disappointed by the rest of Odense. It was like any other small city, lots of shops and nothing out of the ordinary. Jackie bought me a new watch I had taken a shine to whilst window shopping. The watch is a modern digital design made by "Rosendahl" here in Denmark. It was my birthday treat, ok it's not till July, but I didn't complain. We stopped for drinks and a plate of nachos between us. The little bistro was on the corner of a large square, so we watched the world go by and listened to the little fountains pouring water onto the cobbles. It cost us 25 euros but it was enjoyable. We had a photo shoot with one of the many statues of HC Anderson to add to our increasing collection in the gallery on the pc. Another good day.

The bikes came out next day. The cycle routes took us around the outskirts of Odense, passing fields full of poppies, so beautiful. We said we would stop on the way back for a photo session but ended up coming back a different route. Typical, not a poppy in site. Amazingly, what we did see were Camels. We passed by Odense Zoo. It looked a great place to visit, especially for children. We eventually ended up in Odense again, cycling in along the river. This area was all very scenic.

Back at the site, we met up with a couple called Dave and Jean, from Suffolk. They were both retired and Dave was one of those larger than life likeable characters who called a spade a spade, while Jean was the epitome of an English rose. We invited them for drinks that evening. What a small world it is - they had been with a convoy of campervans and knew Sheila and Bob who we had met up with on the campsite near Hamburg. Dave and Jean were touring for eight weeks, Denmark, Sweden and Norway. We had a fun evening with them, exchanging information and hearing about all their many tours, Morocco, Turkey, Greece, all of Europe in fact. We all sat in Belle, it had been a lovely warm day but was by then raining so heavy we thought we were in for a flood.

The following day we waved goodbye to Dave and Jean. Everyone leaves before us, are they trying to tell us something? We were in fact both setting off for Copenhagen, but on different routes and to different campsites. We hoped we would meet them again somewhere in Norway as our dates coincided.

It was a good journey across to Copenhagen. The roads and the traffic were fine and so made for easy travelling. Some of the bridges we crossed were fantastic. The toll to cross over from Funen to Copenhagen cost £42!

The campsite was again an easy commute into Copenhagen, but this time by train. In fact it was only 8km and we could have ridden in on our bikes if Jackie were more confident on the main roads. Still, we enjoy the public transport and the opportunity it gives us to see the locals as they go about their business.

That night we planned our visit into Copenhagen, armed with our Rough Guide to Europe on a Shoestring, and our Eyewitness guide. The Rough Guide is excellent as it gives you price guides and advises where to visit for free. Using a yellow highlighter, we marked the route on our street map, which we had obtained from the site reception. The homework we do pays off when we visit the city centres. We both feel that we haven't missed anything out that we wanted to see. We also have a good idea where we will eat from the recommendations in the rough guide.

Wonderful, Wonderful, Copenhagen. This will prove to be my favourite capital city (although not Jackie's) outside of London and Paris. It is a lovely place with the Tivoli Gardens, (which we didn't have time to visit), unusual coffee kiosks, the mermaid, its grand buildings and atmospheric harbour area. We walked past the Royal Palace to the botanical gardens, which are free to enter, including the magnificent orangery, then onto the fortress and to the mermaid in the harbour. She is a lovely bronze statue, but could easily be missed if it wasn't for the throngs of people taking pictures of her, especially excited little girls. There was also a beautiful domed church, more palaces and interesting old sail boats in the harbour. We eventually found ourselves in Nyhaven.

Nyhaven is a 328-yard canal lined with colourful houses, and known as the new harbour. It is lined with stylish yachts, wooden boats and amidst them is a 19th century lightship, now a restaurant. Hans Christian Anderson lived here, when the north of the canal was a notorious red light district for the visiting sailors. This is now the heart of the trendy, to be seen in area, lined with bars restaurants and crammed with people. We spent some time walking up and down trying to decide which restaurant we would like to eat in, and more importantly, a table in a position that we liked. We finally chose one and sat down for our mid-afternoon meal.

The restaurant/bar was called the 'Skipper Kroen'. It had linen set tables by the quayside and we chose the dish of the day. This comprised of six completely different traditional Danish foods, all in separate dishes but set out on one large plate. There was sliced beef, fresh horseradish and gherkins, herrings in a spicy tomato sauce, plaice in crispy batter with onion and lettuce, chicken breast with bacon and cream sauce, and cheese and beetroot. It does sound rather a lot to eat, but all were very small portions, plenty for us though. This was accompanied by a good bottle of 2009 Pinot Blanc and my beautiful wife who I am still in love with. I told you it was a good bottle of wine!

The whole ensemble and the ambiance is a must do if given the chance. Several wandering musicians entertained us and I even paid for a violinist to serenade Jackie. There was a bride and groom having pictures taken by the quayside and at one stage nearly toppled into the water while trying to strike a pose for the camera man. Now that would have been a wedding with a splash. There was an old gent dapperly dressed in linen trousers and a striped shirt on the next table, who has a trolley with a case of wine strapped to it. There was also a bevy of beautiful blondes behind Jackie all dolled up in white miniskirts. The group started off as two and multiplied to six as the meal progressed. They were having a giggle fest, but not too loud. There were also three elderly American ladies behind me, they all looked like the 'Golden Girls'. They had that lovely southern accent and talked about their purchases and their men. Magical.

Having spent a very pleasant couple of hours we moved on into the busy heart of the city. Eventually, we meandered back down to the harbour before making our way back to the train and the campsite. We were ready for a rest and sat inside Belle with a milky coffee with an amaretto chaser, plus a piece of white chocolate Toblerone for our nightcap. What a day, life doesn't get any better.

Next day it's down to reality as we paid a visit to the local McDonalds for free Wi-Fi so Jackie could post the blog. That done, we then went for a bike ride, following the earth and concrete bastion that was built around Copenhagen in the 17th century. We ended up by the sea and a not too picturesque industrial site. However, we could see in the distance the sky was almost black, it looked as if a storm was on the way. We soon turned tail and rode as quick as we could, full battery assist, no messing, to the campsite.

Whilst at the campsite we met Jeanna and Mike from Shaldon, Devon. For those of you who have never been to Shaldon, near Teignmouth, I can tell you it is one of the prettiest places. Delightful houses surround the bowling green and quaint pub. It is somewhere that Jackie and I would love to live. Jeanna and Mike were travelling on to holiday in southern Sweden, but before leaving, gave us a lot of information and advice as they had travelled all over Europe. They even persuaded us to do some 'wild camping' in Sweden, our next stop.

Jackie and I both agree that Denmark is a very interesting country and a good holiday destination for all. The people are extremely kind and welcoming too. The only downside is that prices for food and drink are slightly higher so it ran our budget close to its limit.

Chapter Eight

Sweden

June 12th to 21st

Gothenburg – Vadstena -Stockholm – Kristianhaven -Karlstad

From Denmark we crossed the 8km Oresund toll bridge (£72) into Sweden and headed directly north along the coast towards Gothenburg. This bridge is another feat of engineering as you rise into the air with ships passing far below and magnificent views. The scenery was really pretty and different, lots of pine trees, pretty little houses made of wood and what I would call Dutch Barns except that we were in Sweden. They also reminded us of some barns we had seen in Pennsylvania when we were there a few years back, visiting friends in the USA.

We headed towards Gothenburg and because of the distance involved, we looked for a place to stay and break the journey, we were in no rush. En route we stopped for a cuppa and something to eat. That's one of the great things with a motorhome, being able to pull up and make a pot of tea and some cheese on toast. We browsed through the travel books and Jackie liked the sound of a place (*not* the name) called Bastad. The book proclaimed it was very picturesque with many medieval buildings and that it was on the coast. The place was also famous for holding the annual Swedish Open Tennis tournament.

We drove though the small town and found a place, just by chance, where motorhomes and caravans were able to park overnight for free. There were already a couple of motorhomes and a caravan parked up. Great! We felt confident for our first taste of wild camping. Jackie had been especially nervous about this and I had made a conscious effort not to force the issue, it had to be both of us that felt comfortable and safe. I can't tell you how big a step this was for us, as we grew in confidence with our life as wandering stars. We had not felt that we were the complete act as we had listened to so many others who were safely wild camping and with confidence (saving loads of money too).

As it was late afternoon when we arrived we had another cuppa and a few biscuits then off for a walk to the beach and to find the medieval buildings. It was a very picturesque place. We passed by the tennis courts, all very modern. The place must have been buzzing when the tournaments were on. It had a pretty marina, some very nice yachts moored up. Couldn't see any medieval buildings? Before long we realised that the medieval buildings were made of wood and don't look particularly old or medieval. As we walked around the village, it did look different to Denmark, not quite sure how. We spotted a red squirrel, sitting on a gatepost. As we approached it ran up a tree and sat very still so we could take some lovely photos, aah, how kind of the lovely little creature, bet it was the local celebrity. We don't see many red squirrels back home.

Back to Belle - oh dear! Where had all the other vehicles gone? We were on our own, I wondered if Jackie would still go through with the wild camping. As it was such a lovely place and there were also very expensive looking houses overlooking the park, we bit the bullet and decided to stay, our first night in the 'wild'. We closed the blinds, about 11.00pm (still daylight) and read for a while, listening for rogue vehicles, wild animals etc. etc. It had just about turned dark when we heard the sound of a vehicle approaching. We looked out of the window as an old VW campervan pulled up about 10 metres away from us. We could just about make out that it was hand painted, black with a skull and crossbones staring at us from the passenger side. It looked as if it was from the set of a horror movie!

I tried to calm Jackie by saying it would probably be just a couple of kids who had parked next to *us* for safety (I hoped). We waited, watched and listened, their lights were on for a short while then they went off. All went quiet. By the way, there was a graveyard at the back of us. It was beautiful, with a memorial garden, which we had walked around earlier. We looked at each other and laughed (nervously), pulled up the duvet and went off to sleep. What a good night's sleep we had, we must have been very tired.

Next morning, just as I had imagined (and to my relief), a young couple emerged from the hippy style VW camper. It was painted in army green with brightly painted patterns and not black with the skull and crossbones we had imagined in the dead of night. They were a young German couple that smiled and waved at us before setting off, obviously they were as relieved as we were to have had company to camp with. Wild camping, yippee we had done it! Bastad, our kinda town, and one small step for man and Jackie.

We set off reasonably early for the drive to Gothenburg and arrived at the campsite just before lunch. Not a patch on the previous campsites and the standard we had become accustomed to. The staff were great, as usual, but the whole place needed some TLC. We decided to stay for just the one night and then head east across to Stockholm.

From the bus station in the centre of Gothenburg, we walked down the main street, which led down to the old town and harbour. We thought it was going to be another Copenhagen; it looked great, with trams, wonderful buildings and pretty gardens. Unfortunately, that was about the best of it. As we walked away from the main street it was all down-hill so to speak. We were really disappointed with the rest of it, just plain ordinary, except for the harbour where there was a ship museum with some interesting boats you could board and have a look around.

We did, however, have a very memorable experience here. We had our first taste of real Swedish meatballs. We came upon an almost identical Market Hall as our very own in Derby. It was oval shaped with a green painted glass and steel roof and wooden stalls. The only difference being that it was full of stalls selling thousands of different sausages, cheeses and other delicious foods. It was alive with people, sitting around the stalls on wooden bar stools eating and drinking. What a great atmosphere. The bar we chose to eat at was called 'Kages'. It was a busy U shape stall with stools all the way around the counter, decorated to an old-fashioned wooden nautical theme. In the centre were several cauldrons on a hot plate, each filled with a different type of hot food, meatballs, boiled potatoes, fish and meat stews.

The meatballs (not sure what meat exactly, could have been Elk!) were served with salad, new potatoes, Lingonberry jam and a rich gravy. We asked our server, a nice young lad, if the Lingonberries were always served with the meatballs. He said they were and that they serve them with just about everything. Very nice they were too. It was one of the most savoury and enjoyable meals we had. It wasn't just the meal, it was the whole experience, sitting at the busy stall, all the hustle and bustle about us, watching and listening to the people who frequented it. We really felt that we were capturing true Swedish life. For us, it was another of those magical moments we had dreamt of. Traditionally, they also served water with the meal, but we already had our beers by then. As we had just caught the tail end of the lunchtime rush, we sat and watched as the servers scraped and cleaned the pots, utensils and work areas in preparation for the next round.

That night we looked in our guide to "Aires in Benelux and Scandinavia" for somewhere else to stay for free for the following night. These places are where you can stay for one night, some are free without facilities, others charge a small amount for limited facilities. Jackie had now built up a little confidence and a taste for wild camping, if we were with others, well in Sweden anyway, as it felt very safe. We chose to stay at a place called Vadstena as it said in the book it was a 'motorhome friendly' town with parking in the centre by a castle and a lake.

The following day, as is the norm now; we stopped off for a cuppa half way through the journey at a place called Jonkoping, quite a large town on the southern tip of Lake Vattern. We drove around looking for somewhere to stop and oddly enough, there were quite a few other motorhomes doing the same. The only place that we could find was a car park by the lake. Not really picturesque. Jonkoping didn't look like it was a place that cried out for a visit, but maybe we just weren't in the right area.

Onwards northeast, the scenery was very beautiful, lots of lakes and pine trees, rolling hills and the roads are very good. Jackie had her eyes glued to the woods to see if she could spot an Elk! Apparently, they tend to appear at dawn to catch the early sunshine. That's it then, we won't see any, too early for us. The vast forests were fenced all along each side of the motorway and main roads to prevent the Elk crossing. Apparently, there are many accidents involving Elk that stray onto the roads, as they have no road sense and have not learnt how to press the buttons on the zebra crossings!

We arrived at Vadstena and just couldn't believe how beautiful it was, and free to boot. We would have paid double any campsite fee, just for the location and the view. We parked directly in view of the fortress surrounded by its moat and had views of Lake Vanern off to our right. The fortress was stunning. Whilst stopping on an Aire you are not supposed to put up an awning or have any tables and chairs outside. However, most people do get their chairs out for a sun bathe or to relax.

Vadstena is a very pretty place with old wooden buildings, an old train yard housing a steam train and coaches and a wonderful old Abbey, now a hotel and restaurant. We were lucky to get a place as the parking spaces were soon filled up as the day progressed. We certainly weren't surprised that we weren't on our own for long.

We, like others can spot a British number plate straight away. Also, a vehicle is noticeable because of the right hand drive. As we were the only British van in the row, an Englishman called Brian came up for a chat. He hailed from Wolverhampton and was on vacation with his son. They were staying in a hotel and were doing some kind of charity cycle ride of 300km, with some 3000 other participants from all over the world. The event was due to take place the following Saturday. They had already cycled 180km the day before and were having a day of rest. Brian had taken early retirement from the Insurance and Pension industry. It amazes me what people get up to, it's only when you get out there that you meet and realise what adventures others are having.

Up and off again, this time to Rosjobaden, north of Stockholm. The campsite was again on the edge of a lake. By now we realised that Sweden is full of lakes. This campsite needed a bit of an update too. Clean facilities, just very old fashioned. Despite this we chose to stay for two nights here, so we could visit Stockholm. We wondered if this is the general standard in Sweden as they do have very short summer seasons, which end mid-August, as the cold weather closes in. These campsites also had workers caravans on, although everyone was very friendly, so no complaints.

I will mention that the guy at reception tried to force us into buying a Camping Scandinavia Card for 14 Euros saying we could not stay unless we had one. We thought it was odd as no one else had said anything. It had its benefits by giving discounts at sites, but there was something about the way he tried to sell it to us. We were on the point of walking out when he relented and let us stay without purchasing one. Obviously, we didn't really need to have one then.

The weather had turned slightly cooler though still very pleasant. We assumed this was because we were further north and similar to the UK, one day warm and sunny, the next cloudy and cool. We caught the bus, just outside the campsite, which took us to a nearby town where we needed to take the metro to central Stockholm. We found that we could buy one ticket that can be used for travelling on the buses, trains, trams and metro, much better than buying several different tickets. Tickets need to be purchased from a shop or supermarket before you travel, as you cannot pay on the bus.

The central station at Stockholm is a very impressive building. We headed straight to the tourist information, exactly opposite the station, to pick up a map of the centre and to check out the best places to visit, not wanting to miss anything. It's always a lightening tour of the city, so we need to know where we are from the start. We were advised that we could also use our bus ticket for a free boat trip across the harbour.

Stockholm is full of very impressive buildings and is in a beautiful setting by the sea. It will prove to be one of Jackie's favourite cities. It's a big city, has a fabulous old town, Gamla

Stan, with beautiful views across the estuary and harbour. Large cruise ships, sailing ships, small pleasure boats, magnificent skyline views, it has it all. We walked down to the harbour and caught the boat across to a fortress island. The island had a pleasure park and ship museum. I managed to take a brilliant picture of the Carousel Swing ride, similar to the ones seen in photographic books. Not to brag but mine is near perfect. It's that good I can still hear the squeals of excitement every time I look at it. We had a stroll around the small island and then back over on the ferry, our tummies were rumbling by this time. Once on terra firma, it was time to look for somewhere nice to eat.

We headed back into the old town and found a restaurant serving up some very eye pleasing food. We chose 'Steak on a Plank' which looked delicious. The steak was in a sauce, surrounded by salad and piped fondant potatoes. Actually, it wasn't that good at all and was quite disappointing. Not a patch on the meatballs. Never mind, you can't win all the time. Our waitresses were very nice young ladies. We chatted to them both, one was from Estonia and the other from Russia. As we were going to visit these countries on this tour, we had a very interesting conversation with them. They were only young and enjoyed working in Sweden. The money they earned was to go towards their future when they would return to their hometowns to continue with their studies at college.

We carried on our sight-seeing, crossing bridges, through arches, across squares with colourful five storey houses, past statues and palaces, all very impressive. We finished off with a tasty treat. We couldn't resist buying a couple of coconut and chocolate covered marsh mellow sticks from a street vendor. Jackie had the white chocolate and I had the dark chocolate, both were yummy. By the time we were back on the Metro we were 'citied out' and ready for a rest. Stockholm is another fantastic capital city and we would definitely go there again.

Westwards we travelled on to Kristinehaven. This town is named after Princess Kristine and situated on, yes, another lake. We arrived too late to visit the Tourist Information, it had closed at 3.00pm. We drove through the town looking for our chosen campsite. We had a choice of two, which actually turned into three. We located the first campsite, which was run by the local council and situated by a river. We were not that impressed. It was just one long line of campers on a dirt gravel area. Thankfully, the young guy in reception, who spoke perfect English, gave us directions to another site just down the road. Unfortunately, when we arrived it was absolutely heaving with caravans and motorhomes, as far as the eye could see. We were told the reason it was so busy was that there was to be a caravan and motorhome rally that weekend. The site was very expensive and the lady at reception advised that because there would be lots of activity and noise, we might be best to move to the next campsite just down the road. Not the one we had just been to, which was a relief for us. We were both ready for a rest by now, so although we fancied looking around the show, decided to move on. We wanted some peace and quiet.

The lady kindly phoned ahead for us and confirmed that there was space. She advised that we could go and choose our spot and the owner would come and see us in the morning. It was about 10km south of Kristinehaven, still positioned lakeside. We arrived at the campsite and took a pitch near the lake in amongst the beech and pine trees, all very picturesque. Most of the campers were in caravans with awnings. They were also very plush with ultra-modern patio furniture. A guy from the caravan behind ours welcomed us. He showed us where everything was. Once again the facilities were in neat log cabins, very basic but clean.

The site had a bar and a veranda overlooking the lake. There was also a small shop. It was nearing the end of June so there was a polite notice on the door advising that they were only open in the height of the season 'July and August'. The setting was idyllic so we decided to stay for three nights to relax.

We were greeted the next day by Leonard, the site owner. He told us he was the farmer from the next village and which was named after his family. Well, when I say village, it was actually just his farm. That was all that was there. He was very laid back, spoke very little English, but had a lovely warm smile. Our lasting impression is of him with his little son beside him on the tractor and trailer cleaning up around the site. We took a day off from sight- seeing and just relaxed in the sunshine. We went for our after dinner stroll down the country paths surrounding the lake. The houses were all made of wood, most painted a red/brown colour. They were very well kept and the gardens perfectly tendered. One unusual sight was a line of around 30 post boxes of all colours, each one about a foot square, perched on top of waist high posts. They stood like sentries on the corner of a track on the roadside. The locals must have had to collect their post as the post man or woman would never have been able to get their job done if they had to wade through the woods to locate the houses nestled amongst the trees, especially in the thick snow. What a picture that must be.

That night there was a howling wind that seemed to last most of the night. We imagined the next day that the site would look like a tornado had passed through it. Amazingly, not one piece of patio furniture had moved. No awnings blown down, all was exactly as it had been. All we could think of was that the noise was the wind blowing through the tall trees surrounding us.

The next day Jackie was having a major clean up and so wanted the person who makes all the mess out of the way. I decided to go for a cycle ride into Kristinehaven. We also needed some money to pay Leonard (no such things as card machines here) and stock up on some food shopping. It was a wee bit cloudy, but still warm and sunny. My cycle ride into town took me across hills, past red, green, cream and lilac painted wooden farmsteads, all very pretty. The trees were a smattering of all sorts, with very few pines, which made for a pleasant break in the landscape. Whilst I was in the supermarket it started to rain so I decided to wait until it stopped. I only had my shorts and tee shirt on. After a short while it seemed not so heavy, so off I set back to the campsite. Half way back the rain started again, but this time, the heavens opened and I got absolutely soaked to the skin. I personally think it was all part of Jackie's clean-up operation. Not only did Belle get a good clean but I had an extra shower as well!

We packed up again and were off looking for another free parking place at Karlstad, our next stop. We went to the tourist information who directed us to a large car park just on the edge of town. It was quite a nice area, near a public park, where we could camp for free. It turned out to be by the estuary, lots of parking spaces but with only one other motorhome on it, which was from Sweden. We went over for a chat and also to ensure that the parking was free. These folk spoke a little English, and confirmed it was free and they were also staying for the night.

We spent the afternoon in Karlstad, a pleasant place with a large railway terminal, but nothing special. We returned to Belle, to find that the Swedes have gone. Must have been something we said unless we misunderstood what they had said. We'll never know. Never mind, by this time there were other motorhomes and a couple of lorries parked up for the night. So again, we felt safe. Our evening meal consisted of local fare, Bratwurst sausage and potato salad. We washed it down with red wine, then coffee and finished off with a dime bar each. Healthy eating, what's that? I down loaded a golf game on our iPad, at one of the McDonalds en route. It gave me something else to fiddle with for the evening. Jackie settled down with her book until it was time for lights out.

The next day dawned bright and sunny and so it's goodbye Sweden. We were still on target with the budget, but only just, as once again food and drink was more expensive here. We had enjoyed our stay very much. The roads had been great to travel on. The people were somewhat reserved but all very nice. We found the scenery to be very beautiful, with many lakes, but sadly, not an Elk in sight. Jackie's 'Elk Monitor' was still on nil. Time yet though, Norway or Finland would surely come up with the goods?

Chapter Nine

Norway

June 21st to July 7th

Oslo – Moss – Fredrickstad – Alesund – Trondheim – Umea (Sweden)

Westward we travelled through Sweden and in to Norway. We were really excited to see what everyone raved about. As we travelled towards the border the landscape began to change, more rugged, hilly without crops of rocks and the roads became more winding. Just over the border we were pulled over by Customs officers. We were waved into a lay-by by a group of five officials. We think they took one look at the GB sticker and thought they would find a stash of booze! We did in fact have very little as we had consumed most of our stocks. Needless to say, they just had a quick look inside Belle, all of 2 minutes and waved us on. Booze was quite expensive in Sweden – well so we thought, till we saw the price in Norway!

It was like turning a page in a book. Suddenly the landscape seemed to open up and beautiful mountains surrounded us. Our first stop was to be Oslo, where our son Howard would be joining us for a few days. Sheila also decided to abandon us as we exited a long tunnel with an intersection at the end. Of course we took the wrong direction, it's what we do best! As we drove into Oslo we noticed the gantries, which are used for automatic payment of tolls in the city, we chose to ignore them. When we were back in the UK we would receive a request to pay the tolls we had accrued, which we duly did.

Howard was due to fly into Rygge Airport, 60km south of Oslo, the following day. Rather than waste time when he arrived, we decided to have a quick reconnoitre around Oslo in the van just to familiarise ourselves with the city. We were so looking forward to seeing him and to have a catch up with how things were back home.

We found a camping stop, exclusively for motorhomes perfectly located on the Marina, just west of the centre of Oslo. The facilities were basic, but we had a prime position with a view over the harbour and bay. We could also see the Olympic ski jump 'Holmenkollen' amongst the mountains that formed our backdrop. Stunning!

Payment was made via a pay machine (10 euros per night), which at first defied logic, well mine anyway. Press green three times, now blue, now red, insert your credit card, press green again. Nothing? Start all over again. You begin to wonder if you have paid for the whole campsite. I was getting very worried about the bill. I felt like a chimp training to be an astronaut, ooh ooh ooh aah aah aah eee eee eee! In the end, two young Norwegian lads came by and hearing my curses decided to give me some assistance. Press green until you get to there on the display, now press blue....easy.... ooh ooh ooh aah aah aah eee eee eee - not for us chimps. I gave them my thanks and went home to sulk. Jackie gave me a banana.

By the end of the day the place was packed full with motorhomes of all shapes and sizes and it buzzed with people. There was lots of activity with yachts being hoisted out of the water or setting sail into the sunset, scrubbing and cleaning of hulls and the clanking of lanyards against the masts. We are about four meters off the decked wharf edge of the harbour. There were tables and benches all along which were soon occupied with campers preparing their evening meals. Despite a few clouds in the sky, it was warm and sunny. Perfect.

The following day we cycled 4km into the centre of Oslo to the Tourist Information. It looked a nice place. We didn't stop, didn't want to spoil the visit with Howard. The weather was good too, far warmer than we expected. We managed to get all the necessary information. Back at Belle, we decided to travel down to another campsite at a place called Moss, not far from the airport and so convenient for us to collect Howard the following day. On the way, we called in at one of the campsites near Oslo just in case it was a better place to stay than the Marina. Not a patch on it, so we decided to go back to the Marina with Howard for another couple of nights on our return. It really is an ideal spot if you have a motorhome.

We had a bit of difficulty finding the campsite at Moss, we ended up on a stately home estate, which included a public park. There was a small sign in the corner saying 'no camping'. We did contemplate on staying there for the night, after being told by another motorist that we would be ok. We imagined the lord of the manor looking out of his window and saying "I say m'dear, just look at those bounders in that camping car. Bloody cheek! Where's m'shotgun?" We turned Belle round and moved on.

After stopping to seek assistance as to where on earth the campsite was, we eventually arrived. Without the directions we would never have found it, it was right on the end of the peninsular. The staff were so nice and directed us to a great pitch. We had spectacular views of Oslofjorden. We could see the cruise ships passing by going to and from Oslo. We imagined all the people on deck, sipping their cocktails, whilst the beautiful vessel slipped quietly out of the Ffjord, continuing on from one beautiful port to another – just like us really, only from one campsite to another. Perhaps a lot less finesse on our part, but much more fun. Now let's not be silly, we certainly would prefer to cruise our way around Europe, if money was of no object.

Howard arrived safely and on time at the airport which was only a fifteen minute drive for us. We scooped him up and hurried back to the Marina in Oslo hoping to get another prime spot right on the wharf again, which luckily we did. Howard loved it too. We had lots to catch up on and soon we were enjoying our first meal together. Chicken curry (again!) on the bbq, which we have appropriately named 'Curry in a Hurry'. 45 minutes start to finish.

Curry in a Hurry (our own take on a curry on the road)
I use the large non-stick griddle on our Carrie Chef, which has a raised lip around the edge
Fry the sliced onions (2/3) and diced tomatoes (4/5) on the griddle in olive oil, add a few dried chillies if you like it hotter.
Add four heaped teaspoons of Pataks curry paste

When softened, add the diced chicken (3/4 breasts worth), which I fry in the centre of the griddle with 5 diced garlic cloves turning until creamy white on all sides
Stir in one plain yogurt and mix thoroughly
Cover with the lid and turn to low heat
Simmer for 20 minutes stirring from time to time
Serve with rice of your choice (We like good old 'boil in the bag' plain rice)

The thing is, the wonderful aroma attracts attention. Jokingly, I was asked if there was any to spare by a German gentleman, Gerhardt. He, and his wife Carmen, came from Bavaria. They were seated at one of the tables in front of us on the wharf. To complete the joke I took them over a little taster of the curry, it was quite hot, but they enjoyed it. Shortly afterwards, we were kindly invited to join them for a glass of Brandy. It turned out to be a great evening, full of fun. Gerhardt's was a real laugh, his favourite line was "I'm Bavarian, no one understands me!" We were all quite merry as we quietly went off to bed, it had been a long day for us all. Howard had the pleasure of being the first to sleep in the 'over the cab' accommodation, which he said was very comfortable.

The following day Gerhardt and Carmen were setting off to travel up to the Nordkapp which is the northern most point of Norway. We wished them well and hoped they would have a fabulous time which we were certain they would, they were full of fun.

Unfortunately, it was raining on and off, but the forecast was for it to eventually clear for the afternoon. Never mind, hardy Brits that we are, we were soon togged up and set off to see the sights. We walked along the sea front into the centre of Oslo, which took about 40 minutes. Despite the rain, the walk was a pleasure as we passed another couple of yachting marinas and the dock for the cruise ships. We passed through the modern office district, which had a lot of electric cars and plug in parking spaces. We continued around the new part of the harbour past the Eternal Peace Flame, which is very poignantly next to the anchor from the sunken German battleship the 'Blucher'. Over the bridge and along the wooden promenade past the many trendy restaurants and bars which were filled by young and fashionable executives, all talking business over lunches, or at least by the looks of things. Then into the old harbour with its fortress looking down from above its walls onto some very old sailing ships, contrasting with the huge cruise ships also docked there. It was a great atmosphere, lots of people posing for photos and the cacophony of noise the tourists created could be heard all around.

We left the sea front area to head for the city centre, which is a mix of new and old buildings. The centre of the city has a street, which runs up to the Royal Palace perched on a hill, surrounded by a beautiful park. After a quick visit and photo shoot at the Palace we descended back into the city and made our way to the shopping district, for a visit to the Ice Bar. The entrance fee was 20 euros each. After attiring ourselves in a thermal hooded cloak and gloves, we entered through sealed doors. You are allowed 30 minutes in the bar and get one drink of vodka or champagne cocktail, served in a block of ice. We were the only ones in the bar for the first few minutes until another family arrived and made it feel a bit more like a bar than just an ice store. Obviously, everything in the bar was made entirely of blocks of ice, the tables, seats, walls and ice sculptures. After swiftly knocking back our drink and having posed for a 'teeth chattering' few photos, we left the bar after about 20 minutes. We all found it far too cold to stay any longer.

The tourist information guy had recommended a restaurant that served traditional Norwegian food. It was a good job he gave us directions, tourists would never find it. It was in the centre but tucked away, just for the Norwegians. It felt very bohemian, being frequented by hip, arty types reading books at the tables and engrossed in heated discussions. It was called Fyet and was situated on the upper tier of a not too trendy building. The inside was more like a pub than a restaurant, festooned with all kinds of ships, clocks, horns, guns and signs. My favourite sign read 'Beer - Helping Ugly People have sex since 1862!

The menu wasn't exactly gourmet and our lovely waitress could barely translate it. Nevertheless, I chose Elkburger.

Have you ever tried to eat a burger with antlers sticking out of it? It can be tricky. Jackie chose Lofotburger which was a steak but not sure what animal, and Howard chose Skipperburger, which sounded too fishy to me. All the dishes were served with salad, no chips, so not too bad on the waist. We all enjoyed the food and the ambience of a traditional Norwegian bistro.

Which brings me to food, drink, and the price of it. Again, not much in the way of really nice places to eat, hardly any decent looking fish restaurants, not that we came across anyway. No fresh fish counters in the supermarkets and we couldn't find any fresh fish in the chilled cabinets either, or if there was any, it was so, so, expensive. £40 for a fresh salmon fillet when it was available. Beer equated to £10 per pint. Need I say more!

Well and truly fed and watered, we made our way back to the tourist information centre and bought a 24 hour travel card, mainly for the trip back in next day. It not only gives you unlimited travel, it also allows you entry into most of the museums for free, so to speak. Jackie and I don't normally go in museums as it takes so much time up but Howard particularly wanted to go to the Munch Museum to see the artwork by Edvard Munch, including one of his most famous, 'The Scream'. Also on Howards list of places to visit were the Olympic Ski jump, Holmenkollen and last but not least, the Viking Museum, which houses several original Viking ships, unearthed in near perfect condition, including fantastic carved wagons, tools, etc. All that to look forward to the next day and very excited we were with the prospect too.

The Munch Museum proved to be a real win for us all. It was extremely interesting. Munch was a very disturbed person, which came across in his paintings. On his death he left his entire collection to the people of Oslo. It was an extensive collection and looked like it contained all of his works. This made me wonder that no one wanted to buy them during his lifetime, which is usually the case. I took a great shot of Howard standing next to the ghoulish character on the canvas with his very own imitation of 'The Scream'. After making a couple of purchases from the museum shop, we made our way outside. It was a gloriously hot day and so we munched our packed lunch in the grounds of the Munch museum which was very pleasant and peaceful, except for the sound of our munching. I wondered if other people munch their lunch at the Munch museum?

Our next port of call was Holmenkollen. To reach this amazing structure, we took the very modern, clean and comfortable tram up the steep summit. During our ascent the tram took us through some of the lovely suburbs of Oslo. This is just what we like to see. Away from the tourist areas we get a real insight as to how the Norwegians live. After leaving the tram we still had to walk up a really steep road to reach the entrance to the ski jump. The ski jump itself is awe-inspiring. Even with TV footage of ski jumping and despite seeing so many photographs of these structures, it still takes some believing when you see the descent and the jump these skiers have to undertake. How anyone can go down the ski run is unbelievable. Brave is certainly the word. There is also a museum area where there are sets of ski's hanging on the walls all belonging to famous skiers from way back when. There were models of other ski slopes depicting the history of ski jumping and how it came to be. Jackie and I have never been skiing, but it is something we would like to try before our knees give way. No ski jumping here though, our knees were shaking just walking up the steps and holding tightly on to the handrails. The views from the top of the ski jump were fantastic, we could see for miles and even spotted Belle in the marina 10kms away.

Hooray! It was here that Jackie spotted her first Elk, stuffed of course! It was a huge great thing, as was the Polar Bear on the next display. Needless to say due to its size, Jackie's not so hell bent on seeing Elk loitering along the roads.

Our final visit of the day was the Viking museum. We had to catch the tram, metro and bus back across Oslo to get to it and time was quickly running out. We managed to get there with just half an hour to have a look round. Again, it was well worth the visit. The long boats were so well preserved and the carvings were very impressive. We were amazed at how open and small they were compared to modern day vessels which sail the high seas. It is remarkable to think how they lived and how far they had travelled in them. Even the burial chambers were intact. It certainly gave us a feel for that era.

Once again we said our fond farewells to Oslo and headed back south towards Moss and Rygge airport. We chose to stop en route at a campsite near a place called Fredrickstad, famous for its old fortified town. On arrival at the campsite, we picked up three identical maps of the local area, one for each of us so we don't get lost. We settled in and had a relaxing evening around Belle. It had been full on up to now so we all wanted to chill out and reflect on our time spent in Oslo.

We woke the following day to blue skies and hot sunshine. After breakfast we set off in search of the old fortress, just a short walk from the campsite. Well it would have been if just one of us had taken the trouble to look at the map properly. Each thinking the other had, we turned the wrong way down the road, went over a huge bridge, no one else in sight. How famous was this place? Ha! Ha! As we looked from the bridge there it was, way behind us, in the direction from which we had just come. Having got that far we decided to carry on into the centre of Fredrickstad, which was now closer than the Old Fortress.

New Fredrickstad was a typical looking town, but with a river running through, lined on one side with busy bars and restaurants. We could see that there was a little ferry going from port to port, so after a beer we hopped onto it. The round trip eventually took us back to the old town and fortress, where we intended to be in the first place. All things happen for a reason. If we had read the map correctly we would never have visited the new town or caught the little ferry and it would have been a shame to have missed it, it was really quite enjoyable. What a pretty little place the Fortress is, with its stone based wooden buildings, brick built barracks all surrounded by earth works and cannons. It was Sunday so all the little shops were closed but it was still well worth a visit. We walked back to Belle, which took us all of 10 minutes.

We decided that for Howard's last night with us we would return to the campsite at Moss. Our last meal was 'an all-day breakfast' and Champagne. We had saved the Champagne that Howard gave us when we left England to have with a nice meal. We didn't think it would accompany eggs, bacon, beans, Norwegian sausage and mushrooms, but it was great. Who needs smoked salmon and caviar anyway?

We had all really enjoyed our first experiences of Norway. The following day Jackie and I said goodbye to Howard as we dropped him off at the airport mid-morning. We then headed northeast making our way over towards Bergen.

It was good weather to begin with but soon it turned to rain the further northeast we drove. We chose to take the tourist route over to Bergen, rather than the motorway. Unexpectedly, the traffic was very heavy. The lorries were nearly all double trailer type, so very long and which shook us up when they drove past. This experience was not as we imagined. We thought there would not be much in the way of traffic at all, if you believe the travel books. The roads were winding and very narrow too, ideal for a James Bond car chase but not really a right hand drive motorhome. To add to this, it began to really pour with rain making visibility difficult. We somehow managed to clip wing mirrors with a lorry at one stage; it was that narrow in places along the cliff edge road. Luckily, we were on the inside of the road, but even then it was frightening. This all added to our journey time too, taking a lot longer than normal to cover a short distance, and a lot more tiring. The bonus was the scenery, which was absolutely stunning. Sadly, there were not many places to stop and take photos or even to sit and take in the magnificent views.

We hadn't planned ahead and chose a campsite for that evening, we just thought we would take it as it comes. We came upon a campsite in a very picturesque setting by a lake. You could also hire pretty little log cabins here. When we arrived there were no other campers or anyone in sight, except for one lady cleaning the loos. It was self-service check in. We had to fill a form with all our details at a small kiosk, pens were provided and there was a phone on the wall to call the manager if any problems occurred. We put the overnight fee in the envelope and placed it in the box as requested. Hey presto! How trusting were these people. Good clean facilities too. It was not long before we were joined by a few other campers and people renting the cabins. Unfortunately, it was still raining. The mist was on the tops of the mountains and rising off the lake. It looked quite eerie at times.

The following day and back on the road, we were getting more and more excited. We were not too far from Bergen. Well about 200 miles! Again we chose the tourist route. Wow! We were soon climbing up the roads and on the tops of the mountains. We were so high we had snow by the side of the road, waterfalls were gushing everywhere, some were that close they were splashing onto the road. Again and sadly for us, it was also very scary in places with our van and the passing lorries. It was also raining heavily again, adding to the hazardous conditions. The roads just got worse, narrow, winding, steep and by the edge of the fjords. It was really breathtakingly beautiful scenery, when Jackie could look at it.

We crossed our first fjord on a small ferry; this was to be one of eight we would eventually tot up on our journey through Norway. It was a great experience for us, which would have been a fabulous sight, if we had a clear blue sky. What a shame, it was grey and overcast which limited our view.

Thankfully, we arrived safe and sound in Bergen. Our chosen camping place (another Aire/Bobil Park) turned out to be a 'no go' for us. We had hoped it would be similar to Oslo marina. How wrong could we be? It was just under a bridge which crossed the estuary, some of the surrounding buildings were derelict and there was graffiti everywhere. Won't go on. We drove in and out as quickly as we could, and were soon on our way to another site from our ACSI book. We arrived within half an hour, settled and satisfied that we had a nice place to stay for a couple of nights. After another long day driving, it was a quick meal then lights out.

The bus stop was just outside the campsite and it was only half an hour into the centre of Bergen. As we imagined there was a cruise ship in the harbour, so lots of tourists buying souvenirs at the many stalls on the wharf. There was also a good selection of foods being sold at the sit down eateries. There was an atmosphere here, with its hustle and bustle. We stopped for a beer at one of the many outside bars along the harbour. The weather was warm, but cloudy and the price of a beer still made us wince. The Bryggen, (old port) was as picturesque and as lively as the tourist books had portrayed. The rest was pleasant, but sadly there was a lot of graffiti and we think it did spoil the feel of a place.

Again, we thought we would try to find a place to sample some more Norwegian food. It seems wherever you go these days you can always get Italian or a McDonald's, which are everywhere. Eventually we found a restaurant that had picture window views of the harbour. It was up a set of stairs and all a bit 'burgundy velvet' and old fashioned. Still, it was busy so we thought it must be ok. It looked as if it was mainly frequented by the very young or very old, so it had to be a bit of a bargain place to eat. We chose the dish of the day, which was called Raspeballer. Everyone seemed to have a plateful, obviously the local delicacy. When it arrived, it looked very inedible. We did eat it, but it tasted very strange. It consisted of, boiled lamb, a portion of smoked sausage, mashed swede and potato dumplings. It was an experience that, once done, was not to be repeated. Still there was a nice local ambience to the place and we felt we had truly tasted another variety of Norwegian fare. Sorry to say, but in our opinion, Bergen was just a tad disappointing.

Next day, we decided to take a day of rest, not just because of the potato dumplings, which are our laugh topic of the day, but because the weather was atrocious, so we stayed in Belle, brought the Wi-Fi from the campsite and caught up on emails, the blog and read our books. We did get out when the rain eventually stopped and had a little walk, which took us to a lake and along some tracks that surrounded the campsite. That evening, we planned our journey further north, hoping for a better drive and to see the fjords in the sunshine. We were experiencing 20 hours of daylight. Thankfully Belle is very 'light tight' so once the blinds were drawn, we were still able to get a good night's sleep.

We woke up to bright sunshine, which always adds a new dimension to scenery. We decided that after the rather hairy scary journey to Bergen we would take the main route north on the E39, all the way up to Trondheim. It was still just a two-way road, no dual carriageways, but at least a bit wider. However, we would need to stop again en route as Trondheim is some 300 miles northeast. We were so looking forward to seeing Sognafjord, which we knew we would have to cross on the ferry. It is one of the largest and most famous of the Fjords. We eventually arrived at Oppedal for the ferry to Lavik. It was a 10-minute crossing and cost us £10, well worth it though. It was so beautiful, a wondrous sight, just as we had imagined it. The sun was still shining too.

Some miles on, we found a gorgeous little campsite. It was by a gushing river, which to say was raging is an under-statement. It roared through the valley, sounding like thunder, very dramatic. We wondered how we would sleep. The reception and facilities were in log cabins, so quaint and immacu-lately clean. We were immediately called upon by a couple of passing Norwegians who were curious about Belle, not having seen this model of motorhome. Shortly after, another young man stopped for a chat as he was passing, en route to the showers as he had just run a marathon somewhere in the ar-ea. He was so nice and could speak perfect English as he had an aunt who lived in Windsor, near London and who he visited regularly. He kindly gave us directions to a viewpoint so that we could get one of the best views of the Fjords. We hoped to take a look the following day. It was a shame we only had the night there, but we had a busy schedule ahead. Needs must!

Fortunately, the gushing river didn't keep us awake, so next morning we are up bright and breezy ready for the jour-ney to Alesund. Oh dear, the weather had changed again. This time though the clouds were nearly touching the top of Belle and the mist hung just above the water. It was such a sight to see, it was as you would imagine the view described in a fantasy novel. The whole area looked magical. Unfortunate-ly, we would not make the detour to the view that our sporty neighbour recommended, as we doubted very much that there would have been one. Even though we were on the E39 the road still ran alongside the Fjords and we still had very dramatic scenery. At one stage we were halted by a group of mountain goats, which had descended from the hillside and blocked the road. After much hooting and honking from all the other vehicles, a baa here, and a baa there and a tinkling of mountain bells, we managed to get through. If they had had a banner 'Freedom for Goats' I would of thought they were on a protest march, they were that stubborn.

We crossed another two Fjords to get to our next port of call, Alesund which is a large town. Luckily, there was a 'Bobil Park', which we had found in our 'Aires in Benelux and Scandinavia' book. Bobil Parks are another form of allegedly cheap stop over's for motorhomes, run by the local council to attract visitors. We were able to stay overnight, along with many other motorhomes, just passing through, at a cost of £20 for the night. The facilities were very limited and basic and not really that clean. We arrived mid-afternoon and were able to park in front of the sea wall and watch the ferries. Alesund is a very busy port, taking tourists to the Fjords. We were only a short walk from the centre, so, after a quick coffee, we set off to explore the town. As with many other Norwegian towns (and Swedish) they were devastated by fires and had to be rebuilt. Someone should tell them not to build them from wood.

Alesund was slightly different, as it was rebuilt using money donated from all over Europe. The architects from each country added their own touch to the Art Nouveau style chosen to rebuild in. Some of the buildings were very beautiful and the harbour area still had a few of the original wooden buildings. Not a lot to see really, but we thought it was quite a nice town.

We set off bright and early next day for our journey towards Molde. Again, we had to take a couple more ferries and drive through lots of tunnels. Tunnels are fine for us, we (well Jackie) would sooner go through a tunnel than up, over or drive on the edge of the mountain. Getting on and off the ferries were old hat by now. What was at first, an amazing experience, it soon got to be the norm. Still we loved every minute of it.

From Molde we deviated to take the road to Kristiansund, route 64, otherwise known as the 'Atlantic Highway'. This is where low bridges and an underwater road tunnel connect small islands and skerries. The highway opened in 2009. It was very picturesque with views of the open sea. Such different scenery. There were many small, relatively flat rocky islands, most having a house and small motorboat moored alongside. The way in which the highway had been promoted, we thought it would go on for miles, but no, no sooner had we gone over the first bridge, than we had driven through. We had to turn around and go back to take some photo's. It was disappointing for us in its briefness. Oh, and the tunnel toll is eye watering as well at £25, although another brilliant feat of engineering.

We picked up the E39 again and drove on to our next site for the night, also chosen at random on the way. It was a strange little campsite, there were lots of caravans and instead of the usual awning as an extension, and they all had wooden huts attached to them. Once again the site was by a beautiful lake and the views were lovely. All the pitches had a decking area, pity the weather wasn't nice enough to sit out for the evening. It had turned a bit chilly too, but we did expect it, we were quite a way up the west coast of Norway.

Our final stop was Trondheim. We found another Bobil Park for Belle for the night, this time it was free. It took some finding though. The site had moved slightly from the description in the travel book, luckily the photograph gave us a hint. It was eagle eye Jackie who spotted our fellow campers in the distance. We were getting quite good at finding things, there is a knack to it like everything, easy when you know how. The site was basically a car park next to a recreation ground on the edge of a huge retail park. According to the travel guide we were using, the site was about thirty minutes' walk from the centre of Trondheim. We felt safe as we parked up alongside several other motorhomes. We had arrived early afternoon and so as it was a lovely hot day we decided to walk into the centre. We walked through the nearby Botanical Gardens, and spotted a bus stop. It was so hot by then, we chose to hop on the next bus going into Trondheim.

We loved the place. For us, there was much more to see and do than in Bergen. The old port is very picturesque and the atmosphere was great. Bars, cafes and restaurants, a real young feel to the place. We spent a pleasurable few hours walking around the streets with their mixture of stone and wooden buildings and along the river around the city. The view down the river is archetypal Norway, lined with the multi coloured wooden warehouses on stilts that have now been renovated and converted into trendy apartments and restaurants. We found a small quirky bistro called 'Bakelandet Skysstation', which was a lovely wooden terraced building in the old part of Trondheim. We had the most superb meal, fresh Salmon, can you believe it? Our last meal in Norway, and it was the best. Although the interior was an absolute delight, we chose to eat outside and people watch as everyone went about their busy lives.

Trondheim had a beating heart that seemed to be absent in a lot of the places we visited in Norway. Quite often as we travelled along, we wanted to stop and have a coffee or a beer as we passed through a pretty Norwegian village, but sadly, we found that most of the villages were a collection of houses spread over a hillside.

All in all, we were ready to say goodbye to Norway. The Elk monitor was still on nil, you really can't count stuffed ones! We both agreed that scenically, it is an absolutely fabulous country and we did like the people. The roads were a bit torturous at times and in places not well maintained. We enjoyed our Motorhoming adventure in Norway without a doubt, but for us, and if we are ever fortunate enough to go again, I think we will float our way around the Fjords on a cruise ship.

We had thought about going all the way up to the Nordkapp, just to say we had done it, but our costs were running at such a rate. We had well and truly bust our budget due to the ferries (which I had not allowed for), the price of food and drink as well as the price diesel which was 1.69ltr euro compared to 1.40ltr euro in the UK at the time. We decided to cut our losses and run for the Swedish border before we died from the lack of alcohol. Once in Sweden we would make our way eastwards for the port of Umea where we would catch a ferry to Finland.

We were so looking forward to going back into Sweden and of course excited at the prospect that we would soon be in Finland. What a change, the roads were so straight, much wider, very little traffic and much flatter terrain. Pine trees as far as the eye could see with rocky outcrops and painted wooden houses dotted here and there. Lots of ski slopes. We passed some of Sweden's best, 'Are' being one of them. It was blue skies and very warm again. There was mile after mile of truly tranquil and beautiful countryside all around us. The pretty river valleys here are a haven for Anglers, they were everywhere, knee deep in the gushing rivers.

We knew we would have to have an overnight stop en route, so chose a halfway point on the E14 near Ostersund. This turned out to be another free car park/motorhome stop, just alongside a lake at a place called Krokum. The facilities were excellent and there was a lovely little café and Tourist Information Centre on the site. Although the parking area was at the side of the busy E road, we had neighbours in another motorhome so felt quite safe.

We had only been there a few minutes when a young Russian couple on a motorbike pulled up and asked if they could use the seating area near to where we had parked, so they could have their lunch. Of course, it was no problem for us. We had our chairs tucked away in Belle if we needed to use them. We chatted for quite a while to Polina and Dimitre. They were travelling to Norway on their motorbike, camping along the way and planned to meet friends in Bergen and generally have a real good time. They gave us lots of information about Russia and St Petersburg, which we very much appreciated. They sat and ate their lunch overlooking the lake. It wasn't long before they were back in their leathers, waving to us as they roared off down the road. How nice they were. We hoped they had a safe journey and a wonderful time in Norway.

We had an excellent journey to Umea the next day. What a surprise too, we crossed the border into Lapland, the Swedish part of course. Sadly, not the 'Lapland' where Santa lives, as we all know, that Lapland is in Finland. I once went to Finland with my job, to visit a paper mill near the Russian border. During the visit and in conversation, our guide said that he had been to Lapland. He said it was a very peaceful and quiet place. I said "How can that be?" He said, "What do you mean?" I said, "Well, with all that banging and clanking going on?" He looked puzzled "There is no noise?" I said "What about Santa's little helpers building all the toys for Christmas, they must make a right racket?" He understood what I meant and we all had a good laugh.

No sooner were we in Lapland we were out, as we were heading east to Umea, rather than north. We arrived at the port, expecting to be able to book the ferry there. We had previously enquired as to the cost and had been advised to book nearer the time. As there was no one in sight and the ferry terminal buildings were all closed, we gave the ferry company another call. Thankfully, we were soon booked on the 8.00am ferry the following day. We decided to stay at the port along with a few other motorhomes as we needed to be up at the crack of dawn and the campsite was a way back down the road close to Umea. It appeared you had to pay to stay in the car park near the ferry terminal, but the machine was not working, so we were lucky to get another freebie.

Shortly after we arrived, we met a lovely couple from Dusseldorf. They had understood from an itinerary they had, that there was a ferry at 10pm. Unfortunately, it was not the case. It must have been a misprint, and so they had to wait with us until the following morning. They weren't able to make a reservation as by now the phone lines were closed, so they just hoped that there would be room for one more vehicle on the ferry. Soon we were chatting and having a lovely time over drinks in Belle. Gerhardt and Monika, had travelled through Norway and were going over to Finland to stay with friends. We had lots of things to talk about and shared experiences we had had so far. They also recommended that we should try

Rumtopft, which is a traditional drink that they make and enjoy especially at Christmas.

During the course of the evening, Gerhardt and I took a short stroll around the port and inspected some giant concrete constructions that were standing on the dockside. They were of German manufacture and we soon realised they were the giant stems that wind turbines sit on, that now cover our landscapes. Quite an interesting sight to see.

Thankfully, Gerhardt and Monika managed to secure their place on the ferry the next morning. We sat together for the entire journey. It was a lovely warm sunny day, but there was nowhere to sit on the deck so we sat inside, chatting ten to the dozen. The ferry wasn't anything like the luxurious Brittany Ferries we are used to, it was more like a 'truckers' ferry. Not that we were complaining, it was a very smooth crossing and only took 4 hours.

Now they do say 'don't mention the war', but Gerhardt brought it up several times as we covered many topics. It was very interesting as we moved from century to century, talking about history. He was reading a book that alleged Shakespeare had not written any of his plays, but that some prince or other had written them. Could it be true? Jackie and Monika chatted about fashion. Monika had her own business making bespoke garments from her own hand woven wool and mohair, very clever lady. Once on Finnish soil, we swapped contact details and said goodbye to Gerhardt and Monika. We hope one day to visit Dusseldorf and accept their kind invitation to call in for a glass of Rumtopft!

Chapter Ten

Finland

July 8th to 27th

Kristinestad –Pori – Rauma – Turku – Helsinki – Kotka - Porvoo

We arrived at Vassa in Finland having had a good crossing on the Ferry. The sea was like a millpond and we enjoyed almost clear blue skies. We planned to head south and follow the coast all the way to the Russian border. The names of the towns and cities were in both Swedish and Finnish. It was near on impossible for us to pronounce some of them. Sheila added her own usual Aussie lilt to them of course.

Because of the linked history of Norway, Sweden, Russia and Finland, their languages have many similarities, a bit like some of our frequently used words in French and German. This was so different and to be honest, we really struggled in all the Scandinavian countries, but perhaps more so in Finland. It's amazing though how you get by with sign language and pointing.

Our first port of call was Kristiinankaupunki (told you they were difficult to pronounce!) or as it is known in Sweden, Kristinestad. As we drove along the coast road the first thing we noticed was how flat it was. You could have mistaken it for Holland, except the trees and buildings were different. The roads were very good and our satnav "Sheila" did a great job, not so much finding places but getting us out of the towns and on the right road, saving us so much time. Sometimes we would go around the houses, but it's a small price to pay for an easy exit. Gone are the days when you go round the same roundabout or street three times.

The campsite we found was excellent. If you think there are many lakes in the other counties, I can tell you that Finland wins the prize, it's full of them. The weather was great and we camped just by a small beach, on the outskirts of Kristiinankaupunki. Haven't we been here before? I think Kristine must have got about a bit! The lake was so calm, it was like looking at a giant mirror. It was great to see the children playing in the lovely soft sand. We felt as though we were finally on our holidays. Everyone was so friendly too, giving us broad smiles and nods as they passed our van. Not sure if we were a novelty as we hadn't seen any other English motorhomes since arriving in Finland.

The campsite was so nice that we decided to stay for a few days. We had also accumulated a huge pile of washing (again) and Belle was really in need of a good clean, inside and out.

We set to next day and managed to get everything done by the afternoon. One thing we were looking forward to was to get back on the bikes. As we weren't too far out of Kristiinankaupunki, we cycled into the centre and had a little look round. It was set on another lake with pretty spouting fountains in the centre. We passed an old windmill and we could tell that it was all very old and quaint. Most of the old buildings were wooden in structure and lined narrow cobbled streets, but again it was all quite a different feel than Sweden and Norway.

On the way back I decided to explore a little further as Jackie went back to the campsite. I carried on past the site and cycled down a wooded path with huge grey boulders strewn about the forest floor, moss and fern and sunrays passing through the trees. I felt like I was in a forest from one of my fantasy novels and expected Elves to appear any minute. It was magical. I came upon a restaurant overlooking a smaller lake. This would be the perfect setting for our evening meal that day, so I went in to try and book a table. As I went through the door, I could see that there was a party in full swing, celebrating an elderly couples wedding anniversary, they were all dressed up in their best clothes. The elderly couple, who looked in their late eighties, were dressed in traditional Finnish costumes. The lady wore a dress with a white lace collar and her husband wore a short jacket and tight pantaloons. They were not disturbed at all by my presence, and invited me to have a drink, I declined of course, as I was in my cycling gear. Unfortunately, the proprietor told me that they wouldn't be able to serve us until around 9.30pm, which was far too late for us. I duly thanked him and declined the offer. As I rode back to the campsite I couldn't help thinking, "how nice was that?"

That evening we met a gentleman and his daughter who were camping opposite in a caravan. Their names were Jouni and Charlotte. Jouni was a Lutheran Minister and Charlotte a pretty, well-travelled young lady. His wife was attending a choir festival in Vassa for the weekend, so they had taken the opportunity to do a bit of sight-seeing. We had a good evening chatting and food tasting with them. Jouni and Charlotte sampled a couple of cheeses we had bought in Sweden. The cheeses were recommended by two ladies who were shopping in the supermarket. As we hadn't a clue what we were buying, we asked them to recommend a strong, traditional Swedish cheese for us. After some debate and some fun and laughter, which of course we didn't understand, they settled on two varieties. We bought both types and they proved to be very tasty and as strong as our English Mature Cheddar.

Anyway, back with Jouni and Charlotte. We sampled their unleavened rye bread, a speciality of the region, delicious it was too. During the evening we found out that Jouni was suffering from Leukaemia and was currently undergoing treatment. He was a very positive man with strong beliefs. We were deeply saddened to hear that he was so ill, he had such a pleasant way with him. Charlotte was a very interesting person too, not quite sure what she wanted to do with her life, like most young people. She was for the moment, enjoying spending quality time with her father.

This was the first night we were attacked by mosquitoes. They appeared to affect us more than Jouni and Charlotte, who just took them in their stride. We soon had our repellents out and were spraying every part of our exposed bodies. They watched us with some amusement as we were continually swatting at the little blighters. It was gone twelve and still quite light by the time we decided to call it a day. As you will have gathered, their English was excellent.

Next day we said our goodbyes. It was then that we first spoke about religion. As Jouni shook my hand firmly he said that whilst on our travels I would find the Bible a good read. Reading books had been one of the topics of the previous night's conversation. Jackie and I expressed our good wishes and sincerely hoped that Jouni would make a full recovery. He looked me in the eye and said, "It's in God's hands, I am at peace whatever happens". For some unknown reason this statement brought to mind one of the lines from a favourite song of ours "Take a chance and enjoy the play God wrote for you". Which I think is exactly what Jackie and I are doing.

We travelled south to Pori, hoping to stay on a nearby campsite Jouni had recommended to us, at Yyteri. We arrived at Pori, to find a jazz/music festival in full swing. Apparently, this was a world famous event, with artists like Sting and Joe Cocker having performed there in previous years. Pori was situated on a river and the festival ran all along the riverside. Crowds of people wandered among the many craft and food stalls. There were stages set up for the artists to perform on, it was quite a fun atmosphere.

Apparently the main festival was being held on the opposite side of the river to where we were. We could see a fenced area and a large stage set up. We sat and listened to a couple of songs that a local group performed with a very nice young Finnish singer. It was the sort of jazz we like, it had a tune to it. We didn't stay long in Pori as we weren't sure that where we had parked was ok, so we were soon heading out of town towards the campsite. At one point Sheila took me down a one-way street the wrong way. I had to back up in the face of oncoming traffic, the Finns took it all in good humour, even if I did cause a traffic jam for a while. It was a bit embarrassing but how was Sheila to know it had recently been changed.

Unfortunately, when we arrived at the campsite, we weren't able to get in as there had been a volleyball tournament on the beach and they weren't taking bookings until later that evening. We didn't want to hang around so continued on to Rauma, a few miles south of Yyteri.

We were shown around the campsite in a golf buggy and were lucky enough to bag a spot on the beachfront overlooking the sea. The campsite had two sauna facilities, one mixed and one men only. These were immediately pointed out to us, as they are a 'must have' in Finland. Once again, we were plagued by mosquitoes, our sprays and citrus candles did give some protection, but still some of the little devils managed to get a meal.

The water in the bay was very warm and the children splashed about having tremendous fun. There were lots of people swimming and sunbathers packed the beach. It had a real holiday resort feel to it.

As ever, we were content to sit and watch the world go by. We couldn't help but notice a little boy, about seven years old, who must have ran past us at least four times, each time going at break neck speed, right around the bay. I can remember when I used to run places. I used to count the lampposts I passed to see how far I could run before having to stop for a break. I found myself thinking, wouldn't it be funny if, as adults, we continued to run everywhere, just like little children. It would be carnage in the shopping centres! Anyway, this little chap was none stop and just kept going, we found it tiring just watching him.

What a little gem of a place old Rauma is, it reminded us of the set from the film Dr. Zchivago. We had never seen buildings like them before. We thought it had a touch of charm and magic all of its own. All you needed was a good layer of snow and a few horse drawn sleighs and you would have been back in 1917.

The old town is famous for its lace making. There is about one square mile of old wooden buildings, mostly single storey, with very elaborately carved windows, facades and door surrounds. They were all painted in bright or pastel colours, usually two-tone. Quite a few of them are shops and restaurants now but many are still family homes. The town square had a rather imposing pastel yellow town hall. The whole place was a delight. We even saw a red squirrel sauntering along a side street, quite unperturbed by our proximity to it.

We chose to eat at a restaurant called "Rosemariini". It had a lovely little courtyard area at the back with comfortable and trendy rattan furniture. The red brick walls surrounded the pale blue and white wooden building. To our amazement, our waitress, Anna, spoke perfect English, so much so that we could only just hear a slight Finnish accent. We chatted to her and she told us that it was her father's restaurant. She and her partner (a Scotsman she had met in England) had just come back to her hometown of Rauma after having lived and worked in Lincoln for ten years. They made the decision to move to Finland to settle down and have a family so had returned to Rauma to give it a go. Anna's father also had a building business and so her partner had no problem finding work. Anna was keen to know if we liked Finland. We said we thought it was a wonderful country apart from the mozzies. She gave us the name of a repellent called 'OFF' that was very reasonably priced and available all over Finland. On our way back to the campsite, we went into the supermarket and bought a couple of the small spray cans. We were ready to try anything!

We had a great excuse to go back to Rauma the following day, we'd forgot to take the camera with us. There was no way Jackie was going to leave without getting some shots of such a beautiful place.

Back at the campsite we relaxed in the warm sunshine that lasted late into the evening. The Finns do need to make the most of the daylight and from what we could see they certainly did, the beach was still buzzing at 11.00pm.

Our next stop was Turku, once the capital of Finland. We pitched up at a campsite just outside, which meant another bus trip into the centre. Not a problem for us, we enjoy these little excursions and for me, it's good not to have to get behind a wheel. Whilst travelling, I do prefer to drive and Jackie is quite content to sit and navigate most of the time. Jackie is happier to take Belle along the straight quiet roads.

Whilst on the bus to Turku, we could hear some French conversation. There were a couple of people seated just a few rows up from us. I say hear, because we couldn't understand most of it and it seemed not quite the same French that we were used to hearing. When we got off the bus, the gentleman and his wife spoke to us in English, with a French accent. They introduced themselves to us as Clarence and Lise. They were actually from Montreal in Canada, and so were French

Canadian, that explained their accent. We thought we were brave touring Europe in a Motorhome, they were cycling around it. They had travelled to Finland through France, Germany, Poland, Lithuania, Latvia and Estonia, across on the Ferry to Finland, then continuing their journey to Sweden and Norway before going back to Canada. All that way on bikes, not electric either. They were staying in one of the chalets on our campsite. Unfortunately, they were leaving early next morning to get the ferry to Sweden, so we didn't see them again, which is a shame, they were great fun and so interesting. We had such a laugh in the short time (an hour) that we stood in the market square chatting.

Turku was heavily bombed during the war by the Russians, so the centre was the usual, four to six storey concrete buildings and not that pleasing to the eye. It started to rain heavily (but it was still very warm) so we made our way to the river hoping to find Finland's oldest restaurant, 'Pinella'. We had seen it in one of the tourist guides and thought we would stop for a coffee and cake. It said it had recently been renovated and so was worth a visit. We had no trouble finding it as it was just across the river from the main city area. It looked lovely and it certainly was. Inside it had a long narrow interior, all the tables were occupied. One wall was bare rock, jutting out at all angles, no health and safety regulations here. It had that ambience about it that made you want to stay, and the food looked good to. Luckily, we were able to get a table outside under the covered terrace. We looked at the menu and at what people were eating and decided to have one of the starters each, instead of cake. Jackie chose the battered squid rings and mayo, and I chose the mini kebabs with fresh tatziki. Not only did it look good it was delicious. What really made it for us, was the bottle of 2010 Chablis, Moreau & Fils, it was nectar, if a touch expensive here.

Well, one thing led to another. After finishing our starter, we looked through the window and saw the steak being served to one of the other diners. It looked tantalisingly good, so our light snack turned into a full blown meal with desserts and coffee. We whiled away the whole afternoon and managed to down another bottle of the Chablis. What better to do when it's raining cats and dogs. Another win was that the restaurant was situated in the old quarter, which we may well have missed, as it wasn't actually in the centre. The rain abated, so we took time to explore the area after our meal.

Next day we walked a mile or so from the campsite and came across a small marina by a bay. We sat in the sun and watched as the boat owners prepared their yachts for sailing. There is something about water and boats that we both find very relaxing. Finland is indeed very pretty with lots of lakes and therefore marinas abound, there seems to be one round every corner. We were slowly falling in love with it all.

Next stop for us was Helsinki. The following day dawned warm and sunny. We drove southeast from Turku to our next campsite, again, just outside the city, but this time a metro ride away. Low hedging made for more privacy and surrounded each relatively small pitch. It was a large modern site and it was full to capacity. The metro station was a convenient five minute walk from the campsite. We bought 48hr travel passes as we also planned to go in the following day, as it was my birthday. We were soon in the centre, which has a great feel to it. Nice harbour, lovely wide tree lined avenues. There were lots of statues and fountains, wonderful architecture and busy café culture.

The Senate square and Helsinki Cathedral are both very beautiful. I had been to Finland many years before with my job, to visit a paper mill at Suma, 14k from the Russian border. It was only when we got to the Cathedral that I could remember any of what I had seen in Helsinki. We had to do a little window-shopping, as the shops here were the best we'd seen for a long while and the sales were in full swing. We go to the 'Sales' in the UK. In Finland they go to the 'Ales' At least that was a word we could pronounce.

Jackie and I had noticed that even though there are big cities in Finland, there are still not many people about. They are busy places, but nowhere near as busy as the cities in the UK. You can easily walk around supermarkets, large stores and through the streets, without dipping and dodging all the time. No queuing for ages at the checkouts either, it's great.

Maybe as its holiday time, most have left the city to go to the Lakeland areas or to the coast.

We had a great first day in Helsinki. The following day was my birthday so Jackie had promised to treat me to a meal. So that morning, after the usual calls, texts, emails and lots of singing 'Happy Birthday' to ME, we set off for another fun filled day in Helsinki. Can you believe it? It was cloudy and had started to rain. It was really warm so we took the brolly, but hoped that it would brighten up.

After a quick walk around in the rain we made our way to a restaurant called 'Juri' where the dish of the day was Sapas. We had read about Finnish Sapas, which are dishes supposedly similar to Spanish Tapas. The restaurant was in a large stone built building. The interior was very nice but quite spartan in appearance. The tables were placed together so that it made eating a communal experience. There were lots of Finns coming and going for lunch which gave it a good atmosphere. When we ordered our Sapas, we were told to help ourselves to the fresh bread, butter and salad, which was set out on a large wooden dresser. Oh dear, our Sapas arrived and it consisted of blackened herring, a small slice of smoked salmon, shredded lamb pate, a few cabbage sticks and boiled potatoes, all served cold. This meal was, in our opinion, very different from Spanish Tapas. Actually, we did enjoy the meal but it really wasn't what we expected.

While we were there we spoke to an Australian lady from Perth, with a lovely name 'Mescal'. She had flown to Europe to attend a conference in Gothenburg and was enjoying a short break in Helsinki before returning to Australia. She was travelling alone and sad not to be sharing Helsinki with someone, but she was of the opinion that you can't stop and wait for things, you have to get out there. We have always been impressed with how independent and strong-minded Australian women are, Mescal was one of them. We had a lovely chat and Mescal didn't waste any time devouring her smoked herring, well it would not do if we were all the same, would it? When we told her what we were doing and how we planned to go back to work she said it was called an 'Encore Career'.

We'd never heard that one before, but apparently, that is what we are now going back to.

We walked around for another couple of hours and found ourselves by the harbour and the oldest market hall in Europe. We went in to have a look, not just to find shelter (yes it was raining again). Each small wooden stall had the original nameplate of the stallholder. Again, lots of people were eating the fresh cooked food whilst sat at the counter tops. They were also selling wonderfully fresh produce on the market stalls. If the stallholders had been in traditional dress, the whole place would have looked exactly as it had been years and years before.

Back outside and a little further along the harbour there were a couple of small boats tied up, selling vegetables. Jackie and I looked at each other and we both said the same thing, "where's the fish then?"

As the boat trip across the harbour was included in our 48-hour travel ticket, we joined the queue to get the next one available. The rain was still with us but at least only on and off, so we decided we would go just for the ride. We sat on the small ferry and watched as a little boy fed his pizza to the seagulls, he thought it was hilarious as they swooped to take the pieces from his hand. His laugh was infectious, he had us laughing too. Some of the older ladies weren't amused though, so they quickly found seats inside. They knew that seagulls weren't bothered where they left their calling cards. Although it was a bit blustery when we were out in the harbour, it was very warm. We really enjoyed the crossing and the Helsinki skyline was definitely a sight to be seen.

Walking back to the Metro the weather suddenly changed, the clouds disappeared and the skies were blue again. So, as my final birthday treat we stopped at 'Café Esplanade' for coffee and cake. It's one of those places you all want to be seen in, on occasion, small elegantly set pavement tables, all very chic. I particularly love the cakes at these establishments, they're just like those that the ladies at the Women's Institute make, which, in my opinion, are to die for. The only difference is that the W.I. sell their cakes at charity events held in village halls, to raise money for the needy. The cakes at 'Café Esplanade' are just for the greedy. It will be a sad day for me if this body of women ever hang up their aprons. Fortunately, for me, our friend Georgina frequents these types of events and knowing my weakness, often buys me a cake. It *was* my birthday and as Jackie said I was worth it, I had a big slab of carrot cake and a latte. Wicked!

As we travelled back to the campsite, we mulled over our feelings for Helsinki, with its beautiful buildings, wonderful domed cathedral, grand squares and street culture. We both agreed that even with the rain, it didn't dampen our enthusiasm, Helsinki is a lovely city.

Our tour of Finland took us east along the coast towards the Russian border. Our next chosen place was Porvoo. Here the campsite was a short bike ride into the centre, so that was good for us, a bit of exercise after all that cake. We had a great pitch, very quiet, so we thought! By the end of the day the site was buzzing. Families in motorhomes and caravans and groups of young people in tents arrived one after the other. One chap was making pancakes on his bbq, they smelled good and as the aroma wafted up to us, we quickly put a note on the shopping list to get some pancake mix. Jackie was also in her element. There was no charge to use the washing machines here, and as the weather was great, Jackie soon had all the laundry on the line. We were on an elevated site so we could just sit and watch everyone setting up and enjoying themselves well into the night.

Next day we rode into Porvoo and locked our bikes up outside a busy little bar on the riverside. We walked around the 'oh so pretty' old town quarter and could quite understand why this was a place often visited by one of the Russian Tsars. Old wooden buildings lined the cobbled streets that meandered up the hillside to the church. We climbed up to the top of one of the steep streets to get the view of the town, then back down again and across the river to the old steam railway. Unfortunately, it wasn't working that particular day but it would have been quite nice to have had a ride to the next station on an old Finnish steam train. We had a short stroll back along the river where we had great views of the dark red wooden buildings on the opposite side. As we walked back through we saw several groups of people with tour guides being herded around, so it is obviously a very popular tourist attraction. Porvoo really is another gem of a place.

Further east along the coast we travelled to Kotka, an industrial town, and to our next campsite. This site was five star graded and it certainly was too. We had a newly laid paved patio area on our parking spot, very nice. The site was surrounded by woodland (where isn't in Finland?), and right on the coast. There were lots of way marked paths through the woods, a golf course, sauna (mixed) and again it was only 8km to the centre of Kotka, so we could cycle in. There were also wide cycle paths which lead all the way into the centre, so it would be safe cycling for us. It was so nice we decided to stay for five nights to just wind down and relax.

We had fantastic weather here too, it was in the high 80's every day. That of course, brought with it a thunderstorm that lasted about an hour and nearly brought the awning down, with the weight of the accumulated rain. At first it was coping well with the water pouring off one end as I had set it on a slant, then the volume just went into overload. I got soaked to the skin in the two seconds it took to wind the awning in. We thought we were going to be washed away but a short while after the sun was out and as hot as ever. It was strange to see little clouds rising from the tarmac as the rain evaporated. We had never seen such a sight before, it wasn't steam, but little white cotton wool clouds floating up in the air.

We had a lovely walk around the coast on a way marked circular path. We went through woodland which had monster rocks strewn all over the ground. Some were so huge we felt like 'the borrowers'. When we reached the beach, the views were stunning. So many little islands lay just off the coast and there were still lots of huge boulders all along the shore. The landscape was so different to anything else we had seen. It really was a pleasant change from walking along streets in towns and cities.

The ride from the campsite to Kotka was very pleasant with some nice views of the coast along the way. Kotka is a mixed affair with some nice parts and some of the more usual urban areas. There was a park by a small harbour, which was very pretty and so quite touristy. There was also a central park area with fragrant flowerbeds and well-kept lawns. As we rode through to the harbour we came across a church on a hill, so we stopped to have a look inside. On entering we were surprised to find that there were guests gathering for a wedding. We were approached by a lady at the entrance who quickly realised we were English. She told us that she was from Kotka but lived in London and had just come back over for her brother's wedding which she had helped to organise. She invited us to stay for the ceremony and introduced us to her brother. How many people would do that. We thanked her for the kind invitation but politely declined as we were in our cycle gear. We did hang around long enough to see the bride arrive accompanied by her proud father. She was a very beautiful young lady. The bridal gown was long, bright red and she wore bright blue shoes and matching handbag. They very kindly found time to pose for a picture for us, give us a quick wave and rushed inside as she was by then respectfully late.

It was whilst we were at the campsite near Kotka that I had a slight health concern and so Jackie thought it wise that I should go and see a doctor. The receptionist at the campsite gave us the directions to the public Medical Centre in Kotka. We did eventually find it, but not before having visited (by mistake) several private clinics along the way. We went into a waiting room, which was obviously full of people waiting to see the doctor. I know a patient when I see one! I joined a small queue to speak to the receptionist seated behind a window. As expected, the receptionist didn't speak any English at all. Why would she. I tried to explain that I hoped to see a doctor urgently. She promptly wrote down a telephone number and handed it back to me. From what we could gather we would have to phone the number to make an appointment. Well, that would be easier said than done wouldn't it.

We went outside to attempt to call the number. We sat on a bench close to the main entrance and were not there long when two young ladies approached to enter the building. They looked like medical workers as they had name badges pinned to their uniforms. We asked if they could speak English. Luckily for us, they did, and perfectly too.

How's this for daftness, if there is such a word. One of them proceeded to call the number. The call went directly to the lady on reception that I had been speaking to only a few moments before, and who had handed me the paper with the number on in the first place. Apparently, it was normal procedure as you cannot make an appointment at the reception desk, you must ring in and make one. The girls thought it was a crazy idea too. They told us they worked at the pharmacy just around the corner, and were delivering some drugs to the Medical Centre. Normally people have to wait 24 hours for an appointment, unless of course it's urgent. I explained we were touring and ideally needed to see a Doctor that day or as soon as possible. They were able to get me past the receptionist and through to a Doctor who spoke good English. I explained my circumstances and she agreed to see me straight away.

Back in reception, another young lady appeared at the counter who spoke English and so proceeded to help with my appointment. Within ten minutes I was sat in front of a very nice lady doctor. She was very thorough and allayed my fears, then sent me for a blood test. Five minutes later the blood test was done and the report sent in to the doctor. I received a diagnosis and given a prescription for some antibiotics. She was very thorough and by the time I left the clinic I felt relieved and also very grateful as I had been so well looked after. On the way out I apologised in English to a lot of bewildered Finns who must have wondered what I was mumbling on about and how I managed to jump the queue!

On the way back to the campsite we took the road back by the port and followed the coast for a while. We stopped to admire a featured waterway with rushes, a babbling brook and some artistic stonework. A lady started to talk to Jackie in Finnish. She obviously thought we were Finnish. She spoke perfect English and asked if this was our first visit to Finland. Jackie pointed out that I had visited a paper mill just down the coast not far from the Russian border. I was called over and what a coincidence, the lady was a worker at Sauma Paper Mill at the time of my visit.

Talking about the mill also brought back some very fond memories of the visit. My colleagues and I were staying in a general's house on an old Russian army base, which was situated on a hill overlooking the camp. The rest of the base had been converted into housing for some of the mill workers and their families. Whilst visiting the mill we were taken to see the trees being felled as part of the papermaking process. It was like watching some pre-historic monster moving through the pine forest. The vehicle moved on caterpillar tracks and had an arm the height of a tree, which it used to grab, strip off the branches and cut the stem into four metre lengths. It was a truly awesome spectacle, at first it looked primitive, but every tree is registered by satellite position, and they can only cut to an agreed pattern. For every tree they cut down to clear the forest, they have to plant three, as this is a sustainable forest crop.

Back at the general's house I was treated to my first sauna, which to the Finns is a must have, in any home. It consisted of a closed room with red hot stones, over which they poured water to create steam. This opens the pores of your skin, thus making you sweat and cleanse the body. Then out for a quick shower to freshen up. There were five guys being entertained on business and we were each given a paper mat to sit on, on the wooden benches, obviously for hygiene purposes. It's amazing how self-conscious you become sitting around chatting in the nude! The Finns take it all in their stride, but we Brits are real prudes. One chap had his beer can strategically placed over his protuberance the whole time we were in there, yet when he was dressed he was the most butch and manly of us all. Nevertheless, it was a good experience, but not one I'd want to make a habit of.

It was October and the snow began to fall overnight. We were treated to a magnificent scene in the morning with icicles hanging from the trees and the chalet style wooden houses. We even went out Skiddoo-ing over a frozen lake. The ice was so thick we drilled a borehole to fish from. One of the guys had recently undergone surgery and so was placed with the safest driver. We were on two-man motorised sledges that looked a bit like jet skis on tracks. Boy, could they go, it was great fun. Anyway, the safest driver hit a rock, hidden by the snow and they were both tipped off. Thankfully, there were no broken bones, just a few bruises.

One other interesting fact to come out of my visit to the mill was that during the winter, the ground often froze for several feet downwards, so there could be no burials. Bodies are kept in cold storage until the thaw and the ground becomes softer and so able to dig. On that interesting note we will move back to our tour and our campsite near Kotka.

The campsite was extremely busy and on this particular evening the bbq hut was alive with activity. Although the wooden hut was about 100 yards away we could see right into it from our elevated pitch. There was a bbq range to one side allowing three families to cook at the same time. All was going well, with lovely aromas of sizzling meats, until a short chubby chap in a brilliant white vest and red shorts arrived (118-118?). He arrived, along with his family, to a fanfare as he had the largest hampers of food and bbq equipment. So far, so good. He began to set up his food and light his bbq, which at first was not going too well, with only wisps of smoke. His fellow bbq'ers were pointing with implements and appearing to give him advice. He then decided to hurry things along somewhat. To this day, I do not know what he added, but there was a whoosh and a billow of smoke. It looked like the entire hut was about to go up in flames! People flew out of every exit. The now red faced short chubby chap was stood by the door with a spatula in one hand looking rather bemused. Inside was Dante's inferno. Anyway, it calmed down in seconds and they all gingerly went back inside, only for it to erupt again with the same results. Third time back in, the two other bbq's in the hut were still cooking fine, his was just a roaring inferno. Everyone else was by now standing watching their food from outside the hut, except for the chubby chappy. As if to prove he was doing nothing unusual, he was inside nonchalantly tending his food. By now there was a growing audience outside. They must have wondered if it was human flesh they could smell burning!

When things eventually calmed, he took the food out to his expectant family, who were quietly sitting down at the table outside ready to eat. *"Dad, why is our meat burnt and where have your eyebrows gone?"* The poor chap looked like an overcooked lobster with an afro.

For our last night in Finland we chose to stay on a campsite a couple of miles from the border, so we could make an early start for Russia and go straight to the pre booked campsite 'Hotel Olgino', 18km west of St Petersburg. Finland proved to be one of our favourite places so far, we were sad to leave, but Russia beckoned.

Chapter Eleven

Russia

July 28th

Russian Border Incident!

We set off early from our campsite in anticipation of it taking some time to pass through border control. It was raining heavily and the black clouds were almost touching the top of Belle. Not a good start to our journey to St Petersburg, but we weren't bothered about a bit of rain. We were eager to get into Russia.

Close to the Russian border we were met with a view of hundreds of Lorries parked up at the roadside, they stretched for miles and so it was quite a sight. We were to learn when we got to border control, that it was due to the time it takes to inspect each Lorries load.

As we approached the border we thought we were at the Russian border control and wondered what all the fuss was about. "How easy was that" we thought. It was just a quick inspection of our passports. How foolish of us, it was actually the Finnish border control. I would point out that sometimes we are not that awake in the mornings, this was one of them. A little further down the road we hit the Russian border with all its trappings. Off to the side of the road stood observation and gun towers, which are now unmanned and in a state of disrepair but still they do look ominous.

The road split and we had no real idea in which direction we should be heading as the signs were all in Cyrillic. We chose which looked like the easiest route, and which took us off to the right. We quickly realised we had gone wrong when we turned a corner and hit another queue of lorries slowly making their way down to an inspection bay. There were about twenty lorries in four rows in each inspection bay, we were waved into one row. Then a guard came to our cab window pointing and frowning, and indicating that we were in the wrong place and should be up over the hill and to the left. He then jumped us through the queue of lorries, which were in the middle of their inspection process. As you can imagine, this caused a near riot. Some of the drivers were furious and began complaining to the officials. They obviously had had to wait some time already and did not take kindly to what appeared to them to be queue jumping. We managed to leave the area unscathed.

Back up across the road we joined the correct queue of cars and passengers all waiting to enter Russia. Once again we are directed to join in the middle of a single line queue of cars and vans. We daren't look at anyone, we knew there would be some unwelcome stares from our fellow travellers. At this stage the queue was not too long so we didn't feel that bad about the situation. We were both a bit stressed out by this stage as the guards were quite intimidating and do not smile or seem welcoming whatsoever.

The queue then split into two as we entered the passport control building, one for Russian nationals, one for other nationalities. We joined the 'others queue' more by luck than the signage, which is very poor for non-Russian reading people. Still that's our fault, is it? The building comprised of a canopy spanning four lanes, two for those entering, two for those leaving. There was also a large office area, again with observation deck. The officers were both male and female in equal proportion and were dressed in a drab green uniform with pale blue shirts. Some of the guards were obviously more senior and had flat army caps that slanted upwards at the front to form quite a peak. There were a few armed guards, but most were for dealing with the traffic and the administration.

We moved to the first kiosk and were asked very impolitely for our passports, which were then inspected and scanned in. Nothing was done at a pace and it was all very thorough and official with no smiles. After a few minutes and a quick telephone call, our passports were passed back and we were told in very abrupt Russian to move on to the next kiosk. Well, that was what we assumed the young lady meant. After some hand waving, we had been dismissed.

At the next kiosk we were asked to open up Belle for inspection. Several guards walked around her. Those who went inside looked in every drawer and cupboard, everything was completely checked. At one stage I got the distinct impression they were all just having a good old nosey, having not seen this model before. More hand waving, without so much of a grin and with the usual abruptness, we were asked to move on to the next kiosk. We were both feeling very anxious about it all by now, especially the total lack of any English, not even one word, and of course the sternness. We had been warned about how intimidating they could be, but it still came as a bit of a shock.

Thankfully, we were still undercover and despite it being quite warm, the rain was coming down in torrents, it was so heavy it was bouncing off the road. At the final kiosk we are asked for our vehicle documentation. The two ladies at this kiosk were very smart, wore make-up and a smile, and so looked much friendlier. As I handed over the documents they both gave me a nice big smile, so I thought things were looking up. Was it? One of the ladies then, from what I could understand, enquired if I had completed a vehicle entry form. I had not. She then proceeded to show me how to complete the form, pointing at instructions on the wall. I duly started to fill it in as requested. Whilst standing outside the kiosk we were joined by a Finnish guy who tried to help us. Back to the ladies, I soon learnt that I had filled in the form incorrectly. I was well and truly told off! She demanded to know why I had not followed her instructions. Well, two seconds of pointing at the form and then at the one on the wall was obviously not enough for me. I think the fear factor of doing anything there had taken over by then.

Back for a second attempt, and still not to her liking, she proceeded to amend the forms for me. Bless her, she did have some compassion after all. Did I mention this form had to be filled out in triplicate? Well it did! They then began to check through the vehicle paperwork. I looked back at this point to find that the queue stretched back as far as the eye could see and I was the cause of it. Shuffling through the papers all seemed to be going well until they got to the registration document, which was a photocopy. They asked, "Where is the original?" One of them was able to tell us that it was blue, and so kept repeating it. It was then that I had to try and explain why I only had a photocopy. It didn't really get through to them, but the following will make it clear to you..............

When we bought the Motorhome, I had asked for my personal number plate to be put on it. This was the first mistake. When we went to collect Belle from Leisure Kingdom we were given all the vehicle documents which included not only the Fiat manuals, but also the Autotrail instruction books, Leisure Kingdom receipts and service information. All this amounted to quite a hefty pack of information. There was so much going on at the time and we were so excited about the whole experience that we didn't discover that the registration document was not in the pack until some days later when we were about to board the ferry to France that we noticed that it was missing. After several calls to Leisure Kingdom we finally established it had been sent out late and would be posted out to our son's address. We were not too worried, as we hoped the only time we would need it, was when we went to enter Russia.

Well time went by and the registration document eventually turned up at our son's house. As we had started the tour, Howard scanned in the document and sent a PDF to us. We went to a Wi-Fi café to print it off, so we at least had something to show if we needed to. We weren't too concerned about not having the original as Howard was due to visit us in Oslo and was going bring it with him. Just before leaving for Oslo, Howard mislaid his passport and so had a fraught couple of hours searching high and low for it. Luckily he found his passport, safely in his hand luggage, ready for the off. Unfortunately for us, he forgot the registration document. Still, we thought, no problem, we have a copy and all the other documentation to prove the vehicle is ours, we should be ok, shouldn't we? So now you know why we only had a photocopy.

We had been very naïve as we had been told by advisors on the MMM magazine forums and by others that photocopies would not be accepted. Apparently, foreign cars can fetch a premium in Russia, so to stop illegal imports they are red hot on this. Still, stupid as you like, we thought we would be ok. With a wink of the eye and a pretty blonde at my side, I thought we would get through, no problem. How wrong can you be.

Back to the main event. We are stood at this kiosk, trying to convince them that the documentation is fine and that we do own the vehicle. Regardless of the fact that we had our visa's, which had cost £240 and also showing them the receipt for the pre booked campsite 'Hotel Olgino', they still demanded the registration document. They then decided to have a discussion in Russian and one disappeared with the paperwork. Now I am not sure at this stage if I should be offering a bribe, but had not felt they were giving the option for me to offer one. I could tell as soon as the lady returned with a third guard that things had taken a turn for the worse. Trying in vain to speak English/Russian they said "Paperwork no good, where blue document"? The look, the stance and the whole atmosphere changed. It was soon clear to us that Belle was not going to be let in. We were told that Jackie and I could go in, not a problem. It was entirely our own fault; we had plenty of opportunity to get the original couriered to us, but we were having such a good time we forgot how important it was. How foolish of us.

Anyway, the long and short of it was that Belle was being refused entry. By this time the queue and the angst of all around us was building. We had been there two hours so far. I kept thinking surely they would take us out of line to allow other visitors to go through. Alas no, we were to remain in line until it was sorted and the guards showed no regard for our fellow travellers being held up. We were eventually told we would be escorted into the exit queue. We apologised again to the group of people who had now gathered around the kiosk. We kept doing this as they had waited patiently with us for the outcome. We had struck up quite a friendly group by the time we were escorted to the exit queue. They were philosophical about it; saying it was quite normal for them to have to wait, up to ten hours in some instances.

Now for the exit queue. The guard who escorted us to this queue explained to the official why we were being pushed in and then left. When we got to the counter at the kiosk we were again asked for our papers, this time vehicle documents first. We showed the lady our photocopy, no good, vehicle document please, it's blue. Well, you could have knocked us down with a feather. We were now being refused exit because our paperwork was not in order. I asked Jackie to go in search of the guard who had escorted us into the exit queue. All this time I was trying to explain in the little Russian I had taken time to learn, which was, yes/no and can we book a table for two! Obviously, didn't make any difference at all.

After a short while Jackie returned with the lady official who had been with us at the start of the documents fiasco. Great, we'll start moving now thinks I. Will we? Well no, of course not! Central command needs to be involved. All this time the queue was growing, and we were both feeling the pressure.

I had visions of news cameras arriving for the border incident, as Jackie and Adrian Rigg are stuck in transit ….

"This is the BBC news".
"Over to the Russian border, to where Jackie and Adrian Rigg have been stuck for seven years, having been refused permission to enter, and refused permission to leave. Mr & Mrs Rigg of no fixed abode and touring Europe for two years, have now been stuck at the Russian border for seven. They also have been declared an official 'Road Block' as they circle continuously from entry to exit. The queue is now as far back as Istanbul to the south and Vladivostok to the north. The Russian officials have refused to comment, but insiders say they have promised to fast track the whole issue as soon as they can. In the meantime, packs of clean underwear and Birds pork pies (Birds is a top class bakers in Derby) have been flown in by friends and family to keep Jackie and Adrian going through their ordeal".

10 minutes later, another lady official returns with who we can only assume is a commander, due the large emblem on his hat and jacket emblazoned with bright bands. Oh dear, now we are for it now. Jackie and I looked at one another, both thinking, "Whatever next?" He looked us over, entered the ki-

osk where the lady had been waiting patiently, albeit with a frown, and said three words in Russian. Whatever he said did the trick. I think the words were "let them go" because there was then a quick flourish of stamping on our passports and the obligatory wave of the hand. With that, and without a moment's thought we were back in Belle and on the move.

Again, during all this time the traffic queue behind us had been growing steadily and the officials showed no interest at all in taking us out of the queue whilst our problem was resolved.

I cannot begin to tell you the relief we felt as we crossed back into Finland. As we did, we both agreed that it was not meant to be. We are both firm believers in fate and we think that someone, somewhere, did not want us to go to Russia. There had been a catalogue of errors that had led to the refusal of entry. We chuckled and gave a little nervous laugh of the slightly insane and decided not to cry over spilt milk. We had no one to blame but ourselves as we had both read and been told, NO PHOTOCOPIES. Still, we were both very disappointed not to visit to St Petersburg as it was going to be one of the highlights of our tour and also the turning point in the tour as we turned back westwards, down through the Baltic states and back westward towards the UK.

The rain was torrential as we headed back to Helsinki. In fact, visibility was so bad we had to stop for a while, it became far too dangerous to drive in those conditions. Whilst we were waiting for the rain to abate, we booked the early morning ferry to Tallinn for the following day. We decided to stay over-night at the campsite just outside of Helsinki again as it was also convenient for the port. During the planning stages of our tour we had decided that if for any reason we couldn't get into Russia, this would be the alternative option anyway.

It goes without saying that Jackie and I were sad not to see St Petersburg, but we were also sad for the Russians too, because had we been able to visit, and had it been even vaguely good, we would have sold it to our friends, family and everyone we met. Surely, they need to be bending over backwards to attract tourists. As it is, we will never know.

At this point I will also mention that we were back on budget having adjusted our eating and drinking habits to suit the Scandinavian way of life. In fact we were almost teetotal... although we did find Finland a lot less expensive than Norway.

Chapter Twelve

Estonia – Latvia – Lithuania

July 29th to August 10th

Beautiful Baltic's 1 – Tallinn, Estonia

It took two hours to cross the Baltic Sea from Helsinki to Tallinn aboard a very nice 'Tallink' ferry. It was a lovely sunny day so we sat on the deck for the whole of the journey. This ferry was different from the ones that cross the English Channel, in that the entire vessel was painted lime green and the interior decor was ultra-modern. There were some reasonably priced bottles of booze on board, so we, along with most of the other passengers, took advantage of the offers. We could see there were lots of young people in groups, laden down with booze. Then the 'penny dropped' so to speak, we realised it was a 'Booze Cruise'. All the 'youngies' (our word for anyone under 35) were popping over to Tallinn for a party weekend. Mind you, that's what we hoped to do.

Upon our safe arrival in Tallinn, we made our way to our chosen campsite at Pirita Marina, 6km east of the city. We reached the marina via what looked like an Olympic approach with a four-lane sea front highway from the city. Along this road we could see a big concrete memorial, we later found out it was there as a memorial to the Russians that were killed during the war. We planned to go back on our bikes and take a closer look. Just after the monument, we spotted a campsite sign (not the one we planned for), so we thought maybe we would see what it was like, after all it would be nearer the centre of Tallinn. We drove up and down and around but couldn't find the site so gave up and continued along the road to the marina.

The marina turned out to be a great location, right on the harbour. It had been purpose build in 1986 to stage the Olympic Yachting and Rowing events. In typical Russian style it was mainly constructed of concrete, which sadly showed its age. The toilet facilities were a rather dated and smelly, but clean and so just about usable. The showers were situated in the huge Olympic building. These were split communally for men and women and you had to pay three euros each for the use of. They looked as if they were originally the competitors changing rooms. Back at the Marina we picked our spot with a great view of the harbour and the beach beyond. Perfect.

It was a very busy place, at one point, over twenty Motorhomes arrived together in a convoy, all from The Netherlands. There was also a reasonably sized grassed area on one side where several tents had already been erected. As we found out a month or so before, when we were lucky enough to stay at the marina in Oslo, they are very interesting places to stay, always plenty of activity of some kind or other to watch and occupy your mind. Boats on trailers of all shapes and sizes coming and going, being taken from or being put back in the water. Here there were a couple of British boats in the harbour, one a yacht and the other a snazzy powerboat. The yacht was crewed by a father and his two sons who were there for a sailing regatta, which was being held at the marina. We never saw the crew of the powerboat, but did see it speeding through the sea, just outside the harbour.

The stone built jetty, which went out to sea had the Olympic rings on it along with the Russian red star. It was easy to imagine how it must have looked during the Olympics and it felt strange walking up the steps to where the medal ceremony would have been held.

"Here is your Gold Medal Comrade Rigg, Adrian. Best in Class for snoring and one for your dear wife for putting up with it!"

I think that America boycotted the event due to Russia's involvement in Afghanistan!

We went out for a bike ride early in the afternoon, just to explore but also to get some food. We rode back down the Olympic approach from the city, which was very impressive. Sadly, the pavements were in a sad state of repair. This would set the tone for a lot of the places on our tour of the old communist bloc. We were also determined to find the elusive campsite. Well, thank goodness we did not find it in the first place, it was really not that nice, just a car park with high walls and buildings surrounding it, very drab indeed. We felt sorry for the people already parked there. We would have told them about the marina, but there was no one around to tell. While out and about we discovered a large modern supermarket just across from the marina. It was well stocked, had a wide variety of produce and the prices were very cheap compared to Scandinavia and the UK. Having been careful with our intake of food over the last few weeks, we embarked on a 'food fest'. You would have thought we had never seen food before. *We had one of them and one of them and one of them, and one of them and one of them. Phew! Then we had some of them and some of them and some of them. Oh and they looked nice, so we had some of them as well.* With all this excitement, we forgot that we only had the panniers on the bikes, to carry all the food back. What a sight we were, with carrier bags hanging and swaying from the handlebars, as we made our way back to Belle.

We hadn't been back at the marina for long before black clouds began to appear across the harbour. Within minutes the rain was coming down in sheets and it continued for twenty four hours.

When it eventually stopped, which was the following afternoon, we took the bus into Tallinn for a quick look around and to locate the Hotel Vana Wiru, where our very good friends, Dave and Jane, would be staying the following week. Dave and Jane had planned to join us somewhere along the way and so the date we were to be in Tallinn fell in perfectly for us all to be together. It also meant that as we didn't get into Russia, we could have a whole week in Tallinn.

Our first impression of Tallinn old town was "Wow this looks nice". Pretty narrow cobbled streets lined with timeworn cream painted buildings with red terracotta roof tiles wound up and around the centre to a beautiful church that overlooked Tallinn. Whilst strolling around for the first time we stopped for a drink at a nice little street restaurant and struck up an interesting conversation with the waiter called Ken. He told us that he had worked in London for two years before returning home.

He said that things were picking up with the economy and that he was glad to be back in Estonia and felt optimistic for its future. He asked how we were finding the Estonian people. We told him that everyone we had met had all been pleasant so far. He thought that the older people tended to be a bit stand-offish, as they had been brought up under the communist regime. They were cautious of chatting in public and even closed their windows at home to have conversations, for fear of being reported to the KGB and being denounced or having their work permit removed. This was changing slowly, but some old habits die-hard.

We in the West do not know what it is like to have lived under this level of surveillance as part of our normal lives. As we were now aware of this fact, we did notice the older generation were a bit reluctant to speak in the streets, even after twenty years of freedom. Ken also said there were a few Russians still living in Estonia who did not leave when the rest did. He said generally they were disgruntled with what had happened and that if we met any they tended to be "not happy people".

Our backdrop, while we were having our little chat, was an Estonian wedding party, gathering for some sort of celebration. The beautifully dressed guests had walked down the street and had stopped at a very elaborate door across the way. The doorway lead into an impressive Masonic Lodge belonging to the 'House of the Blackheads', which apparently was a men only meeting place, but of late rented out as function rooms, and on this occasion, a wedding reception. The newly married couple arrived in a white Rolls Royce, while the guests had walked in procession from the Cathedral.

We didn't see much of Tallinn old town on our first visit. We thought we would leave the rest to explore with Dave and Jane. It had also started to rain again, so we hastily made our way back to the marina.

That evening we met a chap from Gateshead who was staying on the campsite. Mac was in his sixties and he was travelling with his ten month old West Highland white terrier, called Penny. Mac was a great guy and immediately proceeded to tell me his life story.

Mac had been married twice and had two children. He had for many years travelled extensively in a motorhome which he loved. Unfortunately, his current wife did not care for the motorhome holidays, so he travelled alone with his pet dog for company. His wife preferred to stay and look after the home and their business. He had had a hard life early on as his mother had abandoned him as a baby on the doorstep of his aunt's house. Then his uncle had died when he was young and so he became the breadwinner of the family. He began his working life repairing washing machines. One day someone gave him two broken twin tub washing machines, which he decided to make into one working machine, which he sold. He did really well and before long opened his own corner shop, repairing all sorts of electrical items. Back then, we all repaired things, the throw away culture hadn't arrived. From there, he went into house clearance and it was whilst clearing a house for the Coal Board, he had another big break. The Coal Board had offered the entire contents of a house in return for its clearance. The old chap, who had occupied it, had died and had no other living relatives. Other companies had turned down the clearance as there was little or no value in any of the goods, but Mac accepted it as he thought he could sell the wardrobe. It was a while later and whilst moving the wardrobe that he made the discovery, there was a tin hidden in the plinth. When he opened it up, it contained £2,000 pounds. This set him up for life, back then it was a lot of money. He invested in Pet Shops, which was driven by his love of animals, especially dogs. He still owns two shops in the north of England. He retired several times during which he had travelled all around the world, doing all sorts of things, including owning a 40ft Ketch in which he sailed around the Caribbean. He had also been all over Europe in his Motorhome, which looked like Fort Knox from the inside. It had decorative wrought iron bars on all the windows and bar locks on the doors. Mac said he had had an experience when he thought he had been gassed (no evidence of) but certainly had been robbed in Spain during a siesta in his motorhome. Since the incident, he made sure that his motorhome was totally secure. It certainly looked it to us. He had a trailer on the back for his motor scooter, which had a basket on the front for Penny.

What warmed us to Mac was that he was so sincere and loved to laugh. He told us that he had once been a compare/comedian at a nightclub. We could well believe it, he certainly knew how to tell a joke.

The following evening Mac joined us again for drinks and nibbles and of course his lovely little dog came along. Within minutes, Penny was happily chewing Jackie's flip-flop. Not only did Jackie really like these particular flip flops, they were 'Haviana's' and had cost £25 from Australia, not just any old cheap flip-flops then! Mac thought it was hilarious and so did Penny. He did offer to pay for them but Jackie couldn't let him, as he would have thought she was exaggerating the price. Anyway, Penny had so much fun with them.

The following day, the weather had changed and it was back to cloudless blue skies. We decided to walk around the harbour and along the beach. As we set off, we could see that a festival had just started. We were told that it was in celebration of the sea, and so was taking place in the harbour. There was a big old sailing boat with a jazz band on the deck, really giving it some. A procession of giant see-through water bubbles floated along with the help of brightly dressed people who walked around inside them. The main attraction was the float, which carried the Queen of the Sea. She was dressed in a flowing white dress, which covered the entire float, had a silver painted face and smiled and waved at all the spectators as she passed by. It was all very amusing and the families watching were having a great time. We continued our walk around the harbour and to the lovely sandy beach on the other side. This was also where the procession came to an end, so we asked one of the participants what it was all about. He just shrugged and said they do it every year and it was of no real significance. Nevertheless, it was a pleasant start to our Sunday morning stroll.

We walked away from the harbour and along the beach. We agreed that Tallinn should advertise the area more as the beach was lovely soft white sand and very clean, stretching for miles around the bay. There were lots of holidaymakers up to all sorts of activities including making sand castles and digging holes, I nearly fell in one. All along the beach people were sun bathing and swimming and there were changing facilities and seats to rest on. We did dip our toes in the sea, but it was quite cold and there were a few jellyfish, so we were soon out again. There was a great view of the skyline of Tallinn in the distance. We walked all along the beach until we came across the naturist area, we quickly turned around and went back.

For the most part the beach was backed by woods, which offered good shade. We also noticed a cycle path running parallel to the beach through the trees, ideal for a ride around the bay out of the hot sunshine.

The next day we decided to ride along the cycle path through the woods at the back of the beach and then back down around the bay to the war memorial again. We took a coastal path by some very large modern houses, some had impressive looking motorboats moored along-side. One owner was just about to get in his car and we asked if we could get back on to the beach road from where we were. He spoke good English, so we stopped and had quite a lengthy discussion. He was Estonian but his family had fled the country when the Germans invaded. They had moved to Sweden and only moved back to Estonia when the Russians moved out in 1990.

He and his family owned a string of Hotel's in the city and were doing extremely well, due to the boom in the tourist trade. He said we would notice houses in select areas that were sadly being left to deteriorate. The reason for this was because there were disputes over ownership. Apparently, the disputes over who owns what, came about when the Russians left. Of course, many of these are between the same families and are still going on twenty one years later. He said Estonia was doing well at the moment because it had realised the need for tourists and open trade earlier than the other Baltic States. They had also embraced technology as a way of communicating and attracting business.

Back along the Olympic highway we visited the memorial commemorating Estonians, Russians and Germans who had lost their lives during the Second World War. It was so sad to read the names of so many young men, it was also a surprise to see the German war dead commemorated. Once again, the Estonians had realised that things need to move on and that we all need to live together in peace, so had allowed the memorial. The thought of all the misery of a lost one that each name represented was very moving. Mothers of the world should unite and prevent any more *mad* men from seeking revenge or power, and killing their children.

Our friends Dave and Jane arrived safe and sound, and so we planned to meet at their hotel. The weather was perfect for sightseeing and so we were able to amble around the old town all day. We did go back to their hotel for our lunch – a bowl of chips,' Birds' pork pie and a sausage roll. 'Birds' is our local confectioner in Derby who makes the best cream cakes, bread rolls, and pork pies, ever. What a surprise, they wanted to bring us something that we could never get anywhere else in the world. They couldn't have bought us anything better. Delicious!

Tallinn has a beautiful old town built on a hill side, with ramparts, white wash spires and cobbled streets winding up to the Cathedral. It's all very touristy with cafes, bars and restaurants everywhere. It has that street culture air about it, which we like. Tallinn will prove to be one of our favourite spots. The lower town is quite modern, but still worth a visit for its shops, which are up to the standard of any other European city.

Early evening, we booked to go on a KGB museum tour at the Hotel Viru. The hotel had been built in the early 70's by the Russians and was one of the top hotels in Tallinn, attracting many famous people. The tour was conducted in several languages and very popular, so we had quite a wait for the English version. The tour was to see a secret top floor that the KGB had occupied during the 1970's and up until 1991, when Estonia gained its independence. It was only after this, that Floor 23 was discovered. Everyone that worked at the hotel, and the guests of course, were all of the belief that the hotel had 22 floors as that was where the lift stopped. But little did they know that the KGB used the top floor to spy on visiting guests and foreign dignitaries.

There was also a balcony behind the 'Hotel Viru' sign, where they would watch people in the streets below, going about their business. Everyone was on the take, with bribes everywhere, from a job as bottle washer to securing important government positions and contracts. We saw electronic equipment, which had recorded conversations from rooms that had been bugged and drawings of tables, marked out for bugging devices. All this had been going on only twenty years ago, it was amazing to see and hear such things. You could just imagine sitting down for dinner with a daffodil turning to record every time you spoke. *"I say Cynthia did that Daffodil just move?" "Don't be silly, you've had too much to drink Henry".* We all came away with the same feeling. Unbelievable!

We all ate out that evening at a lovely restaurant overlooking the main square, it was a full three-course meal, and very tasty and very reasonable, about half the price it would have been in the UK.

The following day, Dave and Jane caught the bus to the marina, to see just how we were living in Belle and our surroundings that we had been raving about. They too thought it was an ideal spot. It was hot and sunny again, so we walked along the beach then back to Belle for a bbq.

It's always nice to see our friends and a chance for Jackie and I to catch up with the gossip back home. On our last day together we went sightseeing again, but this time on one of the tour buses. It was a good tour as we saw both the old and new Tallinn. Just a slight problem with the audio equipment, meant that we didn't hear most of what the tour guide was saying. *Crackle, crackle, pop…. "over there, and this monument is dedicated to"…. Crackle, crackle, pop… "and his followers, and this wooden house…*
Crackle, crackle, pop… "from the 16th century"….. and the winning lottery numbers for tomorrow are… crackle, crackle, pop…?

The latter part of the day Jane and Jackie dragged Dave and I all over Tallinn looking at Matryoshka Dolls. They were everywhere, as was the Amber, which the Baltics are famous for. The dolls are known as Russian nesting dolls, hand painted, traditionally in sets of five, decreasing in size, one inside the other. Eventually, out of sheer desperation Dave and I decided to join in the hunt. We eventually found the shop with the designs and colours that they wanted and at the right price. The dolls range from 5 euro's to 2,000 euro's depending on their quantity, size and artist. The girls chose the hand painted ones, signed by the artist and which depicted a traditional Russian fairy-tale. Obviously, Dave and I were immensely happy for them!

For our last evening together, we decided to go to an Indian restaurant to sample the Estonian taste in curry. To our surprise we found two restaurants to choose from. The one we chose was authentically decorated and we enjoyed the meal but it was disappointingly not up to UK standard, which we think is very high at the moment. We have lots of Indian restaurants in Derby that serve superb curries. Now, I am a bit of a curry fanatic and self-proclaimed connoisseur, so my expectations are always high as I have been frequenting curry houses in Derby since the early 1970's. Tallinn went up in my estimation just for the fact they had two curry houses. How sad am I?

We'd had a great time with Jane and Dave, it was so good to see familiar faces after three months away from home, and also it felt like a real holiday. We said our fond farewells before flagging down a taxi back to the Marina.

The next and final day at the Marina, we met our new neighbours Walter and Gloria, from The Netherlands. They gave us lots of advice on campsites and websites for the other Baltics and further afield. We also met a great guy from New Zealand called Franz, who lives in London. He came to see us in Belle and spent a while chatting to us, again exchanging experiences and offering good advice. He had retired and was travelling around Europe with his wife on a similar tour to us. The difference being he hoped to continue on for a few more years, lucky thing. Franz persuaded us to visit Turkey, as he said he found it very friendly and safe. We said we would definitely think of including it in our tour for next year. They also used their on board facilities (toilet/shower) rather than using those on any of the sites they visit. They just use the sites to top up with water and for waste disposal. Perhaps Jackie and I will adopt the same idea one day. Still not there yet though.

We said our goodbyes to all we met and hoped to meet up with Mac and Penny again in Riga as he was travelling back through the Baltic's en route to the UK.

All in all, Tallinn is a city well worth a visit. Old Tallinn is very pretty, we loved every minute of it. For anyone who hasn't been to this part of Europe, we would recommend a week here. Take a cheap flight into Tallinn and use it as a base to see Helsinki, (2hr ferry over to Helsinki plus overnight in a hotel). Back to Tallinn for another couple of nights and then pick up a cruise to St Petersburg for a 72hour return visit, visa's all included, fly back home from Tallinn. Perhaps we will go back and do that, and hopefully get to see St Petersburg.

As we drove through Estonia we found the roads were reasonably good, at least while we are on the main roads. The countryside had changed again to flat wooded vistas, rolling into the distance. There were a few farms and villages on the way, all well-kept and looking prosperous, we were pleasantly surprised. En route to Riga we decided to stop halfway and overnight at a little campsite near Parnu. We set up our pitch overlooking the river, the facilities were very basic, but clean. The campsite had a rowing club in the grounds. It was interesting for us to watch club members arrive and take the boats out on river.

We cycled into Parnu for a look around. It was quite a small town, but very pleasant. We were also very lucky that the town was holding a street market all along the central street. It was full of local craft stalls, very interesting, from cut glass to a working iron forge. Jackie liked the look of the handmade wooden cutlery, especially the small butter knives and so decided to splash out and buy one, 3 euro's. It turned out to be a great buy too. We called in the Tourist Information and picked up a leaflet, which directed us along a red painted tourist route taking us through the streets of Parnu. We found the mixture of wooden and stone built buildings very pleasing to the eye. There was also a lovely domed church, typical of those we would see in the Baltic States. We also came across the Estonian liqueur called Vana Tallinn here. Our friends had recommended that we buy a bottle. Somehow we missed seeing it when we were in Tallinn. It is served with coffee and as a nightcap, so we decided to buy a bottle. Yes, thanks Mike and Yvonne, it is very nice drink.

That evening, just as we were about to go to bed, two young couples decided to pitch their tents next to Belle. They proceeded to make quite a lot of noise, not that we minded, they were having such a good time, all we could hear was laughter. Eventually, it went quiet and we went off to sleep. What we didn't realise was they must of gone off into the town for more fun. In the early hours of the morning, the music started again and so did the laughter, until someone on the site shouted for them to shut up, which they did immediately, and without any retort.

When we got up the next morning, we were treated to the funniest of sights. What had caused their laughter the night before was that one of the couples had bought an inflatable mattress for their tent, obviously without checking the size. Unfortunately, it was far too big to fit inside the tent, so they had pitched the tent up on top of the mattress. The other tent was so small the zip was open at the bottom and two pairs of feet were sticking out. We just had to laugh. There was no movement from either of the tents until just before mid-day. The girls were up, washed and dressed. Typically, the boys were much the worse for wear. We were ready for the off and still chuckling at the sight of them all as we left the campsite.

Beautiful Baltic's 2 – Riga, Latvia

Driving in the Baltic's was quite a different experience with the roads having a hard shoulder either side. Vehicles use this to pull onto, to give overtaking vehicles more space in both directions on the road. A bit scary at first, but you soon got used to it. There were very few dual carriageways and the drivers were reasonably well behaved.

We found 'Riga City Camping' without any problem and were soon pitched up. No sign of Mac and Penny. The campsite was in the grounds of an Exhibition Centre, open from September to March, then used for camping April to August. The site was within walking distance of the centre, however, it was so hot, we decided that we would catch the bus in.

Riga is a very large city, full of fabulous Art Nouveau buildings. Not much in the way of really old buildings, apart from in the town square. Again, most of the centre was devastated during the wars. Having said that, it had been re-built to replicate most of the old buildings during Russian control, and to a high standard. We enjoyed our day in Riga as there were lots to do and see and it was very interesting walking through the extensive and well-maintained park with its beautiful flower displays, fountains and visiting the churches. It would appear the Baltic States are very religious as there is a church or cathedral around every corner of some denomination and size. The centre was buzzing with people sightseeing, drinking and eating outside at the street bars and restaurants.

The Latvian people are very friendly and welcoming and quite a few in the service trade spoke good English. While walking through the central boulevard we were greeted by a bevy of beautiful young ladies, all in wedding dresses. There were all sorts, from sexy miniskirts and suspenders through to traditional Latvian wedding gowns. We stopped for a while and tried to get into the photo shoot (well I did), while taking some of photos of our own. It was all very friendly and I managed to kiss nearly all of the brides, "watch your step" says Jackie "you will trip over your eyeballs". Sadly, there were no grooms for Jackie, so she had to make do with me!

Once again we ate out as the prices were very affordable. It was great for us as we were now well under budget. We had two freshly made pizzas, a cocktail and a beer in the busiest part of town for less than £15.

Back at the campsite we spotted a British number plate on an old Peugeot 203 with two young dudes sitting in it. I decided to wander over and make contact. Adam and Ed were from the UK and touring Europe in Isabelle. They were students and had bought the car and a tent and just decided to go for it. They were on their way to Russia with paperwork that looked as dodgy as ours had been. What amazed us is how unfazed they are by it all and unconcerned. They had stopped at Riga on their way out and gave us some good advice about Poland, where they had just been.

It rained all night and we were thinking of them in their little two-man tent. We need not have worried, they were both recovering from huge hang over's having spent the night on the town. Jackie had declared the day as a washing day again, as the laundry bag was full and it was very cheap at this particular campsite.

Adam and Ed set off the following day, but before leaving they bought us a tin of Heinz Beans for our kindness (we had given them a few bits of food and chocolate) and expected nothing in return, but how thoughtful was that? We wished them a safe journey and truly hoped they have a fabulous time.

That day a very old blue VW camper parked next to us. We didn't see the owners until that evening. Innes and Peter came from Bremen, Germany. They were holidaying with their beautiful dog, Flicka who looked like a St Bernard (one of those mountain rescue dogs that have barrels under their chin), she was gorgeous. We had a great night chatting and a good few glasses of Vana Tallinn, which we introduced them to. Peter worked for an Adventure company that took people to see rare and interesting animals. He had just come back from two months in the Tibetan mountains looking for Snow Tigers. Peter had my sort of humour. He said that usually on the expeditions they saw plenty of turds and a few glazed eyes on the night vision cameras, but that was it. Innes, his wife was a very attractive lady with a very gentle disposition, very apt as she was a social worker. Innes also had a good sense of humour and so the evening was filled with laughter and merriment as we exchanged stories. We said our goodbyes in the small hours, as they were off early in the morning. When we got up the next day they had already left. Under our doormat was a hand drawn sketch of us all sitting by our van. They had also left a little bunch of flowers, which Innes had made up for us. All we could think is that there are some beautiful people who walk this planet and we were so privileged to be meeting them.

One other interesting thing on this site was the German Hotel Bus, which turned up on the second day. Basically it looked like a standard single decker bus, but slightly taller. It accommodated around twenty people with on-board sleeping quarters and loos. When it stopped at each campsite, the drivers set up seats outside with parasols and the bbq's. They prepared and cooked the food and then served for their guests. It was all very civilised and the holiday makers seemed to be having a great time chatting and laughing over their wine or beer. However, the thought of all that snoring in a confined space would put us off that idea somewhat. We had never seen anything like it before, but Innes said it was quite normal for German people to go on such tours and is a lot cheaper than staying in hotels.

Beautiful Baltic's 3 – Vilnius, Lithuania

We travelled southeast from Riga, across to Vilnius. The road journey was good and much the same as the other Baltic States. We didn't venture off the main roads so have no idea what the small country lanes would be like. It was very scenic with rolling countryside. We were amazed to see lots of black and white Storks feeding on the crops in the fields, it was quite a picture. Their nests were huge and sat perfectly on top of the wooden telegraph poles. They were obviously looked after by the locals, as there were man made nesting platforms at most of the farms we passed. The few farms and villages we saw en route to Vilnius were well maintained and looked in good condition. Should this surprise us?

We chose a City campsite for its convenience, as it was just another short bus ride away from the centre of Vilnius. Once again it was next to an exhibition centre, so quite easy to locate. Sheila's on the ball again. This site used portacabins for the loos and showers, which were both clean and relatively new. There were some more Brits on the campsite in a caravan, the first one we had seen in Scandinavia or the Baltic states. The chap looked a bit fed up and had one arm in plaster. Unfortunately, we didn't get chance to speak to them.

Once settled, we took a walk to the local shops, which we found at the entrance to a high-rise apartment block estate. The shop was a bit basic, not much in the way of provisions and only accepted cash, but we managed to get all the things we needed. The people were curious that there were English people in their local supermarket. Nevertheless, they were warm and friendly towards us. We also found where the bus stop was for the next morning. The area was very nice, well-kept and modern.

For the first time using the public transport we managed to get slightly lost. We received some instruction from the chap running the campsite, but we think we probably caught the bus going the wrong way! This can be difficult when relying on someone who is not that fluent in English giving you directions and may get things mixed up from time to time, unlike us of course! The way we went meant we had to change buses, whereas, we later found out, the other way was a one-stop ride. Never mind? There were very few English speaking people about and we had only learnt how to say 'please' and 'thank you' in Lithuanian. After three bus rides and 1 hour later (should have been 20mins), we finally found our way into the centre.

Far from being a bad experience, and getting lost, this turned out to be just another part of our adventure. On the first trolley bus we caught, we ended up at a terminal having travelled on the city ring road. When we arrived at the terminal we sat there for a few minutes bemused thinking they had just stopped for a break. No this was it, so we got off and went into the office to seek assistance from the transport manager, who was a lady. She was very smartly dressed, middle aged, with piercing blue eyes and a lovely smile. When we entered the office, she was sitting at her desk writing in what looked like a time keeping ledger for the buses. We tried in vain to explain that we wanted to get to the centre of Vilnius, showing her a map out of our travel book, which detailed the main attractions. As she couldn't understand or speak any English whatsoever, she drew us a diagram of where we needed to go. She then led us out to another trolley bus, sat us on board and had a chat with the driver, who then pointed to his watch.

Well we were either being told he was departing in 7 minutes, we were to get off in 7 stops or we were on a no. 7 bus or 7 was his lucky number? We thanked and waved to the lovely lady who had assisted us as she went back to her office. We set off again only this time in the opposite direction. The instructions she gave us said we should get off at a large island and catch another bus going from the bisecting road on the left. After seven minutes and not an island in site, we knew that must have been wrong. Seven stops later and we still were not at the island the transport manger had drawn for us. By now we were worried as the driver kept pointing to 7 o'clock on his watch at each stop. What should we do? Eventually, we reached an island and the roads around looked like the ones the lady had drawn for us so we decided to get off. The driver seemed to think that we should stay on the bus and still kept pointing at his watch. What he was on about we will never know, perhaps we should have stayed on the bus for 7 hours, luckily the lady's instructions were spot on.

Whilst on the bus travelling around the ring road we were shocked to see just how many grey concrete high-rise blocks of flats there were. Not easy on the eye at all, we thought this must be the Russians idea of housing everyone communist style. There was plenty of green space surrounding the huge structures, but no recreation areas visible. This big urban conurbation of high-rise accommodation may be explained by the fact that as we had travelled through Lithuania, the villages were few and far between, so we thought perhaps that most people must live in the cities. These buildings seemed to cover the outer ring road and most looked as if they were in need of some maintenance. We eventually caught the bus the lady advised on her diagram and we were in the centre of Vilnius within no time.

Compared to the surrounding area, the centre of Vilnius is very beautiful and once again as with the others we were really impressed by this city. I don't know what we were expecting, but it certainly was better than we had imagined and really well worth the visit. The churches are magnificent and in most cases very ornate both inside and out. Again, the people were very friendly and helpful with the majority of the service trade speaking some English. The old town has a street culture and is very clean and scenic with a backdrop of modern skyscrapers to one side. Gathered outside the Tourist Information were about twenty British scouts on some kind of exchange adventure tour. Despite being very excited, they were very well behaved.

The old buildings are all very well maintained and impressive to look at. Our first refreshment break was a snack and a beer at a café restaurant, which overlooked a beautiful church. We had Lithuanian potato cakes. Two guys at the next table were tucking into them and they looked rather tasty so we asked the waitress what they were and she recommended the best ones for us. They were a local favourite, which are fried in a light batter and served with sour cream, delicious. After eating and people watching, we walked through some very elegant streets to the main square, which had many statues and what appeared to be a 'non-leaning' tower of Pisa in it. We were taking the circular route, which also took us into the new part of the city. Here were good shops and what was noticeable was the absence of graffiti, so it was all very clean and a pleasure to peruse.

The evening was drawing in and we had come full circle on our walk. Time to eat again, so we set about trying to find a suitable restaurant. We were looking for one that offered traditional fare and spotted a nice place in one of the many picturesque squares. The restaurant was called 'Gabi' and had a pretty cobbled courtyard. We sat ourselves down on a very old, wooden wagon, which had been converted into a bench and table.

We had a bird's eye view into the kitchen and so able to observe the meals being prepared and cooked. The chefs were all ladies dressed in white blouses, checked trousers and puffed hats. One lady was rather plump, one was tall and slim and the other was quite petite. At first glance all looked well until after a while I noticed that two were buzzing around like bees on a honey pot, while the short one appeared to be doing bugger all. Now, I don't know if there was an industrial dispute, but the sound of crockery being plonked on tables in the kitchen was mounting. Eventually, there were some stern words and the small one disappeared. I told Jackie not to have the Sweeny Todd pie! Jackie had country chicken and I had 'the peasant meal' which is a kind of sausage with potatoes. It was all washed down with a carafe of wine.

Whilst enjoying our meal, we were joined at the table by some more very nice, interesting and fun people, Teaude and Heinz who came from Munich. They were currently on a bus tour of the Baltic States but were well travelled, having been all over the world. We whiled away a couple of hours talking about travel, food and our experiences, good and bad. If we do get as far as Munich (it is on the agenda for next year) then we hope to accept their kind invitation to look them up when we get there.

Trying to get back to the campsite, the fun started again, but in reverse. We were rather late leaving the restaurant and it was by then quite dark. We made our way back to the bus stop across from the one where we had alighted earlier in the day. We checked out the timetable (which we should have done before we walked into Vilnius, take note). Well, there were that many conflicting times for the bus we thought we wanted to catch, we were not sure what to expect or even if it had stopped running for the night. The people in the queue didn't speak any English and only added to our confusion with pointing and gesticulations. There were buses arriving all the time, but not the one we wanted. Just as we began to think about ordering a taxi, we had a stroke of luck.

Two young people got off one of the buses and proceeded to have a kiss and a cuddle. (We remember it well!) During a break for air, they saw us looking at the timetable and heard our conversation which by now was about a taxi. The next thing, the young guy came over and in broken English asked us if we needed any help. We did indeed. After much fun and entertainment with the rest of the people, who were still waiting for their bus, he managed to confirm that our bus was still running and that we should wait for it. We had a little chat to them both and they told us that they had been to visit her aunt, somewhere out of the city and on their return had to catch another bus to get home, then he was heading back to his student accommodation, which was in Vilnius. His name was Christophe and he was our St Christopher! Once again we were really impressed at how helpful people were here. It did make us wonder if these people would be as well treated in the UK if they couldn't speak English.

What was also very interesting for us both, were the trolley buses, not trams that ran on lines, but buses which receive power from an overhead power line via a pole on top of the bus. It was a touch of nostalgia for us both as they used to have them on certain bus routes in Derby. Jackie's dad used to be a conductor on the trolley buses years ago, when there was both a driver and a conductor/ess to collect your fare on every bus. They used to be a bit unreliable at times, as the pole would occasionally come off the power line, thus halting the bus while it was reconnected. Derby's buses were double-deckers with the entrance via an open platform at the back. In those days you could smoke on the bus so the driver was put in an enclosed cab at the front to prevent being overcome by smoker's fog. The Baltic States versions are single-decker, reasonably modern with the driver doubling up as the conductor/ess, but with no smoking, of course.

We eventually arrived back at the campsite safe and sound and over a coffee reflected on our experience of the Baltic States, which some people and literature had said could be risky places to visit because of the crime. We had just walked back along a dimly lit path, through a wood and urban area to get back to the campsite, no problem whatsoever. We both agreed that in the main, the people had been very friendly and courteous. Whilst being extremely conscious of our security at all times, we had never felt threatened at any time or been approached by dodgy characters, unlike some places in the UK we could name. So on reflection we both felt we would be able to recommend that anyone visit the Baltic States. The capital cities are surprisingly beautiful and the surrounding countryside is also very nice. The only caveat I would put on this was that we did stick to the main roads whilst travelling and also made sure that we travelled in daylight.

Off to Poland next, and to the Big Posh Polish Wedding of the Year!

Chapter Thirteen

Poland

August 10th to 29th

Sopot - Gdynia - Gdansk – Torun – Bydgoszcz – Warsaw – Krakow – Auschwitz - Wroclaw

Poland was the one destination that had been on the agenda from the start as we were due to attend my brothers step daughter's wedding in Bydgoszcz on the 20th August. We had also arranged to see our fiends Clive, Keith and Eddie in Gdynia, to enjoy another few days together. They had also been invited to the wedding, so it was all set to be a great family occasion and friend's reunion for us all.

As we entered Poland it became quite clear that this was a country still recovering from a long time of occupation. Poland is a large country and it is obvious that it will take them longer to renovate and restore than the smaller Baltic States. You can, however, tell that it is moving forward, if not quite at the pace the locals would like. It's only twenty years since they gained their full independence and it is clear to see that they have made great strides in a relatively short time. We passed many construction sites and areas where renovations were under well under way. It would be interesting to visit in another twenty years' time to see just how much progress has been made.

We had been warned, so it came as no surprise, to find that the roads were really bad in places, and so we were reduced to travelling at 20 mph. We had to dodge large potholes and deep ruts made by the huge heavy goods Lorries. In other parts the roads were well maintained and looked like they had only just been resurfaced. I think the worst thing for us was that some of the roads were so rutted from use by heavy goods vehicles, it caused Belle to snake alarmingly and we felt very unsafe. What was a surprise to us was that the roads were as busy as in the UK, if not more so, and the drivers just as aggressive.

The landscape was pretty much the same as parts of England, becoming more open with rolling vistas. There were lots of small farms dotted about amongst green hedgerows. In general, it all looked well-tended. As we travelled along, we still had the company of our old friend, the Stork. Quite a lot of the houses are built using grey breezeblocks, without the outer layer of rendering, which made them look unfinished. There were also some very grand houses in amongst all of this. There was certainly a mix.

Our first campsite in Poland was in the north, close to the Great Mazurian Lakes. It looked a really pretty area but we were too tired that evening to walk into the small town or even take photos. The drive, which we estimated would take us four hours, had taken us seven. We would learn to double any expected travel times due to the state of the roads and also take into account the very heavy traffic. The campsite was well set out and maintained and an inspection of the toilet facilities revealed a clean modern set up, but at reception we found they spoke very little English.

Later that evening, when it was dark, there was a knock on our door. We wondered who it could it be at that time of night. When we opened the door, there was a guy holding a bag of what looked like smoked fish. He was trying to ask us something in Polish. We weren't sure if he was selling the fish, or if he wanted us to cook it for him! We politely declined whatever it was he was after and off he went. Was this the norm on Polish campsites?

Next day we were up early and off to Sopot, a popular holiday resort on the north coast between Gdansk and Gdynia. According to our guidebook, Sopot had great beaches, and in the 20's and 30's it was frequented by the rich and famous.

Sheila decided to throw us off course, taking us down side roads which were no more than unpaved tracks, but obviously still well used by the locals. Boy, was it a long day again. Once back on the main road, there were road works everywhere, some were repairs to the existing road surface, whilst others were the construction of new motorways. So we would fly along one piece of modern new road only to meet a traffic jam a few kilometres later. These hold ups caused queues of traffic for miles, especially around Gdansk where the main artery along the front was undergoing repairs to the tramlines. It was a nightmare, two hours to travel ten kilometres. Finally, we arrived at the campsite after another gruelling day travelling. The campsite was located near the sea front and so ideally placed for both a walk into Sopot, and also a five minute walk to the little station for the regional train into Gdynia and Gdansk. We received a warm welcome at reception, but again, very little English spoken. At first sight, it all looked a bit grubby, as some of the caravans were very old and dirty. Although the caravans looked like tourers, we think that they were actually left on the site all the time and rented; out to families coming to the site for their holidays. They were definitely in need of some TLC. However, after our usual inspection, the site was all very clean where it needed to be.

The following day we went for a walk into Sopot, through the woods and along a picturesque block paved promenade, which backed the lovely white sandy beaches. It was really busy with holiday makers skateboarding and cycling along. It was a family resort with lots going on for children and it all had a pleasant ambiance. It was easy to see why it is still a very popular holiday resort. Also along the promenade were beach bars and restaurants and when we reached the centre of Sopot the beach widened and was really stunning. There were street sellers here as well as a covered walkway with many jewellery stalls. It was very up market and the place was buzzing with people. There was a very impressive hotel on the front, aptly named 'The Grand', where a wedding was taking place. All the guests were very well dressed, even an Afghan hound, which had obviously been invited as it had had its cream silky fur plaited, it looked amazing.

Before going back to the campsite, we called at the nearby shop. This was our first visit to a Polish food store and it was just like any UK corner shop. It was a busy little place, holidaymakers stocking up with essentials and children running around with ice-lollies in their mouths. The variety of food on offer was very different to the UK with lots of pre-packed stuffed dumplings, salads and processed meats. All the food was very inexpensive. We bought a ready-made Lasagne for 8 zloty, which was about £2. It turned out to be very nice and full of meat, what kind, we weren't quite sure, but nevertheless, very tasty. It was cash only at the tills, but at those prices who cares. As the shop was across the road from the station we also took the opportunity to check out the train times for our visit to Gdynia the following day. We were so looking forward to seeing our friends there. We spent the rest of the day relaxing in the warm sunshine and watching the campsite slowly fill up with caravans and motorhomes from all over Europe. Across from us were two old caravans occupied by two young Polish families. They set up two long tables and proceeded to fire up the bbq. Before long they were having a great time enjoying their meal and playing with the little children. Once the children had been tired out (that was our trick to get some peace) and put to bed, the party moved up a gear and lasted well into the night. We lay awake listening to them, they must have been telling jokes as every few minutes they roared with laughter. When we got up next day, all was very quiet. Left-over food and empty bottles of vodka were everywhere, just as it had been left. We had to smile. What are holidays for if you can't enjoy yourself?

We bought our tickets, (75p each) from the automated ticket machine, and then caught the train, which was every ten minutes, into Gdynia to rendezvous with Clive, Keith and Eddie at their hotel. The small trains were very old fashioned and slowly clanked and clunked along the tracks. We really did feel that we were in what must have been a very poor country.

Gdynia is a large port but also another busy seaside resort. We walked through the main shopping area to get to their hotel. Our friends had positioned themselves at various points outside, so as not to miss our arrival. Luckily, Eddie spotted Jackie's blonde hair as we entered the hotel and so it was hugs and kisses all round. If you can recall, when we met up with them in France, they were the guinea pigs for my soups and here they were, back for more! The hotel was ideally situated not far from the beachfront, was large, modern and comfortable.

It was very hot and sunny so after some well-needed refreshments at a nearby bar, we made our way to the beach. There were crowds of people gathering around a huge stage that was being erected, in readiness for a rock bands performance that evening. It was 13th August, and so the height of the holiday season. The place was alive with bikini-clad girls and hip young guys eyeing them up.

Our friends had arrived in Gdynia a couple of days before and so had had chance to have a look around and get a feel for the place. They were as surprised as we were by how nice it was. They had already tried out a few restaurants and were particularly impressed by an Italian one, so took us back there for lunch. It was their treat too .How kind was that. They never said, but we did wonder if they were worried that we might suggest they came back to Belle for more soup!

Before leaving them, we made arrangements for us all to get on the same train to Gdansk, the following day. They were to get the 12.00 noon train and we would get on it as it passed through Sopot. We had timed the journey there, so it was due to arrive in Sopot about 15 minutes after leaving Gdynia. Clive was supposed to stick his head out of the window as the train approached the platform, so we could see him. He sent a text to us to say they were on carriage no. 2. When it arrived, no head appeared and all the carriages were no. 2 anyway, so we didn't get on it. We waited for the next train and just as it approached we got a call asking where we were, they were all in Gdansk! We eventually arrived in Gdansk and there they were, standing on the platform, clapping and cheering loudly. Cheeky things! What we wanted to know, was, where was Clive's head? And, how on earth were we to know which carriage to get on when all the carriages were number 2? What a bunch of fools we all were, no.2 meant 2nd class. What a laugh though.

Gdansk is something to see. We arrived just as one of the main thoroughfares was in the midst of a street festival. The buildings are so beautiful, very ornate, five and six storey high. The facades were brightly painted, many were edged with gold. It was another hot day and heaving with people. We had a wonderful afternoon as we sat listening to a children's choir on stage. Lots of restaurants lined the streets with alfresco dining. Winding our way through the narrow streets, we came to the Harbour front. There was an old galleon which sails up and down the waterways in the harbour. Actually, it was a bit of trick as it was motor powered... *"I say Horatio, the Spanish are getting damn close"*. *"Don't worry Hardy, switch to motor power"*. *"What's motor power?"* *"I don't know, but if the Polish have it, we should have it!"*

Thankfully, we all managed to get on the same train back. We said our goodbyes as we neared Sopot station. The next time we would see them would be in Bydgoszcz, where the wedding was to take place. We also looked forward to seeing them again as it was Keith's 70th birthday and unbeknown to him, a surprise party had been secretly planned.

When we got off the train at Sopot we realised we had got off one stop too soon. It was fine for us, we looked forward to the walk back along the promenade to the campsite. To our delight there was another street festival in progress, how lucky was that? The place was absolutely rammed with people enjoying themselves and the cacophony of noise was unbelievable. We were treated to a traditional Polish dance troop on a stage with a supporting band giving it their all, as well as a rock group playing on the beach. We eventually reached the campsite, well and truly shattered, and so it wasn't long before we were both in the land of nod.

As we left Sopot, we chose to ignore Sheila for once and so avoided the roadwork's along the front at Sopot/Gdansk. We were right to do so and so had a great journey down to Bydgoszcz. The motorway was newly surfaced, as was the road into Bydgoszcz itself. Clive, Keith and Eddie, however, left a little later than us and chose to follow the seafront road around Gdansk, even though we had warned them about the roadwork's. They spent four frustrating hours in the traffic there and so arrived in Bydgoszcz later that day, much the worse for wear.

We decided to go straight to the Hotel Pod Orlem, which is in the centre of Bydgoszcz. All of the wedding party were going to stay there, some arriving before others during the week leading up to the wedding on the Saturday. We had also booked ourselves a room for three nights over the wedding weekend. It was rather foolish of us not to have booked a campsite near Bydgoszcz but we were certain there was one close by, so not too worried. Jackie went in and asked the receptionist for directions to the nearest campsite. The receptionist was very helpful and spoke good English. After consulting the Internet, she found the nearest campsite for us, and kindly phoned them to tell them we were on our way.

We journeyed on a few miles east of the city until we came across the campsite signs. Oh dear! The road in was horrendous, I thought Belle would break in two it was so full of potholes. We arrived at the campsite and Jackie's eagle eyes spotted a rubbish heap just at the entrance to the site. Our suspicions were raised. We were met by a young boy of about ten years of age, who said we could go and choose our spot, which we did. It looked ok, in the middle of woods, there were other people about and little chalets made out of wood were dotted about the site. We pitched up and had something to eat, then decided to go to the reception to book in.

Oh my goodness. As we approached we could see that it was in need of some real TLC. Well, actually, that was a complete understatement, the whole place needed demolishing. I went to inspect the gent's toilets and showers, which were in a disgusting state as they were awash with water. To my horror, I pulled the chain and the water gushed out the back of the cistern and toilet and onto the floor, it looked like a scene from the 'Slum Dog Millionaire' movie. The kitchen area was just as bad and that is no exaggeration. It was a complete health hazard. We were totally speechless. It looked like the site was aimed at canoeists and fishermen who would make use of the lake and who probably would put up with that level of cleanliness, but I'm not sure. I would gladly have thrown a hand grenade into the toilet block sooner than use it. I had also looked into one of the chalets, which appeared to cater for young couples wanting more privacy. They were just as bad, with old stained mattresses on chipboard bases. I told Jackie not to look. It makes my skin crawl even now, just thinking about it.

Consequently, you have never seen anyone move so fast. Belle was packed and we were out of there before you could have blinked an eye. As we were leaving, the camp manager came over to us. I'm sorry to have to admit, but we had to tell him a white lie. We said we had taken a call and were urgently needed in Bydgoszcz, so sorry, we could not stay. Shame on us!

Just down the road and well out of sight, we got out the lap top and the ACSI campsite software and found a campsite in a place called Torun, an hour's drive from Bydgoszcz. The train station was only a few minutes' walk away, so no bother at all for us to commute for the wedding.

We arrived safely and wow, what a difference, it was five star compared to what we had escaped from. We advised the receptionist that we would be staying for one week and leaving Belle for the three nights over the wedding weekend. That was no problem, so all was fine. What a relief!

The following day we planned to go into Bydgoszcz early evening because we were to attend the surprise birthday party for Keith. That left us with the whole day to explore Torun. We had never heard of the place before the ACSI guide had thrown it up as the closest campsite to Bydgoszcz. It was quite touristy, which is why there was a campsite nearby. The small town of Torun is situated on the river Wisla and was founded by the Teutonic Knights in 1454. Its main claim to fame is that it is the birthplace of Nicolas Copernicus, the famous Astronomer. It is a beautiful town, has good shops, lovely restaurants and cafes, and still retains its medieval character and layout with fortress walls facing the river. We were very impressed with our little gem of a find again and spent a pleasant day wandering the streets, old market square and taking in the views down by the river.

One interesting point was the re-appearance of the pad locks complete with messages, attached to the railings on the bridge which spanned the Wisla. We had first seen these at Montmartre in Paris. We would see this new form of graffiti in other Polish cities. Some of them are quite unique with messages like 'Piotr woz ere!'

After having a light snack, we caught the train into Bydgoszcz. The journey took about an hour, so different from our earlier journey and very relaxing. It made about ten stops on the way and so we got chance to see more of the Polish countryside and suburbs. It was a mixed bag, with well-kept places in the main, but a few places where suburbs needed raising to the ground. The trains look a wider gauge than ours with the carriages having more space. We were on one of the regional trains and all the carriages appeared to be marked 2nd class, we never saw 1st class. The carriages were all open plan, having double seats to each side, very basic. They had been built to last but by now were old and rickety.

Well, back at the Hotel Pod Orlem it's a big family re-union as everybody was gathering for a fun few days before the wedding. We met up with my brother Keith and his wife Ela and Keith's children from his previous marriage, William and Phoebe. Ela came to England thirty years ago from Poland and has two lovely daughters Urzula and Monica, also from a previous marriage. Urzula was to be married to Craig, which was the reason for the gathering in Bydgoszcz, which is Ela's home town. So the main contingent was from the UK with Ela's mother, sister, brother and friends making up the Polish contingent. Our son Howard and his girlfriend Amy were due to arrive later that week, so it was destined to be a great time for us all. After a few welcome drinks we were all relaxed and ready for the evening's main event.

Keith (not my brother) had no idea that it had been arranged and when he came down into the foyer, we were all there singing 'Happy Birthday'. We soon learnt that he, Eddie and Clive had been for a drink at lunchtime. Keith had one too many and couldn't understand why the others weren't celebrating his birthday with him. He even told them that he thought they were boring old 'fxxts'. Not realising of course that Clive and Eddie were trying to preserve him and themselves for the evening ahead. He was really pleased to see everyone and it was a total surprise for him. We met up with more of the wedding party that had arrived during the day and made our way to a lovely restaurant called 'Villa Calvados'. The restaurant was a ten minute walk from the hotel and set in a Romanesque garden with a mini coliseum and pencil firs. The inside was luxuriously decorated throughout with antique furniture and paintings, all tastefully done to create an ambiance of opulence. There were fourteen of us and we all sat down at a long dining table decorated with fresh flowers, perfectly set out cutlery and sparkling cut glass wine goblets. There were chandeliers at one end of the room, and a large painting of a Polish knight fighting the Ottoman's. Keith was so overwhelmed by it all he went back to the hotel to fetch his credit card, he insisted that he would pay for the evening. It was one of those magical moments where you think you have gone back in time and are playing out a part in one of Tolstoy's novels.

The food was some of the best we have ever tasted, so fresh and expertly presented, the choice on the menu was top notch too. The chef had recently moved back from Paris to set up his own restaurant and he had done a bloody good job, it was very impressive. We called for a taxi at 10.30pm to make sure we were at the station to catch the last train back to Torun. It was difficult to leave as everybody was having a riotous time.

Bydgoszcz station was just the same as any of our train stations, late at night, with the young ones messing around, playing jokes on one another, full of fun. This train was very old fashioned, similar to the ones we remember when we were children. The carriages had narrow corridors and compartments for the travellers. They even had curtains at the windows.

The following afternoon we went back to the station, to get the train into Bydgoszcz, as we had been invited for tea and cakes at Ela's mother's house. We waited and we waited, then there were announcements, that we couldn't understand a word of, coming over the PA system. Eventually, the train arrived, an hour late. When we eventually got to Ela's mums, we were told that there was a one day strike which affected the regional railways (just like UK). We were lucky to get on the intercity train. We enjoyed the cakes and Earl Grey tea out in the garden at Ela's mum's as the weather was nice again.

Then came the Vodka! The Polish people always drink Vodka and fruit juice, morning, midday and evening, it would appear. Regardless of the Vodka, we still couldn't properly converse with the family, having to rely on my brother's wife Ela as the interpreter. Ela's niece, Angelica, could speak some English so kindly checked on the trains for us. Luckily there was one train, but again, we had to leave early to ensure we caught it back to Torun. It was a tense moment for us on the platform as there were more announcements and we were the only people there, but eventually the train did turn up. What a relief that was!

Things were hotting up for the wedding. Jackie had to go into Torun to get her hair done. Well, it was about time, the last time she had it done was 15th April. Oh girls, you can imagine what her roots were like, despite being out in the sun all day! Jackie went to the Tourist Information to enquire where the nearest hairdresser was and also for their recommendation. Another stroke of luck, there was a good one just around the corner. Even though none of the ladies could converse, the lovely girl did a great job and Jackie was well pleased, it cost half the usual price.

Jackie went into Torun on her own, that's how safe it felt, and I joined up with her after she had had her hair done. We had a meal in one of the street restaurants and whiled away another afternoon. On the walk back we decided to have an ice cream served at one of the street side ice cream parlours. We sat outside and waited for service which never came, so in the end we went in to order. We were choosing which flavour ice cream to have when we noticed the iced cakes up the other end of the counter. They were a living mass of wasps. It looked like the honey comb you take out of a beehive to extract the honey. We both looked mesmerised at the spectacle in front of us. The young girl behind the counter just carried on as if nothing was happening. We sat outside eating our ice creams watching the wasp infestation inside. As we were about to leave I asked the waitress, "How much are the iced wasp cakes?" She said "We don't sell ice wasp cakes", I said, "Well why do you have them on display then?" Ha! Ha! Just joking, I wish I could have said it though.

Next day we were up and packed ready for the week-end ahead. We just popped into the reception on the way out of the campsite to remind them that we were leaving and would be back on the Monday. Good job we did. They asked us to move Belle. Why? Because there was some sort of Vintage Car Rally taking place over that weekend and there would be hundreds of people on site and of course needed the area to be clear. We packed up and moved Belle well out of the way before setting off yet again. Great, we missed the train of course. We had to wait another hour and a half for the next one. By this time, hunger got the better of us and so we had to have a Kebab. No wonder we haven't lost any weight, despite all the cycling and walking. They allow food kiosks on the platforms which sell all sorts from hot dogs to burgers and chips, it's all very different. No buffet cars on their trains perhaps?

It was only about a twenty minute walk from the station, but we were fully laden with bags and clothes and it was a blisteringly hot day. We were far too hot and bothered by the time we reached Bydgoszcz so we took a taxi to the hotel Pod Orlem (translated means 'Under the Eagle'). You can see as you approach, the great big Golden Eagle on top of the building. This time we were stopping for three nights and not just asking for directions. The Hotel was old and beautiful with oak panelling and burgundy furnishings. At the back of the foyer was a grand sweeping staircase and crystal chandeliers hung from the ceilings. Our room was very spacious and had a shower and a bath, in fact it was superb. As soon as Jackie saw the bath she was in, and so was I, err not at the same time you mucky people, we hadn't seen a bath in 3 months! We do have a shower every day, thank you, and back home I usually prefer only to shower, but Jackie does enjoy a soak in the bath, so it was an added luxury for her.

We met up with all our family and friends again and also the rest of the wedding party who had since arrived. Howard and Amy had arrived the evening before and were actually slightly worse for wear having been out on the town with the soon to be wed, Craig and Urzula. We persuaded Howard and Amy to come and have a look around the centre of Bydgoszcz with us. Over coffee, they told us that as Howard had had strict instructions to bring Jackie's hat and my suit with him he tried to carry the hat on the plane in a carrier bag, but the Ryanair staff said he could only take on one item of hand luggage. No problem for Howard, he put the hat on, hey presto, one piece of hand luggage and one very camp looking young man! All a bit ridiculous really, but rules are rules.

We were all pleasantly surprised with Bydgoszcz. It is very modern and the immediate area around the main square had been recently renovated. Parts of Bydgoszcz were still in need of an uplift, but what they had achieved up to now was of a very high standard. They had also made the most of the river, which ran through the town, with seating areas and landscaped gardens either side. That evening we took Howard and Amy to Villa Calvados, the restaurant we had been to for Keith's surprise birthday party. We wanted them to see just how good it was. They thought it was superb too.

Before we knew it, it was the big day. The weather was good, a bit windy, but warm and sunny, perfect. The Polish do things differently. All the ladies were elegantly dressed and all wore hats, while the men were in their best suits. It was a traditional white wedding with top hat and tails for the groom and his party. The wedding carriage waited for the bride at the entrance to the hotel. It was a magnificent cream and black carriage with two white horses. The bride came down the golden staircase, accompanied by my brother Keith (her stepfather). After a brief stop for a photo shoot, they continued out to the awaiting carriage. Urzula looked absolutely stunning. She had said she wanted to look like a princess and she certainly did. It was just like a wedding from a fairy-tale.

When the carriage had left with the bride and her stepfather, it was the turn of the Best Man, the Ushers and the Bridesmaids to leave. They were whisked away in open top limos to Bydgoszcz Cathedral, where the ceremony was to take place. The rest of the wedding party then walked from the hotel, through the town to the Cathedral, which was just off the main square. The ladies had to hang on to their hats all the way as there was a slight breeze. We eventually arrived at the

Cathedral and the inside was a magnificent affair, all in a lovely powder blue and gold theme.

Urzula walked down the aisle to the traditional wedding march being pumped out on a magnificent organ. The wedding ceremony itself was conducted in English and Polish, so we could understand some of it, but not all. It had a wonderful feel to it, with the incantations and rising and falling of the Priests words backed up by a choir. We both find wedding ceremonies very moving and find ourselves wishing Craig and Urzula the happiness we have found. (We only had a registry office affair and then back to my parents for tea and cakes). Luckily there were no hymns as this would have proved a riot in English and Polish!

Sorry digressing again, back to the wedding ceremony. Within no time, there was the commitment from the Bride and Groom and they were man and wife. Afterwards the photos were taken in the centre of Bydgoszcz in the park by the river and Craig and Urzula let fly two white turtle doves, as a memento of their marriage. It was then back to the hotel for the reception, another pleasant stroll as we took in more of the sites Bydgoszcz had to offer.

The reception was in the banqueting hall and the place settings and flowers looked magnificent, much the same as we have in the UK, but there the similarity ends. We had the first of many main courses, the speeches, then more courses, mainly meat, the live band and dancing, then more courses. Next came the games, including 'musical chairs' and 'guess whose feet you are smelling' (a Polish favourite). Followed by more courses and finally supper/breakfast at 6.00am in the morning!

No wine at the tables, only vodka and assorted flavoured fruit juices. My brother Keith assured me that if you only drink vodka you will not have a hangover. Well, we certainly had a thick head in the morning. It was all a memorable experience, especially the conversations between English and Polish under the influence of vodka. It's amazing what you think you understand with the waving of arms and gesticulations. Breakfast was at 10.00am which saw none of the younger generation turn up for, but the stalwarts of the older group all made it, having gone to bed at around 2.00am, ok we cheated a bit. The young ones appeared at various times throughout the day and all looked rather worse for wear having tried to keep up with the Poles, and mixing the drinks. During the reception and while I was still sober, I had a rather interesting conversation with a young Polish mother. She had worked in Germany before coming back to Poland to marry. Her husband was a builder who had also worked away in England before returning to Poland. I asked how they were coping back in Poland with their newly born son. She said it was very difficult making ends meet and that although things were a lot cheaper in Poland it was all relative to the wages paid, which were very low. Their expectations for the future were high, but they wished prosperity was happening now. I asked if she was planning to have any more children, she said that they could not afford another baby as they wanted to give their son every educational opportunity they could. She said they were contemplating working abroad again as the wages were so much better than in Poland.

After the wedding on Saturday, Sunday was a day of quiet meditation, a casual walk around Bydgoszcz and an evening meal with all the family, which turned out to be a curry, once again, nice, but not up to UK standards. On our way back from the restaurant we saw a real live beaver nestling amongst the reeds in the river Brda that runs through Bydgoszcz. Amazing sight.

We said goodbye to everyone on Monday apart from Howard and Amy who came back to Torun with us. They wanted to see a bit more of Poland and to see for themselves how lovely Torun was, especially as we had been raving on about it! It was also a good experience for them to travel on the public transport which was so different from ours.

Howard and Amy enjoyed their time in Torun and it was sad to put them back on the train. Although they were sad to be leaving us, they were also pleased as it proved to be the 'Night of the Mosquitos'. The campsite was alive with them in the evening as we arrived back from sightseeing in Torun. We attempted to sit out and have some drinks and nibbles before Howard and Amy departed. Poor Amy was bitten all over, despite putting on loads of the repellent we had bought. Perhaps Polish mosquitos can't read what it said on the spray. It was the same on the platform at the station, they were attacking in swarms. It was quite amusing, for all the wrong reasons, to see people swatting and wafting and running about to avoid getting bit. It looked like people had been afflicted by a case of St Vitus dance!

We were soon back on the road heading east to Warsaw. We were really looking forward to it, although some people had said it wasn't such a great place to visit and that Krakow was far better. Regardless, we were determined to go and see what Warsaw had to offer.

The campsite wasn't anything to shout about, but it was ideally located for the short ride into the centre on the bus. We were on the outskirts of Warsaw and just next to our campsite was a state of the art shopping centre which looked like it had only just been built. It had a Carrefour as well as an M&S and other international retail shops, including the obligatory McDonalds for Wi-Fi.

We caught the bus into the centre having bought our tickets from a local convenience store and then validated on the bus. We are soon in the centre and remembered to take note of the landscape and bus stop for the return journey. We absolutely loved it, right from the word go. There is a very modern part to the city, and also a beautiful old part. We headed for the old part first, which had been reconstructed under the Russians to its previous glory. We walked to Plac Zamkowy down impressive wide boulevards and came across a monument to the Jewish ghetto that was created by the Nazis in 1940 and destroyed in the 1943 uprising while the Russians stood idly by some 30km away. There is a metal track in the pavement tracing where the enclosing wall used to stand. Across the road is an old building which used to be a bank at that time, which bears the marks of the uprising and is one of only a few surviving buildings.

Plac Zamkowy is a magnificent square, as is the surrounding area with its battlements and Royal Castle. It was pulsating with tourists, as are all the little back streets, cafés and restaurants. We wandered around the streets and avenues admiring the classical architecture and buildings. As with many of the eastern bloc countries there was a beautiful church around every corner. We discovered a little museum selling Thai puppets and for a while I toyed with the idea of buying one, but as Jackie pointed out we had no home to put it in. They were exquisite though and reminded me of the film 'The King and I'.

We did take a look at the new part of Warsaw before finding our way back to the bus stop. Again, we were impressed; we saw the embassies and business area. The shops were chic and modern. It was a great day and we really enjoyed Warsaw and were so glad not to have missed this marvellous city.

Back at the campsite next morning we couldn't believe our eyes when we saw another Autotrail Motorhome a few pitches down from ours. It belonged to Gordon and Janice from Durham who were retired and visiting Poland for the first time. They had been to Krakow (our next stop) and had arrived in Warsaw late the night before, so we exchanged travel notes. Gordon had put an engine management chip on his Motorhome, which was bigger than ours and claimed he was getting around 30 miles per gallon compared to my 25. I will look into this for next year as he has given me the address of the company who supplied it. They recommended a campsite for us to stay at whilst we visited Krakow. They seemed to be smitten with the place, so we were really excited to see it too.

From Warsaw we drove south towards Krakow, staying at a lovely little campsite on the way, as it's too far for one days travel and we were not in a rush anyway. It was located by a lake just a few miles off the main highway. It turned out to be another win from our ACSI guide with its map on the lap top. After a good night's rest we were up and on our way again.

The countryside was very open and flat with low rolling hills, mostly farmland. True to their word the campsite proved to be as good as they said it was. So clean and well-kept by the young students working there, they were clearing leaves up all day long. There were pots of geraniums between each pitch to keep the mozzies at bay. There was a local shop just a short walk away so we stocked up with provisions.

Right next to the campsite was a huge outdoor swimming pool and it was packed with Polish people enjoying the heat wave. We sat and relaxed outside Belle, enjoying the sunshine and a few drinks. It really is too much like hard work at times...

Krakow was a very compact old town centred on the largest market square in Europe. We entered by the river and the castle which overlooked the town. The main square is magnificent and was a hive of activity with school choirs singing on a stage and surrounded by bars and restaurants. In the centre of the square is the Cloth Hall, which is now an arcade and houses all sorts of craft and jewellery stalls. There were also plenty of little kiosk selling all sorts of traditional Polish snack foods including sausages, roast meats, Pierogi (little dumplings with various fillings) and Bigos (cabbage and sausage stew).

It is reputedly one of the most beautiful cities in Europe and whilst we did agree it was very beautiful, we both preferred Warsaw. It just shows that there is truth in the saying, 'each to his own'. It was so hot, about 95 degrees, we had to sit under the trees in the park that runs around the old city, whilst the sun was at its hottest.

We spent the rest of the afternoon exploring the city. I even bought Jackie a sun parasol, it was that hot out in the full sun. Back to the main square where we spied a little bar selling cocktails. We sat down and proceeded to get a little tipsy, I sampled the Black Russians and White Russians while Jackie had her favourite Mahito's. Once again there was that lovely atmosphere with the sound of people enjoying themselves so we sat and quite literally drank it all in. We decided we better move while we still could as the cocktails are going down far too easily, as they do when they only cost £2.50 each. Feeling peckish, we took off to look for a Tapas that I had found in our DK Eyewitness guide. After several minutes exploring we asked a waiter if he knew where it was as we thought it should be where we were? He said you are in the right place but it's now a trendy European restaurant, so we decided to eat there. The food didn't disappoint either.

Back at the main square things were hotting up as the school choir had been replaced by a traditional Polish skiffle group, banging out popular tunes, on the stage. Sometime later they were replaced by a "Rock Band" who looked as if they had come out the ark, not one looked younger than 70. They were dressed very similar to our London Pearly Kings, a bit Chas and Dave. Still they begin to bash out a good Status Quo type sound which the audience seemed to know and sang along to. It was getting really quite late by now so we wandered back to the bus stop.

During the day we had noticed that there were lots of girl guides and scouts mulling around. As we went back by the castle, there must have been some sort of world jamboree going on. There were hundreds of scouts and guides enjoying a large event being held by the river. We obviously missed that one. We were however, never without some sort of different scene to entertain us. It was great.

We spent the next day relaxing at the campsite while Jackie caught up with washing again. We also planned our next stop.

One of the reasons we travelled to the south of Poland was so that we could visit Auschwitz, well me to be specific, I don't think Jackie would have gone by choice. I had always been very interested in the Second World War and had read many books on the subject. I had always found the subject of the death camps and the factories for slaughtering humans both fascinating and very disturbing, so felt a macabre fascination and magnetic attraction to go to Auschwitz, lest we forget.

Entrance to Auschwitz is free, but the car park is not. You can pay for a guided tour, which we chose to do and would recommend if you want to make the most of it.

We arrived mid-afternoon to take in the tour not realising there were two parts to it. The first is Auschwitz 1, which started off as a place for political dissidents or anyone the Nazi party felt they should get rid of. Life expectancy was three months for women and four months for men, all meticulously documented. Words cannot truly describe the horrors that we saw. We went into the only surviving gas chamber and cremation area, the horror of being there where thousands died was palpable.

Part two of our tour included a bus trip to Auschwitz II, Birkenhau, the death camp. This was the purpose built camp where the Jews were bought in by train and sent to their deaths. Men, Women, old folk and children, altogether one and a half million. You can see the remains of the habitation blocks where they were kept before death. The tour guide later told us that the reason he worked there, was because his grandfather had been imprisoned in Birkenhau at the end of the war, so luckily he survived.

As you walk around, it brings home to you, the horrors one human being can inflict on another. It is some of the smaller detail that is the hardest to come to terms with, rather than the numbers, which defy imagination. I'm afraid this is where human beings become animals and not worthy of the title human. I am talking of the planners, architects and willing participants of the holocaust, not necessarily some of the innocents who had no choice in their actions. And yet it is still disappointing for humans to this day, to know that it's still happening, all be it on a smaller scale as we saw in the break-up of Yugoslavia. It is sad that one human beings colour, religion, politics, sex or country of origin, cannot be tolerated by another.

Jackie and I stayed at a campsite nearby, which was a centre for prayer. Built specifically for people to go and remember those that had suffered. Needless to say, we had a very disturbed night with little sleep, as we contemplated the scale of suffering, that took place close by. I wholeheartedly think Auschwitz should be visited at least once by everybody.

Next day, eastwards toward Wroclaw, our final city in Poland. By now we had had our fill of the little Pierogi dumplings and the cabbage and sausage stew, Bigos. This was again a campsite which was part of an Olympic site a few years back. I won't go into detail, but it had seen better days. We only intended to stay one night and would use our own facilities if need be. We did manage to use the toilets, but not the showers; they were just too old and rusty. There is always a silver lining as we met a great young couple from Australia, Matt and Steph. They had known one another at school, but did not particularly like one another then. It was only later, as Matt was preparing to leave to work in the UK as an electrician in London on the 2012 Olympic site, that they realised they did in fact like one another and started their romance. Matt had called Steph over to London when he had finished his work so they could tour Europe before going back to Australia. They had bought an old Ford Escort van for £285 and kitted it out for their road trip. They had been to France, Spain, Germany and now Poland; they were heading to the Tetra Mountains in Poland, which are supposed to be magnificent. We spent an evening chatting in the back of Belle with beers for the boys and wine for the girls. We chatted into the small hours, exchanging travel information, talking about favourite films, music and life in general. During the course of the evening a big yellow Sherpa van pulled up next to Belle and out spilled seven more young Australians and New Zealanders also touring Europe. So out we went and had a little chat with them too, but it was getting late and loud, so we four scuttled back into Belle and continued our evening. In the morning we exchanged details with Matt and Steph and hope to keep in touch with them.

Prior to entertaining with Steph and Matt we paid a brief visit into Wroclaw as it was only 15mins by tram. The tram system was very modern and a joy to use, as we could pay on entry. Wroclaw has a lovely old centre which we walked around in an hour before going back to the campsite. The environs were the same as any large city - a bit grim from what we could see.

That's about it for Poland; we really enjoyed our time there. You get a lot for your money, food and drink is inexpensive. A really good meal out for two with wine only cost about £20. The language barrier was quite a problem, most seem not to be able to speak English, and why should they. We wondered if some of them had been mistreated when they had come to work in the UK, as there is definitely an edge to some of them, although most seemed friendly enough.

The Polish are a proud, hardworking nation and are aspiring to better things, as with the rest of the old Eastern Bloc. They are enjoying their freedom, but want a good life style today, not tomorrow, which we think frustrates them. Culturally, there are some amazing places to visit and we only saw a few. We hope to go back sometime in the future and see what more Poland has to offer.

Chapter Fourteen

Germany 2

August 30th to September 25th

Dresden – Spreewald – Berlin – Hanover – Hertz Mountains –
Frankfurt – Rhine Valley – Mosel Valley

As we travelled from Poland across the border into Germany, we were quite excited to be back. Not only because the roads are fantastic, but we had so enjoyed being in Germany earlier in the tour, when we had visited Bremen and Hamburg.

Our first stop was to be Dresden, which is situated on the river Elbe. It had, at Stalin's request been flattened by the British and American bombers at the very end of the war in 1945 and to this day remains a very controversial subject. Because of this, we were not sure what type of welcome we would find when we visited the city, as we assumed most would have lost loved ones. We need not have been concerned as the welcome we received was very friendly.

The nearest campsite we could find was one just outside Moritzburg, a bus ride into the city. The campsite was really big, well laid out and surrounded by beautiful countryside, very much like England. The receptionist was very friendly but only spoke a little English. The facilities here were of a high standard, as we had come to expect from the Germans. There was just one small problem, in that the water pipe on our pitch didn't work, but it wasn't of any inconvenience, there were plenty of others to use. Other than that the site was perfect. Not only had it lots of pitches for motorhomes, caravans and tents, there were pretty wooden chalets dotted about in the woodland.

We were soon set up on our pitch in the forest and decided to explore on our bikes. It had been a while since we had been on our bikes as the Eastern bloc countries didn't have many cycle paths, so that was another thing we had been looking forward to in Germany, where they do cater for cyclists. The weather was a bit overcast but perfect for a bike ride. We followed the track out of the site. Where we were off to, we had no idea, but whizzing along through the fields was exhilarating.

We soon found a peaceful little village and followed a horse and trap, carrying a few tourists, through the centre. There was also an old small-gauge steam railway winding its way through the hills in the near distance. It was so picturesque. Unfortunately, there was no village pub, so nowhere to sit in the sun and have a quick pint. No bother, we turned round and rode back the way we had come, back to Belle for tea.

When we arrive at a campsite, we always ask the staff for as many directions and information as we can. Usually, they are able to give us print out of local bus timetables, shopping areas etc. Most have display racks full of information on the local attractions. So armed with our timetables and information, we set off the following day to get the bus at the end of road, to take us into Dresden. While we were waiting for the bus, I took the time to find a stick and knock a few conkers off the Horse Chestnut trees that lined the road. One was a beauty and I would have loved to have played conkers with someone, as I was sure I had a winner in my hands. Jackie wouldn't oblige, she had just manicured and painted her nails. Spoil sport!

We arrived at the Bahnhof Station Dresden - Neustadt, not the central station. As there was not a Tourist Information office there, (there usually is at the main stations), we asked a young lady for the walking directions into the centre, which we knew wouldn't be far away.

The young ladies name was Anka and she spoke perfect English. She was going into the centre herself and asked if we would like to walk in with her, rather than her direct us. As we walked along, which took about 15mins we passed large elegant properties, she pointed out places of interest to us. What a kind lady. Dresden was her hometown and we could tell she was very proud of it. She didn't mention that we had flattened it during the war, but that the reconstruction was nearly complete and had been done by skilled craftsmen.

Dresden is split by the river Elbe. We had walked through the new modern city to reach the bridge. It had spacious avenues, fountains, good shops and with landscaped gardens to walk through. Anka said farewell as we crossed the bridge into the Old City. On the other side of the river, the old part was very close to being completely renovated to its original grandeur. It was all very beautiful with the Theatre Square being the centrepiece. There were some very imposing buildings, our favourite being the Baroque style Zwinger building, which has a central garden, many sculptured fountains, one not unlike the Trevi off to one side in an annex all of its own.

The weather was warm and pleasant, but a bit overcast so perfect for sightseeing. We spent several hours wandering around the streets and craft fair before we felt peckish. We went to Neumarket Square where there were several restaurants and cafes. Whilst we were sampling the traditional German fare we took the time to do some people watching.

It was here that Jackie pointed out a man dressed in a very smart suit with dark shades, standing outside a very smart jewellers shop, looking at the door expectantly. Jackie said he had been there some time stood facing the door, not moving or turning around. Occasionally, he would look at his mobile and take a quick look around the square. We thought that he was waiting for some very wealthy person/s, maybe celebrities – The Beckhams? Princes Michael? or Michael Schumacher? Someone must have gone into the shop to buy a very costly item of jewellery to be in there *that* long. We waited with bated breath, who could it be to demand such vigilance?

We must have been at the table for at least an hour and a half (good excuse for a few beers!) and the only movement he made was to put his sunglasses on and change his stance from one foot to the other. By now it had turned into a really warm day too, and so we began to feel sorry for him. What were his employers thinking of leaving him standing outside in the heat like that? Disappointingly, nobody came out of the shop, so as we were about to leave, Jackie asked the waitress who he was waiting for. "Oh nobody", she said, "he's just the security guard, and he stands there all day, every day". What a job!

Back at the campsite that evening we chatted to an English guy, who recommended that we go into Moritzburg, which was just over the hill from the campsite. He said there was a beautiful Schloss (Hunting Lodge), which was well worth seeing. Ray and his wife had been holidaying in Rugen on the northern coast but travelled down to the area to find a relatives grave. Ray's mother was a German lady who came from Dresden and had met his father whilst he was stationed there just after the war.

As we reached the crest of the hill, early the following morning, we were greeted with a stunning site. The Schloss was bathed in sunshine with its refection in the lake. The lodge all resplendent in a yellow/cream which is more like a Palace, is surrounded by a lake/moat and fabulous ornamental gardens. We parked up and took the time to have a walk around the lake. It was free entry to the gardens too. It was whilst we were walking around that I start lamenting to Jackie about the lot of the poor peasants who must have had to build this for the Lords and Barons, while they lived in real poverty. It's then that Jackie hit me with a stunner. "Well, if there had been no peasants to abuse there would be no magnificent buildings for us to walk around". Durgh!... It's so obvious it hurts! And that goes for all the castles, cathedrals and other fabulous buildings on this earth. They were all built on the backs of poor people, many losing their lives in the process. In honour to them all, all we can do is admire their workmanship. I now philosophise to Jackie, thank god they abused those goodly peasants so that we can walk around these magnificent buildings. Right...which one of you said turn coat?

From Moritzburg, we travelled northward towards Berlin. Having studied the map and read about the area south of Berlin in our DK guide, we chose to stop on a campsite at a place called Lubben, in the Spreewald area. The area is famous for its little canals and rivers that crisscross the countryside and also for growing gherkins.

Once again the campsite was excellent with friendly staff and friendly campers. The weather was kind to us, it was the beginning of September and still hot and sunny. We were soon sorted and off on our bikes for a visit to Lubben, only 5 minutes away. Lubben is a little tourist town, very pretty too. On our way in to the town we got our first view of the canal system and the boats that ply their trade on them. These small river/canal boats are the German version of the Venetian Gondola. The little boats were manned by two men, both dressed in white shirts, black trousers, with a captain's hat and neckerchief. They operated as a team with one man serving and the other propelling the boat by pole or out board motor. The boats hold from four to ten people, subject to size, and were quite wide, sitting two by two across the table(s). You could hire them and they took you to explore the canals and river whilst enjoying a meal or they would moor up at one of the many drinking and sightseeing opportunities. We didn't hear much singing though; they were all too busy eating at the tables, complete with vases of flowers. What is the German equivalent of "Just One Cornetto" anyway?

As usual, we called into the tourist information centre and picked up a couple of cycle routes so that we could explore this fascinating area. We also felt the need to get back into the wide open countryside as we felt a bit 'citied out' again. We are taking each day at a time now, as we have no deadlines to meet and we could just do what we like. Also, we could tell we will like the Spreewald, it had that feel to it.

Out on our bikes again, we took a packed lunch on both days and really enjoyed seeing the area, cycling the Gherkin trail. You can get Gherkins in every variety of flavours, chilli, garlic, vinegar, oil, etc. and they are a real speciality of the region. The Germans were snapping them up by the tub load. We have to admit that they do compliment the German sausages. Some of the cycle paths took us through marsh-lands on narrow boarded paths, luckily we managed to ride over them without veering off and falling into the marshes. Other paths are wide and nearly always by a canal or the river, it was a real pleasure and we could see why it was so popular. Jackie was getting the hang of balancing the bike so much better these days, after such a nervous start, I even catch sight of her practicing riding hands free!

Sadly, we received some bad news. Jackie's mum has been taken into hospital and it all sounded very serious. Jackie wanted to get back to the UK as soon as possible. So it's back to the maps again, to find a campsite just outside Berlin and not too far from Shonefield airport. Ryanair fly from there direct to East Midlands airport, which is a half hour drive to Derby. We decided that Jackie would visit for 5 days, to get some quality time with her mum and also see if we needed to curtail the tour. I would stay at the campsite, at a little place called Mahlow, near the airport and await instructions.

We arrived at the campsite, it was by far the best facilities we would have on the entire first part of the journey. Five star could even have under rated it. Just one negative, which actually wasn't to do with the site, was that it was fifty minutes' walk to the station in Mahlow and this was where we needed to go for the metro into Berlin. Not that that bothered us really, because we like walking, but when you have been walking around a city all day, the thought of a trek back to the campsite from the station, is a bit daunting, especially if it's late and cold.

I dropped Jackie off at Shonefield Airport for the afternoon flight to East Midlands airport. I planned to go into Berlin for a couple of days, have a good look around, so that on Jackie's return, we would know all the best places to visit. Well, all good plans…….. Unfortunately, whilst Jackie was away the weather in Mahlow took a turn for the worse. It rained every day, sometimes very heavy and prolonged. So I was holed up in Belle, and yes, I was missing Jackie very much. It felt very strange, after four months being together twenty four seven, to be all alone. I did manage to get in a couple of bike rides along the wooded cycle routes around Mahlow, albeit getting completely soaked on both occasions.

I had always thought there was a book in me, so rather than feel sorry for myself, I got the laptop out and began to write. Jackie had been keeping a journal and also a web blog for our friends back in the UK. So armed with these and the pictures we had taken so far, I began to write. Hopefully, if you are still reading this now, it has been published, and if you have got this far it is readable!

After five days Jackie was back again and it's a happy reunion. Her mum would be in hospital for several months, and it would take a long time for her to recover. Jackie came back knowing that she had had lots of laughs, hugs and kisses with her mum. Another comfort was that she has seen for herself, that her Mum was being well looked after by the staff at the hospital and of course by her wonderful father, brother, sister and family. But the biggest relief after finding out Jackie's mum illness was treatable, was that our Adventure could continue......

We were both really excited about seeing Berlin, me especially so, because I have always had a great interest in its history during WW1 & 2. Also, because in the eighties its night club scene was supposed to have been one of the best and we had wanted to visit but never managed it for one reason or another.

We had an excellent day in which we managed to pull in all the places on the agenda. When you have read about something for so long and then you are there, it suddenly feels very real. I found parts of the visit strangely haunting, as if I could see the past in the structures, statues and buildings. As we wandered through the Brandenburg Gate to the Reichstag and then onto the Tiergarten, we visit the Holocaust Memorial. We then spent some time trying to locate Hitler's Bunker, which for obvious reasons is not well advertised. We finally found it a few hundred yards from the Holocaust Memorial, which in a strange way, is quite apt.

We then made our way to a section of the Berlin wall which was close to the museum "The Typographie of Terrors" (free entrance). The museum was situated where some of the Nazi Party Headquarters and government buildings used to stand, including those for the Gestapo and SS. The museum conveys the history of the rise of National Socialism and the atrocities it committed as the Nazi Party. In the beginning, they got rid of all German dissenters and anyone who spoke out of turn or they did not like, this continued throughout the war. They then moved onto bigger things. I reflect that the Germans have come to terms with their past, as the common people were victims of the Nazi Party too, and so also paid the full price.

Jackie and I thought Berlin a very nice city, lots going on, wonderful buildings, and friendly people. We stopped for a coffee at a street café, a few steps away from Checkpoint Charlie, watching the tourists, of many nationalities, posing for photographs with the American soldiers. We continued onto the Unter Den Linden which is the main boulevard running through Berlin, then on to the Museum Island in the river Spree. There were street venders selling all sorts of hand-made crafts and it appeared to be a hive of activity and the hub of the city. We came upon a riverside bar which had a decked area for dancing. For those who wished not to get up and dance, there with tables and chairs set out all along the promenade. We sat and watched couples expertly dancing the Argentine Tango. The ambience was something else. It's at times like that, that we wish we had gone to Ballroom classes.

Time to move on again and still lots to see, we left the river area and walked back down the Unter Den Linden to find somewhere to eat. We walked through the famous Bebelplatz (the burning of thousands of books during the war) and onto a street full of restaurants. We chose the restaurant called "Luter & Wegner". It was very smart, and the waiters all wore black suits and long white aprons, very 20's. The food was delicious. We asked our waiter 'Wolfgang' how he felt about life under the West as he was an East Berliner. We were surprised by his answer, "It's not all good, we enjoy our freedom, but some things have got worse. There is a lack of job security, which was very much felt by the old people" And while he certainly would not want to go back to Communist rule, he did miss the comfort of the old system, even though there was no get up and go in it.

We had just finished our meal as it started to rain, then thunder, which then turned into the most terrific storm. Jackie and I were dressed for a hot summer's day, no coats or brolly. We waited for ages for the rain to stop, but it didn't, it wouldn't even get lighter, it was torrential. It was getting late by then and we had to get back to the train station. I had tipped the waiter and so didn't have any euros left, so a taxi just wasn't an option. The rain lessened slightly so we made a run for it, dodging in and out of shop doorways back on the Unter den Linden. We were slowly getting drenched to the skin. Luckily, about an hour later, we did manage to find a tourist shop that was still open and that sold brollies. We quickly purchased one, which added to the those back at Belle meant we had five! Despite the rain, we did some window-shopping along the way, and I saw my next car, a Bugatti Veyron, it looked fabulous. Well, I can dream!

When we got back to Mahlow, it was still throwing it down. Thankfully, we found a cash machine and quickly hailed a taxi. No way could we have walked home, even with a brolly.

Whilst still at Mahlow campsite we met another great couple from Australia, Marcus and Natalie. They were in an old Ford Transit van which they had kitted out for their travels. It was all flip flop tastic with a Kangaroo on the back. They had lived and worked in the UK for a while and were touring Europe so making the most of it, before they headed back to Australia to settle down. We went into Berlin on the metro with them but they were back at the campsite before us, so were kind enough to take in our washing when it started to rain. The next morning we said our goodbyes as they were going over to Hamburg and we were heading south to the Harz Mountains.

We have beautiful views of the countryside as we snaked along the motorway and into the Harz Mountains, a winter ski resort. A few years ago, I had had to visit a Printing Plate manufacturer for work, which was in this area. I remembered how lovely it was, so Jackie and I decided to visit together. It is a very pretty area, gently rolling hills backed by the mountains and beautiful wooded countryside. The roads become steeper and narrower as we drove up in to the mountains. While on one narrow stretch of road we come across two horse drawn gypsy wagons full of tourists on a sightseeing tour. It set the scene perfectly, very natural with a beautiful mountain backdrop.

We chose to stay overnight at a place called Weringerode. It turned out to be our first stop on a Stellplatz. We had by chance, stumbled on it whilst we were looking for a proper campsite. Stellplatz are everywhere in Germany. These are places for Motorhomes and campervans to stop for the night, usually in the centre of towns and villages. They are well sign-posted and nearly always full of other Motorhomes, so are quite safe places to stay. Some are free, others are a few euros. Great for our budget. This one was in a public car park, but was behind a barriered gate, as you had to pay to use the facilities. It was five euros to get in and another one euro per 40 litres of water, no toilet facilities though. There were about 10 motorhomes on the site and all were German. As ever, all the folk were friendly and went out of their way to explain how everything worked. Opposite the Stellplatz, there was a row of very nice modern houses. Not much of a view for the people that live in them, but we felt safer than ever in this environment.

The next morning dawned warm and bright, although a bit cloudy. It was only a few minutes' walk into Weringerode so no rush to get anywhere fast. First we crossed a bridge which has a great view of a steam railway, with quaint little coaches in cream and red. It's called the Harzquerbahn and linked all the villages between Weringerode and Nordhousen in the Hertz mountains. We were given a great puff of steam and a loud whistle as a train passed under the bridge while we are on it.

Wow, Weringerode is an absolutely picture of a place. As we walked into the centre square we had views of a castle on a hill, with its round turreted spires. The central district has narrow cobbled streets with terraced timbered cottages with pastel coloured walls and flower boxes at every window. The flowers are in full bloom and it added a magnificent splurge of colour to the narrow streets. The central square itself is drop dead gorgeous with market stalls and street bars, restaurants and a grand civic building. We stopped for bratwurst and coffee at one of the street vendors, before visiting the Tourist Information Centre who gave us a map with all the places of interest listed. We spent the afternoon looking around before revisiting the square to sit and people watch over a beer. Later its back to Belle for a 'curry in a hurry'. What a perfect day.

Next stop, Hannover. However, before we left the Stellplatz I had a slight concern, as I could not see a button to press to open the barrier to let us out. We wondered if we have to pay to get out as well as in. Worry over, the barrier lifted automatically as we approached. We had many little learning curves like this along the way.

Again, Hannover is a place I had to visit for my job (didn't see too much of the city), so I wanted to take Jackie to see it. The roads are a joy to use and we have no trouble locating our next place to stay.

The campsite was fine, but the downside again was that it was very rural and a good 45 minutes' walk to get to the suburb before we could get the tram into Hannover. Whilst settling in we met a lovely couple from Lincolnshire, John and Joan. We invited them round for drinks and nibbles that evening. They had been retired for some time and were touring this area of Germany for the first time. They gave us lots of information and advice as they had been touring for many years. We mentioned the Stellplatz we had stayed at and they recommended just the book for us, the 'ReiseMobil Bord Atlas book of Stellplatz in Germany and Europe'. That night with John and Joan we had a really good laugh. Our conversation moved onto the time when we could drink and drive. I had once had six pints of beer and driven 10 miles home, no wonder there was carnage on the roads back in those 'good old days'. You could smoke on planes and public transport, "eeee... when I were a lad". We also talked old money, when there were three parts to any sum... 'Pounds', 'Shillings' and 'Pence'. What confusion it would be now..... twenty shillings to the pound and twelve pennies to the shilling. Also coins like the 'Half Crown', which was two shillings and six pence. Not forgetting the Three Penny coin, which people called 'the thrupenny bit' or 'thrupence' where we lived anyway. It had a lovely ring to it, 'twelve pounds, six shillings and thrupence, or as today, twelve pounds and thirty three pence. Now what about the very old 'Guinea', which was twenty-one shillings, now who thought that one up? It was all quite simple back then, because we all bought a dozen (twelve) eggs, and there were twelve inches to a foot, not three hundred and ten millimetres. Then came decimal, those arty smarty Europeans who made it so simple with ten of everything. But you still get eggs packed in six, even in Europe, because nobody has figured out how to pack them in five's.

My mind wanders. I think the Government must have asked Jeeves and Wooster to come up with the units of weight and measurement back then......

"I say Jeeves, what names shall we start with for weights?"
"Well m'lord we could use Stones, Bricks and Pebbles for units of weight, because they all weigh differently".
"Tosh Jeeves, that's far too easy., We'll give them something far more complicated. Stones yes, but what about pounds of flesh and then something smaller?"
"What about One m'lord, Stones, Pounds and One?"
"Not quite Jeeves, what about Ounce, it's kind of One with a bit more pizazz!"
"Jolly good m'lord, and what about numbers to go with the names?"
"Well, I've always liked the number fourteen and I kinda like sixteen as well, so we could have fourteen pounds to the stone and sixteen ounces to the pound. Now that should jolly well confuse Johnny Public, what?!"
"Absolutely m'lord! Now, what about measurement?"
"Well, I usually use my hands and feet to measure, so we could have Feet, Hand, Finger and Toe!"
"That could be confusing when at the doctor's m'lord?"
"Oh well thought of Jeeves. Well what about Pace? I'm always pacing the yard."
"I like the sound of Yard better m'lord and I also like the word Inch, now you don't come across that every day".
"Absolutely top ho, Jeeves, so what's an inch?"
"Exactly m'lord, I've no idea."
"Right then Jeeves, my good man, we've got Yards, Feet and Inches, so what bally numbers can we give them?"

"Well we haven't used twelve yet, so how's about twelve Inches to the Foot.

"So, was that Foot or Feet Jeeves?"

"Well one Foot is twelve Inches m'lord and two Feet are twenty four Inches."

"Oh great guns Jeeves, and we can give them three Feet to the Yard, even though no one has actually got three feet!"

"Absolutely spiffing m'lord!"

"I say Jeeves, I like this kind of work, we could take it up for a living. Now what have we in mind for Decimal?"

"Ahh! There I'm afraid you have me m'lord........!"

"You sound positively Ten-tative Jeeves!"

Where were we? Oh yes, we could take our bikes and leave them at the tram station as it was 45 minutes away, but we weren't sure what the area would be like, so decided to walk. It was a lovely walk, along way-marked paths through the fields. It was a warm and sunny day, but we remembered to take the brolly with us, just in case.

Hannover is a pleasant city with a mostly modern centre and the usual pedestrian shopping area. The Rathaus (Town Hall) is a really impressive building, which is how I had remembered it. There is a display in the main entrance hall, which shows how Hannover had been in the past and how it is today. It consists of four models of the city in large glass display cabinets. One showed the city in 1689 when it was a small village on the river Liene. One in 1939 as a large vibrant city. The next one depicts the city as it was in 1945 virtually flattened, except for three landmarks, which were needed so the British and Americans could use as points for the bombers to aim for. The fourth cabinet showed how it had been rebuilt to the present day modern city.

Hannover also still has strong links with our Royal Family with a Palace that Prince Charles and Diana had visited as part of their marriage tour. There are also the magnificent gardens at Herrenhausen, close to where the old Palace once stood. It was here that the name "Ballroom" was coined, as they used to clear away the tennis court which was in the ball room, to make way for the dancing. Also the word "Marmalade" was coined here. This came about after one of the princes had an orange and lime grove planted outside to hide the smell of the latrines which were thought to be causing Maladies (illnesses). The subsequent jam produced was called "Marmalade" and was thought to help with the curing of illnesses.

Hannover was ok, but somehow did not quite live up to my previous memories of it. Jackie wasn't very taken with it either. We did however, manage to buy the Stellplatz book. It was twenty one euros, which at first we thought was a bit steep, but we knew we would easily reap that back with just one night stopover, rather than paying campsite fees.

The walk back home didn't seem at all bad; it was a lovely evening, as we had only stayed in Hannover for the afternoon. The freshly ploughed fields were so pretty and the birds were singing. There was still the odd Sunflower scattered here and there, which were the remnants of a previous crop. I picked three for Jackie along with a few other wild flowers and a poppy; surely the farmer wouldn't miss them. They looked beautiful in Belles kitchen after Jackie had done her flower arranging.

On our way back we were passed by a very old couple who look in their eighties on motorised bikes. The bikes made a loud noise as they drew near and they are quite literally normal bikes with a motor strapped to them. The couple turned out to be on our campsite and were from the Netherlands. We said hello as we passed their motorhome. We hope we are still hacking it when we are their age. We also see another couple of British registered motorhomes and caravans on the site, but make no contact with the owners. We did see many more British people on the German campsites we would visit. It's a very popular place and we know why.

That evening we re-appraise our remaining journey through Germany and then onto France. Jackie and I had planned to tour all over Germany during September. Two things changed our plans, firstly, because Jackie had gone back to the UK to see her Mum, which had taken a week out, and secondly because we began to realise the size of Germany. There are so many wonderful places we now wanted to visit, we realised that we could not do it all in one go. We had planned to visit the Rhine Valley but now also wanted to do the Mosel, thanks to John and Joan, who had shown us two fold out maps of the rivers. We had hoped to travel to Dusseldorf, and call in for a glass of Rumtoft and catch up with the lovely people we met in Sweden, Gerhard and Monika. Unfortunately, it was too far West for us to do this time. We did email Gerhard and Monika and hope to visit them on next year's tour.

So we decided to head south from Hannover to Frankfurt. Now armed with the Stellplatz books, we found a place called Fritzlar, which sounded very nice and where we could stay for just one night on the way for free.

Fritzlar proves to be another gem. The small town is situated on a hill with its near complete medieval wall, watch towers and bastions. We soon found the Stellplatz which was a small car park, sitting just outside the wall. There were some public toilets as you entered the town through an archway, but apart from those, there were no other facilities at all. We were in beautiful surroundings, horse chestnut trees lined the car park. The leaves were turning autumn gold and there was a spectacular view over the river valley, only a few strides away. After a bit of manoeuvring, we soon had Belle levelled up on the chocks. We needed them here as we were on quite a slope. Once settled in, we made our way into the town centre. We couldn't wait to see it. It was so picturesque, almost as lovely as Weringerode. There were cobbled streets, with very old half-timbered houses and a beautiful Rathaus. We wander through taking in the views, it's just so lovely. We always say that we wished everyone could be with us to see such amazing sights. But then, what is amazing to us might not be to others. In this instance, no normal person could dislike what they saw. In this gorgeous place, of all places, we ended up eating a kebab! We could see lots of people tucking in to them outside a Turkish restaurant, we just couldn't resist. It was a very pleasant change for us. We don't want to go on about food all the time, but it is an important part of the tour. Not only are we intrigued by the people, the architecture and their customs, we are keen to know just what they eat. Everyone thinks Brits eat roast beef and Yorkshire pudding. Of course we don't. We eat a great variety of food, the majority of which is excellent. We, like others, assume that all the Germans eat is Sauerkraut and Bratwurst. Nonsense, you can get a McDonald and a kebab in all the best places!

Before leaving the following day, we thought we would take a last look at Fritzlar again. In the centre by the Rathaus, a small stage had been erected and there was a ladies accordion group playing popular waltz music. We stopped to sway along to a couple of tunes, along with quite a large audience. Then moving on and out of the walled town and down to the river. Here we had totally different view of the town. We could see the roofs and chimney pots peeking above the wall at the top of the hill. The church and its spires dominated the scene. We were sad to leave Fritzlar, a very pleasant interlude between big cities.

From Fritzlar, we travelled southwest through more picturesque rolling countryside towards Frankfurt am Main then on to the Rhine Valley. Our revised plan was to have a quick look at Frankfurt and then on to a place called Rudesheim at the southern end of the Rhine Valley. From there northwards we would make our way to Koblenz, then south west down the Mosel, to Trier. This way, taking in as much scenery (and wine) as we possibly could.

For the very first time, we parked Belle on a busy main road, a few hundred metres from the centre of a city, this one being Frankfurt. We were a bit nervous at leaving her there and as we walked away we hoped she would still be there when we got back. It was only a ten minute walk to the main train station and then another few minutes into the city centre. We didn't plan on being there for long as we knew it was going to be a huge modern metropolis. Frankfurt is a very modern city with many skyscrapers. It is renowned as being one of the main economic centres of Europe. The shopping area was alive with people, it looked as if retail therapy was certainly thriving here. The usual street artists abound. It had been a while since we had seen a proper one man band busker with his drum strapped to his back, his mouth organ and kazoo at his mouth, a horn under his foot and another between his knees, a banjo in his hands and still managing to belt out a recognisable tune!

We were able to find the old part of the city with its medieval square and statues. We stopped for the obligatory beer and people watch. There were some Japanese people at the next table who were in deep conversation with an American guy and the topic was cars. It was then that I remembered that the Frankfurt Motor Show was taking place at the time. I would have loved to have gone, but it was not to be, maybe next time.

We were only gone about three hours, so we were soon back at Belle and she was still there, untouched. We had no need to worry after all.

Our next port of call and overnight stop was supposed to be a short drive to a place called Eltville on the Rhine. Another free Stellplatz for us, but here we soon realised that not all Stellplatz are the same. This one was a supermarket overflow car park and in the middle of a concrete jungle. After filling the water tank, as there were facilities here, we decided to move on. This was a mistake, as we had already had a full day and were both a bit techy and hungry. We then spent the next two hours trying to locate a campsite we both liked. By that time we were well and truly knackered. In the end we spied some motorhomes parked up in a layby which we think was only for tour coaches. It was just off the main road and we were not sure if we were supposed to be there, it was dark by then so frankly, my dear, we didn't really give a dam.

We woke the next day to find that another Motorhome has joined us, so we felt quite at ease with the whole situation. After breakfast we thought we may as well go in and take a look at the village behind us. There were lots of people coming and going by this time, so thought it must be some sort of tourist attraction. It turned out to be a one street affair with a pretty white painted church. There were vine groves all around the village and it was right on the banks of the Rhine. We spotted a coach load of people entering a building along the street and so thought we would go and investigate. This was a stroke of luck, as it was to be our first German winery called Weingut

Basting Gimbel. Downstairs the wall was lined with barrels stretching to the back of the long narrow room. The ceiling was festooned with lights and all the Germans are sitting at candle lit trestle tables, tasting the various wines being offered by the young waitress. It was only 11 am but we thought if they can do it, so can we. We made our way to the bar where we are told that we were very welcome to taste the wines, but that they were busy serving the coach party. We had a small glass of Riesling, and to be quite honest it was a bit too sweet for us, so we thanked them and left without buying a bottle. I don't think they were too worried, they were far too busy with the coach party.

We drove along the Rhine taking in the beautiful views of the grape vines on the hillside, pretty villages and castles along the way. We crossed the river on a ferry at a place called Rudesheim, where we had planned to stop, but because it was still early in the day we decided to travel on a bit further up the river. We eventually chose to stay at a place called Bacharach. Don't think this was where the famous Bert was from!

This Stellplatz was on the banks of the Rhine and a short walk across the road into the village. As we arrived there was a motorhome pulling out, so we got a front row place. We couldn't believe how lucky we were to get such an idyllic view. The motorhomes were several rows deep with some unable to get a view at all. There were huge river barges carrying all sorts of cargo, cars, gas, oil etc. There were also canoeists, speed boats and all manner of boats floating along the river. We are also a short walk away from where the pleasure boats docked, taking tourists to the many lovely little villages and of course to the fabulous castles dominating the vine covered hillsides.

Bacharach was a very pretty little place, typically German, with half-timbered houses. We decided to stay a few days and do a short river cruise and also get the bikes out and cycle to the next village. The river cruise took us to a place called St Goar. It was a short cruise only fifty minutes up river and a little longer back down to Bacharach against the flow.

Unfortunately, it rained, and Jackie and I had a few words for some reason or other. It was a shame as it was such a romantic setting. That's life!

The cruise was lovely. We reached St Goar, which was quite a tourist attraction because of its castle, Burg Rheinfels, and also its location on the Rhine. We were both a bit disappointed because most of the place was closed and not at all as nice as Bacharach. We didn't stay long as we were both still sulking a bit, so it wasn't long before we caught the next boat back.

St Goar is also ideally located for its proximity to a famous large rock which rises steeply above the Rhine.

Legend has it that a fair maiden called Loreley sat on the very top of the rock and sang so sweetly, that she attracted many passing sailors, on hearing her voice, they tried to find her, but alas, all were drowned on the treacherous rocks below.

Years later a well-known song, composed by Heinrich Heine, became famous. Our captain played the song as we passed, it was quite eerie.

The following day the weather had cheered up somewhat and so had we, so we set off on our bikes for Oberwesel about 6km away. One really great thing about the Rhine is that the cycle paths run alongside the river so you could ride almost the entire length. This little place had Schonberg Castle towering above it and also the ramparts around the village. We secured our bikes and walked along the wall to take in the views. Oberwesel was a very pleasant little village and occupied us for an hour. We rode back to Bacharach, which in our opinion, is the jewel of that particular stretch of the Rhine. We sat outside Belle and watched the Rhine and life flow by.

The part of the Rhine which we planned to cover was only about 50miles long from Frankfurt to Koblenz. We both agreed that the scenery was breathtakingly beautiful with all the castles, villages and vineyards on the slopes of the hilllsides. We were on our way to Koblenz to have a quick look at the famous 'Deutsches Eck' (German Corner), which is where the Rhine and the Mosel join, and then head off down the Mosel. Several of the people we had met during our travels had said how lovely the Mosel was. Having just been on the Rhine, we thought that surely we couldn't see anything as beautiful. Well, as the saying goes 'You know what thought did'!

Once on the Mosel we chose to stay on a campsite, this time at a little place called Winningen, just down from Koblenz. This was so that Jackie could have the luxury of doing the washing in a washing machine. She did think of taking it down to the riverbank and giving it a good scrub, but there were too many tourists about!

Whilst at the campsite, we met some more very nice English people, Roger and Carol who were touring in their caravan. They had had their caravan three years and it was absolutely immaculate inside. They were very proud of it and so Carol never cooked in it. We had another fun filled evening, chatting and hearing all about each other's escapades.

The village of Winningen was a few minutes ride through the vineyards surrounding the campsite. Such a pretty little place, vines hung across nearly every street. Similarly, the Vintners on the Mosel also had their wineries along the little streets. We came upon one such merchant who had just off loaded the first harvest of his grapes from the very hillside we had just ridden through. We asked if he just harvested the grapes to sell on or if he made his own wine. He said he made his own wine and then I asked the rather amusing question, "Do you sell any?" There's always one, isn't there? He gave a right chortle, of course he did. His name was Richard Richter and he had won many awards for his wines, which were named after him.

As you may know in the Mosel, the grapes are all eventually made into the local speciality, Riesling. He gave us a small guided tour through his wine making facility and a talk on how and where the best of the grapes are grown. It was very interesting. I told him how the first wines we sampled back in the seventies had been German Riesling, Piesporter and Tigermilch, but all were a bit sweet for our taste these days. He said they now all produce a dry wine called Trochen and that he had three classes of wine. The grapes from the top of the hill, which were his best and the most difficult to harvest. The grapes from the middle of the hill, which were a good quality and those from the bottom of the hill, which are also a reasonable quality, generally producing the cheaper bottles of wine. I asked which wine he would recommend for us, expecting him to choose the most expensive bottle in the place. But no, he recommended we try a middle of the hill wine which is one of his best at 12 euros a bottle. It was called "Bruckstuck" and was a Riesling Spatlese Trocken. He gave us a sample to taste, our verdict was that it was certainly quaffable for us.

Back at Belle we had an idea to add wine tasting to our daily routine and try the local wine from each place we stop whilst on the Mosel. This would add an extra interest to our tour of the Mosel, as well as an excuse to drink some more wine, as if we needed any! I am surprised at how nice the dry white is, as I am usually a red wine drinker and only like very few whites. So far, Richards wine held top spot but as Jackie quickly pointed out, we had only tried his.

As we travelled down the Mosel, the views were absolutely stunning and for us, actually topped the Rhine. The Rhine is wider and on a grander scale, but the Mosel is more 'in your face' gorgeous. We were also treated to our first sight of grapes being harvested, some by hand, and some using machinery. Rails wound their way up the hillside carrying small motorised seats and a container in which the grapes could then be sent back down the hill to the tractor and trailer waiting to take them back to the vintner. Most are still handpicked and we could see the gangs of people picking them high up on the steep slopes. There were lots of small tractors moving up and down the winding roads with their loads of grapes, it was very busy and slow going if you got behind one. Unbeknown to us, it was a big win visiting this area in September, as it was not only the time for picking the grapes, but also the time they celebrate the harvest.

Our next stop was at a place called Cochem. All these lovely places are on the banks of the Mosel and as we travelled along the roads we could see each picturesque village either side of the river. We stopped at a Stellplatz across the river from the town right next to an official campsite. There were no facilities at this Stellplatz, but there was a sanitary station outside the neighbouring campsite, so we were able to fill up with water and dispose of our waste for a few euros. We debated whether we should stay as we had already seen some of it when we drove through to the Stellplatz. After a quick cuppa, we decided it probably was worth a proper look, so we set off on our bikes for a short ride to the bridge. We locked our bikes to some railings and walked across the bridge into the town centre. The town is overlooked by an imposing castle, one of the most pleasing to look at on the Mosel. The town is once again very picturesque with its obligatory painted half-timber buildings, cobbled streets and Rathaus.

We did a bit of window shopping, along with hundreds of tourists all doing the same. We spied a shop selling wines from their own vineyard, there were plenty of others too of course. We went in just as they were shutting up shop for the day, but instead of ushering us out, they let us taste some of wines. We both agreed that the one from their vineyard tasted the best for us, so we bought three bottles and got a special late shopper offer, 5% off. Back at Belle, the official wine tasting commenced. This wine was called "Heidrich" Riesling Trocken 2010 and after the first bottle was emptied, we decided that it would go into second place after Richard Richter's.

For no particular reason, our next chosen place was to be Brauneberg. Talk about being in 'the right place at the right time', we arrived at the riverside Motorhome park late afternoon. The village of Brauneberg was a few minutes' walk along the narrow road that backed the site. It was a really busy site, compared with the others we had stayed at and had seen on the Mosel. We were amazed at how many Motorhomes arrived after us and wondered what the attraction was? As we sat talking outside and whilst peeling the spuds for our evening meal, we could hear bagpipes playing? We looked towards the village and there were two Scottish Pipers, in traditional Scottish dress, giving it some. I do find "Scotland the Brave" inspiring on the pipes. A little later, and with curiosity getting the better of us, I walked over towards where they had been playing to see if there was anything going on. There was indeed! It was Saturday night and there was to be a 'Wein-Strassenfest'. I think translated, it means, Wine Street Festival. Covered bar areas, table and seating was being set up all along the road and through the village. Now that explained why there were so many Motorhomes.

At around 7.30pm we took a stroll in, well, one has to, doesn't one? Just after midnight we strolled back. What a brilliant time we had had. Each stallholder sold wine produced from their own grapes, grown on the vines on the hills surrounding us. We sampled quite a few and tried to keep track of our scoring system. There were hundreds of people there, everyone was having such a good time, and it was a great atmosphere. The best thing for us was to see, hear and swing along to, the many 'Oompah Bands'. There were six in total and the music, dancing and swaying, was a real spectacle. The grand finale was when all the bands played together as they left the festival. Jackie and I couldn't have wished for a better way to experience the Mosel. The wine tasting had proved a big success as we could not remember the name of any one of them.

Back to our two Scottish bag pipe men, on the way in to the fest, we spotted them chatting up a couple of wee German lassies, while giving instruction on how the pipes worked. A bit later, there they were again chatting up some more ladies. As we walked by we overheard them comment that they thought their luck was in with these ladies, only by this time the ladies and the Scots looked very much worse for wear, and it looked like there were four people fighting with two octopi, with the octopi winning. At the end of the evening I spied them propping up the bar with their bag pipes playing dead and not a woman in sight. As we passed by, I couldn't resist making a request, and bless one did make an attempt at "Mull of Kintyre" only to wheeze to a sorry end. His final comment was "there's nay puff left". I think the German ladies had come to the same conclusion!

After a rather lazy start to the day, we travelled along to another small village called Mehring, As we entered the campsite we followed a track looking for a place to park as it was quite full. I finally drove Belle to the river front as I thought I could see an exit along the track. On turning onto the river side I realised I was actually on the walking and cycle path and no longer on the campsite. Not only was there no exit, there was no end in sight. By this time all the German campers who were out enjoying the sun were now quietly amused as I had to reverse slowly back down the very narrow path. It was then that I hit on the idea to disguise our error. I told Jackie to go into the back of the Belle, open the window and start shouting loudly "Get ze ice creamnze heren" while I play Mr Whippy music loudly. Maybe not, they didn't look as if they would be fooled that easily!

We eventually found a vacant pitch and parked up. The bikes were soon off the back of Belle and so off we went to blow the cobwebs away. It was all really nice, cycling through the little villages along the way. A good way down the river, we decided to turn back as we were going nowhere in particular. It was a good job we did. One of my pedals started to act up and so became difficult to use. The bearings had broken up causing it to stick in one place every now and then. As we rode through the next village, and to our amazement, there was a bicycle shop, and it was open. Not one other shop was open in the place. The guy was so nice and replaced the pedals there and then. I must say we were really disappointed that we had such a problem as our bikes had not been that heavily used.

Our final stop on the Mosel was Trier, just a short drive further on down the river and close to the border with Luxembourg. We drove into the city and parked up, but not before going down a one way street and ending up in the town's main square, much to the amusement and mayhem of the Germans. We stuck out like a sore thumb as we tried in vain to leave the area, only to find that we had to go back out the way we came in. I tell Jackie its plan B again as we pretend to be ice cream sellers. This time there are a few takers, so I have to speed up, so they can't actually make an order. One does make it to the window, *Cornet bitte...we've sold outen...ice lolly bitte....we've sold outen....have you got anythinken.....Nine, its hoten und ve hav eaten zem.* It was one of those moments you wish the earth could swallow you up; it's a bit difficult with the size of our Belle. *Vat are ze English doing, don't ze realize ziss is pedestrian only, dum koffs!*

We walked back into Trier having found some where to park and visited the square we had just driven into by mistake. It had calmed down a bit since our tour de force and fortunately no one recognised us. Trier is very nice, and still has one of the oldest Roman gateways, the Porte Nigra at one end of the city. It's also the birth place of Karl Marx and we managed to find his house. However, it's not anywhere as quaint as the little towns we had visited along the Mosel. After a few hours sightseeing we went back to Belle and off to find another Stellplatz for the night.

We had no trouble finding it as it was just over the river. It was run by the local council and basically just another car park. There was a difference here as each pitch was metred for electricity and although quite a substantial area, which could easily accommodate a hundred motorhomes, it only had two well used toilet and shower rooms.

We got on our bikes for a last ride along the Mosel. This part of the river was not anywhere near as scenic as the rest. The sun was out so we had a pleasant afternoon taking in the different views. The hillsides were now in the distance and the landscape changed to fields and farmland.

For anyone who hasn't been to the Mosel Valley, it really is well worth a visit and we would thoroughly recommend it, particularly at this time of year. The Mosel and Rhine Valleys were an unexpected and memorable highlight of the tour. They are so beautiful. We can imagine that during the summer the villages and the roads must get extremely busy with tourists. The Spreewald was also another highlight for us and we think an often missed gem along with the Harz Mountains.

As with anywhere, the weather makes a difference. We were so lucky that it had been hot and sunny for the most part during the days we visited. It was now definitely starting to get colder in the evenings; we could tell autumn was just around the corner. We are sad to leave Germany as it was all so nice and friendly. We plan to go back and see a lot more next year, especially Bavaria and Dusseldorf.

Last but not least, the winner of our wine tasting was Richard Richter, with his rather expensive Bruckstuck 2010, the Riesling Spatlese Trocken.

Luxembourg here we come....

Chapter Fifteen

Luxembourg

September 25th

Luxembourg is the land of the petrol station as it is one of the cheapest places in Western Europe to buy petrol. Currently the price for Diesel in the UK is £1.39 litre (25-09-11) and in Luxembourg £0.99 litre with an exchange rate of 1.18eu/£. Our first sight after crossing the border was.................. wait for it.......... lots of petrol stations with queues of cars and lorries waiting to fill up. I was running rather low on Diesel as I had been keeping my eye on fuel prices via the web at www.drive-alive.co.uk. So, I waited until we got to Luxembourg to fill up as well. It actually took us some time to find a petrol station without a long queue of vehicles. Jackie and I had in fact, driven through Luxembourg some years before, on our way to Lake Garda in Italy. We remembered that back then we only stopped to fill up with cheap petrol for the long journey ahead.

Luxembourg is a small principality which nestles between Germany, France and Belgium. It is said that it is one of the wealthiest place in Europe and also the most densely populated. Having crossed the border we are soon heading into the capital. The wide dual carriage ways were lined with very modern high-rise office blocks straight out of a designers sketch book. The approach looked all very slick.

Once in the centre of the city, we had the usual problem of finding a space to park Belle as she is 7.2m long. After trawling quite a few back streets, we eventually pulled up in a leafy suburb on a residential street with some rather strange looking parking display signs. We weren't sure if we should be parking there, or if we have to pay to park there. The houses were very similar to those in Belgium, mainly small flat fronted and in terraces, fronted by small flower filled gardens. Fortunately, a car with a man and his children parked up next to us. He was very well dressed in a smart grey suit, all very business-like. We asked if there were any parking restrictions. He did, of course speak perfect English, and he said we had to pay at the machine at the end of the road. He also advised we were only fifteen minutes' walk to the city centre. He took the time to explain all this, even getting a map out at one stage, and was very interested in where we were from and what we were doing.

We made our way through lovely tree lined residential streets and into the centre of Luxembourg. We also passed through the Embassy area with its grand buildings, shining brass name plaques and flags. Only the American embassy had a guard post and dark glass observation area. We passed through a nice park before finding ourselves in the city centre. It was lunch time and the streets were crammed with business people lunching at the numerous cafes and bistros. The majority of the men were very well dressed with suits and lap top bags and the ladies also looked very business-like elegant and chic. It was plain to see that we were indeed in a very wealthy country.

Throughout the book, we haven't really mentioned in any depth about how people dress. In general folk seem to have dressed much of the same where ever we have been. That is, very casual, with jeans, shirts or tee shirts along with all manner of jackets, certainly in Scandinavia and the Baltic States. We did come across a few elegantly dressed ladies and smartly dressed men, but surprisingly, not many at all. When we passed through business districts they did of course dress accordingly. The only exception being France where we find the majority of people do take an interest on how they look.

As we wander through the streets we agreed Luxembourg had a really nice feel to it. To one side of the city centre, there is a valley, where you get magnificent views down and across the rocky wooded expanse. From one vantage point you can see caves in the rock side where people used to live in times gone by. We walked back in and around the Court Houses and back to the main square where we had a quick snack, one of our favourites, Croque Monsieur (cheese and ham toasty).

We took a leisurely stroll through the shopping area before making our way back to Belle.

We were so pleased that we made the time to visit this lovely city. During our tour some people had made the comment that there was not much worth seeing but we would very definitely beg to differ.

Next, our beloved France, Oo la la!

Chapter Sixteen

France 2

September 27th – October

Stenay – Fontainebleau – The Loire Valley – Moelan-sur-Mer

We were both sad, and glad, to be back in France. On the one hand, we were sad that our journey was drawing to an end because we had enjoyed it so much. On the other hand, we are so glad to be back in France as we feel so at home here.

We planned to visit Fontainebleau en route to the Loire Valley and then on to our final destination, Moelan sur Mer in Brittany. The countryside and little villages we pass through are as ever, quaint and very peaceful. Of all the countries, France still has that special something, not just for us but for many other Brits as well.

The small town of Stenay was just across the border from Luxembourg and perfect for a one night stopover. The campsite was just outside the town and situated on a river. It was only 10 euros a night and had good clean facilities. It was split into two areas, there were marked pitches on a car park and others in a field across the river. We chose to stay in the car park as it was literally right by the river and close to the little 'Bar du Port' so much more convenient.

We parked up next to another British plated motorhome. The owners were already set up and sitting relaxing by the river. Alan and Beryl were both retired and came from Coventry. They too were seasoned Motorhomer's, having been, here, there and everywhere. They told us that they were travelling on to the Mosel for a few weeks and that it was their first time in the area. What a treat they had in store.

During our chat with them we came round to the usual topic of conversation, toilets and whether or not to use our on board facility. They could not believe that we had never used ours and tried to persuade us that we should. They gave us a handy tip that instead of using expensive chemicals we should use washing tablets, they even gave us two to get started with. Up to date they are still in the packet.

It was a lovely evening so we went to sit at the tables by the river and have a pint from the bar. The barman/owner was lovely and friendly but did things in his own time. He took his time to finish his conversation with an old chap at the bar before serving us. For some impatient Brits this would have been seen as ignorant, for us it's one of the reasons we love the French. Where is the rush? When he eventually finished his chat he apologised for the delay and took my order and then said he would bring the drinks out to us. Sitting by the entrance door was a little white dog somewhat smaller than a Scottie, but which was quite aggressive. As I left the bar the dog took a bite at my shoes but I shook him off with some fast footwork. Some French expletives followed from the barman which quietened the dog down. It was a good job it wasn't a Rottweiler or I would have been minus one foot!

Not long after, an overall clad chap from the next table got up and strode over to the bar. He had obviously just finished work and as many French workers do, had popped in for a beer with his mate on their way home. As he entered the bar we could hear snarling from inside. The guy re-emerged carrying two beers, one for himself and one for his friend. It was at this point the dog also took a dislike to his boots and attached himself to one. There then followed a tug of war, as the chap tried to hurry back to the table, with the dog attached to his boot and without spilling the beers. There were now some real French expletives as even I recognised "merde". The owner eventually came out and detached the dog from the boot accompanied by laughter from all around. These French landlords are very cunning, they train their guard dogs to stop their customers leaving!

Anyway, entertainment over, we returned to Belle and spent the rest of the evening watching the sunset by the river.

Whilst crossing the Champagne region on our way to Fontainebleau we came across the Navarin memorial to the French and Americans who died in their thousands in this region during the 1st World War. The countryside here has a chalky base with straw coloured grass and low rolling hills and we can see for miles. It was easy for me to imagine the view back then as there were still shell craters dotted here and there. If my memory serves me right, this was where the French first used their version of the tank because of the hard ground to support its weight. While sad to see, it does make people remember those who gave up their lives. The farmers of the region still unearth bones which are kept in a crypt below the memorial.

We arrived on the outskirts of Fontainebleau and soon found a campsite nearby for the night. The lady owner of the campsite was English, so we had a good chat about the area and she gave us directions to the Chateau and the parking area. The following day we drove in to the centre and parked up on the designated tree lined street parking, just a few yards away from the entrance to the Chateau. The weather was still on our side with the sun shining and creating sunbeams through the trees. The Chateau is truly magnificent and the gardens were quite stunning. It was a pleasant surprise that we could walk round the gardens and grounds for free. The Chateau is a few steps away from the centre of town and as it was by then lunch time, there were lots of young people eating their food, sitting on the grass amongst the flower beds that filled the gardens. What was also nice to see was that they didn't leave any litter behind. Not surprisingly, they must have been very proud of their town and wonderful Chateau.

We left the Chateau grounds and pottered around the pretty tree-lined streets where we bought a freshly baked French loaf to have for our lunch back at Belle.

We had visited The Loire Valley a year or so before but had driven along the river from Nevers to Orleans, which was still lovely, but lacked the Chateau's that it is famous for. This time we were following the river from Orleans to Tours which turned out to be every bit as scenic as the Rhine and Mosel. To be honest, we don't find the river itself that picturesque, but the villages, the Chateau's and the surrounding area is stunning.

Again, for no reason, but convenient for us, we chose to stop at a small town called Beaugency on the Loire. We found the place from the Bord Atlas Stellplatz book. It was free to park for one night. There were no toilet facilities but there was waste disposal and fresh water supply. The Motorhomes were all crowded up one end of the car park towards the river. We timed our arrival just right as we took the last but one vacant spot. We chatted to a friendly French couple in the next Motorhome. It's amazing how much you can make yourself understood with a bit of arm waving, you might have thought we were landing planes on an aircraft carrier. We didn't plan on going anywhere that evening, but they told us the town was very nice and that we should make time to go and have a look before leaving.

After tea, we walked into the town and it proved to be just as picturesque as our French neighbours had described it. It was turning dusk as we made our way in which made for some atmospheric views along the cobbled back streets. Everywhere was neat and tidy. There was one narrow street with houses either side and a pretty fenced in stream running right through the middle and down into the Loire. The lighting and reflections made for some good photo opportunities next to the bars and restaurants. Incorporated into the centre was a medieval walled town with a magnificent church that had towers and spired turrets.

The next day dawned bright and warm and we were soon off following the river side road. By midday we were at Blois which is situated by an ancient arched bridge and according to our guide book had a beautiful Chateau. We were lucky to find a parking spot a short walk from the centre. We found that if we weren't on a campsite, it wasn't always easy to find somewhere that would accommodate the length of Belle.

We spent a pleasant couple of hours walking around Blois. At first, because of the hilly nature of the town we had trouble finding the Chateau. It was only after I decided to follow a sign to the public toilets, that we discovered it. How can anyone miss a building of that size! It was a fabulous place. As with all of these wonderful buildings, we only viewed it from the outside due to our time schedule. It was whilst we were in Blois that we bought a fold down map which detailed all the Chateau's on the Loire. We hadn't realised how many there were. Sadly, we knew that we would not be able to see them all this time round.

Our next stop was Amboise, with its beautiful bridge and fabulous Chateau. Jackie's favourite to date. We only had one night here, as the campsite was closing for the season. Many do in France. Bizarrely, there was a Stellplatz that our book listed and it was right next to the official campsite, both cost exactly the same. The difference was the facilities. The campsite had every facility, was very modern and clean, whilst the Stellplatz only had fresh water and a chemical disposal unit. The Stellplatz (called Aires in France) listed site was full, whereas the official site was almost empty, which was why we ended up in there. What a lucky break that was.

We were soon set up and relaxing in our parkland setting with only another ten motorhomes occupying a site that could easily have held two hundred. Before long, two four by four vehicles with trailers drove through the sports field next to the campsite and proceeded to unload a large basket and hot air balloon. We sat watching the whole spectacle while eating our evening meal. Within the hour the brightly coloured balloon was ready for the off. It always amazes me how the flame from the burner creating the hot air does not set the balloon on fire. Once its passengers were in the basket, it lifted up into the sky, moving quietly away towards the Chateau in the near distance.

As the evening drew in we walked across the bridge into the centre of Amboise. As we crossed the magnificent arched bridge, the river was gushing and there was a guy with waist high waders fly fishing in the river. With the views of the Chateau and its reflection in the river and the fisherman, it all looked picture book. This Chateau sits proudly above the streets of Amboise. We passed several restaurants and cocktail bars and were sorely tested not to pop in for one or two. But no, we thought better of it as we are running tight on our budget.

Amboise is beautiful by day, but even more so at night as the lighting added a different dimension to its beauty. As we walked along the café lined streets with its beautiful people and babble of French conversation, it certainly had that wow factor for us. The smells from restaurants were also very tempting and the food did look delicious

Our taste buds were tingling again by now so we went into a little shop and bought a bottle of the local red and a few nibbles. The bottle of red wine was a Domaine Dutertre Touraine Amboise 2010 and proved to be very quaffable back at Belle. We couldn't believe how good the weather was as it was still very warm at eleven o'clock. We sat outside again reminiscing about our tour and thinking how nice it was to sit out without having to squat mosquitoes. To have toured the river valleys of the Rhine, Mosel and Loire, back to back, it had been the icing on the cake for both of us. They each had a beauty all of their own and had given us the perfect ending to our tour.

The next day we were up late and had a bit of a rush to vacate the site by twelve due to it closing for the season that day. As we drove along the river again, it was possibly the most picturesque part as we moved from one side of the river to the other. Sheila wasn't navigating as we attempted to stay as close to the river as possible to get the views and that wasn't always the way our Sheila wanted us to go. I do not know what we would have done without her though, as on most occasions she proved to be the star in getting us to and from not the easiest of places to find. But occasionally she had to be ignored in order to make the most of the views.

It's a good job that Sheila and I couldn't communicate for real. I think the conversation would go something along the lines of:

"Turn right at the next junction".

"No, I'm going straight on because there is a lovely view of the river"
"Turn right at the next junction".
"No, I said I'm going straight on"
"Turn right at the next junction you Pommy twit"
"Who are you calling a Pommy twit, you Aussie floosie"
"Re calculating"
"What for?"
"I need some new words to call you"
"I've got some new ones for you as well"
"Turn right at the next junction"
"I'll turn you off "
"You'll get lost!"

Our final stop on the Loire was to be Compteceaux which is hard to pronounce and even harder for me to spell. Sheila, as usual makes an Aussie meal of it with her translation, and has us in fits of laughter. Yet another pretty village, perched high above the Loire. It took some getting up to the village but when we got there, we had magnificent views of the river. The stopover parking place was just behind the tourist information centre at the back of the church. There was one other Motorhome there when we arrived, but within an hour or so, we were joined by a few more. It was a popular spot with lots of people coming and going to admire the view of the river. From the car park it was only a few minutes' walk through a small wooded area to a viewpoint. It was quite a famous place as there had been a medieval village there, some of which could still be seen, albeit in ruins.

We cooked a chilli for tea and not long after we have finished eating it, a gorgeous little kitten appeared at the door. She was so cute and we weren't sure if she was a stray or not, but we gave her something to eat and drink. She drank a whole cup of milk and ate two plates of minced beef. The beef was actually left over from the chilli so Jackie gave it a good rinse to wash away the hot chilli pepper. Kitty didn't think much to the kidney beans though, she left them in the dish. That was to be the final day of the first part of our tour of Europe.

The following day was Jackie's birthday, October 1st, and amazingly for the time of year, the weather was still hot and sunny. As we drove back along the motorway we looked forward to seeing our good friends back in Moelan-Sur-Mer, Brittany. We stopped for a break half way through the journey and unfortunately, so did Belles water system. We could hear that the pump was still working but there was no water coming out of any of the taps, shower etc. and yet we knew that the water tank was full. A quick call to Leisure Kingdom revealed the likely cause was the syphon pipe that had come lose in the water tank, so not allowing the water to be drawn into the system. They gave their permission for us to have it repaired as soon as possible. Although we were annoyed that we had the problem, we thought we were lucky that it had happened at the end of the tour and not when we were half way round.

Was it Belle telling us it was time to go home?

Chapter Seventeen

Conclusion

The Travellers Return
(A Rigg)
He's happy yet sad
Down the road there is a gate
And then a door
The welcome is hearty
A hug and more
He has a story to tell
His shoes are soon off and by the door
Ready for when he's off once more

Some 9000 miles later and around £1000 under budget, we arrived back in the UK in time for Christmas. This gave us some time to reflect on the first part of our journey. Looking back, it was even better than we had both anticipated. We were lucky not to have had encountered any life threatening situations and had felt safe all of the time (apart from the killer sheep!). Which just goes to show, that if you have a positive attitude, you should not be put off by what people say, especially those who have never been there or done it. Listening to some of the advice we received, we would have never left the house. That's not to say we were not vigilant most of the time. Perhaps we had not encountered any problems because we had listened to the good advice we had been given.

We met some great people along the way and feel we have gained a small insight into the cultures and way of life of the countries we visited. As strange as it sounds, we as people, are all very much alike, mothers love their children and fathers want to provide as best they can. All want a better life for their children and would also like prosperity now, not later. It's the political and economic backdrop that provides the main difference along with where they are located on the map. For the most part they have all been very friendly and welcoming to us. Very rarely, language proved a barrier as we always managed to make ourselves understood in some way shape or form. English is spoken in most places and it appears they would sooner speak to us in English than hear our feeble attempts at their languages. It made us feel very humble and lazy at times.

We've been to some magnificent cities, towns and villages from modern to ancient, from small to large. The breadth of difference in the buildings we have seen has been amazing and a testament to human achievement and diversity. We are truly blessed here in Europe to have such a wealth of architecture and cultures right on our door step and must be the envy of the world. In some cities there was a church or some kind of place of worship around every corner. Just when you think there can be nothing more magnificent than the last building, another one appears. We've also seen a few blots on the landscape. Unfortunately, these have been where people have had to live, a sobering contrast which keep things in perspective.

The countryside has at times been breathtakingly beautiful with views to die for. From well-maintained hedged farmland to rolling prairieland, from flat plains to rugged mountains. From woodland to forest, from stream to river, to lakes and inland sea, the diversity of the landscape has kept us looking forward to the next day and what we may discover. This has been coupled with the wildlife that has inhabited these ever changing environments. I think the most memorable and surprising was the wild Beaver nestling on the river bank right in the city centre of Bydgoszcz in Poland.

I think the question most often asked since our return, is, "If you had to pick one place to go back to where would it be?" It's extremely difficult to answer, as there were so many memorable experiences and wonderful places which we had seen. Thinking of one invariably conjured up another. In answer, we took out the whole of France because we just love the place. However, not being ones to sit on the fence, we chose to put it into four categories:-

	Jackie	Adrian
City	Stockholm	Copenhagen
View	Norwegian Fjords	Mosel River Valley
Emotional	Auschwitz	Auschwitz
Place to eat	Pinella,	Villa Calvados
	Turku, Finland	Bydgoszcz, Poland

Another frequently asked question is, "Did we pick the right Motorhome?" Without a doubt for us, the answer is a big "Yes". First and foremost we managed to get a good night's sleep most nights, as the rear bed is so big and comfortable when made up. Because we were away so long we needed to maximise on the living space, while keeping the length of the motorhome to an acceptable minimum for parking. Belle (Autotrail Apache 634U) proved just right in both departments, as well as having the right amount of equipment and storage space.

During our journey we received excellent after sales service from all concerned. I had informed Leisure Kingdom what we were buying the Motorhome for and that we must be able to rely on their support if anything went wrong. There were two occasions when we thought we would have to have small repairs carried out immediately in mainland Europe, and not in the UK. Leisure Kingdom quickly secured approval from Autotrail for us to have the work carried out under warranty. This was a huge comfort factor. We also had good telephone support from both Gaslow and Oyster when we encountered minor problems with their kit during our journey.

As with all things new and so complex Belle did have a few snags that we made note of along the way. All minor except for the water pipe to the main tank which came away in France at the very end of our journey. I had updated Gayle, our contact at Leisure Kingdom from time to time, by e-mail during our journey. Gayle, in turn, very kindly consulted with Autotrail. It was pleasing to know that all the snags, but one (a tiny hole in the floor covering, which we were too late reporting) would be covered under the warranty. We dropped Belle off at Leisure Kingdom on our return to the UK and Martin the Service Manager assured us that all the faults would be put right, and more importantly to our satisfaction. Did we learn anything along the way? Well, yes plenty, but mainly 'we are all the same'. It's Politicians, the media, newspapers and religions that cause most of the problems by feeding on our differences and phobias. What mother wants to see her son go off to war? Also, there is a big friendly fraternity out there. Almost a secret society that we have now joined, called the Motorhomers and Caravaners. What a friendly and happy bunch they are, and from all nations. The general order of the day is to wave at one another as you pass by, because we have a big secret, we are happy doing it. You just know if you have a problem, large or small, they'll chip in to help as we are all in the same boat, so to speak.

Finally we have been asked many times, "How did you get along together?" It was not all plain sailing of course, what partnership is? We do enjoy each other's company, and we have both survived to tell this story. We are very much looking forward to Part 2, so that in itself should answer the question. You see, for us it's been a very enjoyable and fun fulfilment of a dream. We can't wait to be on our way again.......

To finish off, we hope you have enjoyed reading about our adventure and hope it may inspire you to do whatever you dream of doing.

To end, we will quote an oft said phrase from our very good friend and my mentor, Dave Coley.

"Cheerio now, places to go, people to meet"

List of Campsites, Aires and Stellplatz in order of our route

UK

Castle Donnington - Kingsmill Camping – Nicely located campsite, basic clean facilities. Close to our home in Derby.

Somerset - Cornish Farm – Friendly staff, excellent facilities, toilets and showers. Recommended by others.

France 1

Mayenne - Ambrieres les Valles – Friendly staff, good clean facilities. ACSI.

Paris – Bois de Boulogne – Convenient for visiting Paris. Good clean facilities. Very busy. Found on web and by recommendation.

Bryeres - St Amande les Eaux - Lovely site, surrounded by woodland with cycle paths. Friendly staff, very clean. ACSI

Belgium

Brussels - RCCB Camping Paul Rosmant – Warandeberg 52 - Wessembeek Oppum –Small untidy site, friendly staff, toilet/showers clean but in need of refurbishment. Caravan Club (CC)

The Netherlands

Rockanje – Molecaten Park Waterboss - Excellent, extremely clean site and facilities, close to beach. Friendly staff. ACSI.

Edam - Strandbad Camping - Excellent location for Edam, Volendam and Amsterdam. Good clean facilities. ACSI

Dokkum – Harddraverspark Campsite - Excellent location for Dokkum and surrounding villages. Good Clean facilities. ACSI

Germany

Oyten - Near Bremen - Knaus Camping - Excellent facilities, Friendly staff. ACSI.

Nr Drage/Winsen Hamburg - Stove Strand International - Large site, good clean facilities. ACSI.

Denmark

Tonder - Tonder Camping - Excellent location. Friendly welcoming staff. Good facilities. ACSI

Asperup - Baringskov Camping - Friendly staff. Clean facilities. Some areas in need of refurbishment.

Odense – City Camping – Excellent location for visiting Odense. Good clean facilities, friendly staff. ACSI

Copenhagen - Rodovre DCU Absalon Camping – Excellent site, good clean facilities. Convenient for train into Copenhagen. CC.

Sweden

Bastad – On the main road through the town - Close to centre of small town and beach, first time wild camping in a field. Would say very safe. Not in the books and is overspill parking for the tennis, there is a pay machine for high season of 10 euros.

Gothenburg - Krono Camping – Facilities clean, but dated. Staff v friendly. Some residential caravans for workers. Bus stop outside campsite so very convenient for city. CC.

Vadstena - Fabulous free place for parking, right in centre of village next to the castle. No facilities - Other campers, v safe. All the Aires in Scandinavia

Stockholm - Rosjobadens Camping – Very clean but needed refurbishing as old facilities. All staff young eastern European men. Site on lake but not much to do. Bus stop outside camp for buses to the train or Metro into Stockholm. CC.

Kristinehamn - Lakeside at Vanern - Revsand Camping - Pitch, overlooking the lake. Woodland, very quiet, nice people. No shops or bus stop. Very secluded campsite. Facilities in need of refurbishment. This campsite was recommended by another campsite from CC book as they were full.

Karlstad - Wild parked in car park by the park and marina - Felt safe, recommended by Tourist Information. Within walking distance of Karlstad. Nice area.

Norway

Olso - Sjolyst Marina - Fab position overlooking the marina. Motorhomes only, large car park but so convenient for Oslo. Facilities - mixed and only 3 toilets and one shower - we showered in Belle. All the Aires in Scandinavia

Moss - Nes camping – Lovely site, beautiful views of Oslofjorden. Excellent facilities. Too remote. Nice staff. From Tourist Information Oslo.

Fredrickstad - Motel & Camping - Good campsite, close to old town within walking distance. Good facilities. Pitches very uneven. CC

Nesbyen - Liodden Camping - En route to Bergen. Fab location. Self-service. Toilets and showers clean. Washing up area in the open. CC.

Bergen – Bratland Camping – Good facilities and location for visiting Bergen by bus. Road noise. Pitches not that good. Nice picturesque area. CC & ACSI

En route to Alesund - Jolvassbu Camping - Located by picturesque river and mountains. Nice pitches. V good clean facilities. V friendly staff. Noisy gushing river. Found by chance, not in books.

Alesund – Aire in the centre by the sea and harbour. Short walk into the town. Toilets only. All the Aires in Scandinavia

On route to Trondheim - Unknown Campsite where the wooden huts were attached to the caravans and we had decking on the pitch. Also beautiful setting by a lake. Not in books.

Trondheim Bobil park – Car park area near a commercial estate. All the Aires in Scandinavia.

Sweden 2

Krokum - Bobil park – Free overnight parking. Lovely area by a lake and tourist information/café. All the Aires in Scandinavia.

Umea Port – Overnight parking for ferry. Pay at machine. Not in books

Finland

Campsite at Kristiinankaupunki – Pukinsaari Camping. Excellent facilities by a small beach. CC

Rauma – Poroholma Camping – Excellent site, good facilities by beach. CC

Turku - Ruissalo Camping – Good facilities, convenient for bus into Turku. CC

Helsinki - Rastila Camping – Good facilities, convenient for metro into Helsinki. CC

Porvoo – Camping Kokonniemi – Limited clean facilities, convenient for Porvoo. CC

Kotka – Large 5 star campsite, Excellent facilities, coastal. Recommended by other tourists.

Campsite near to the border of Russia. Small, facilities not good! Found in one of the Finnish camping books given by Tourist Information.

Estonia

Tallinn – Pirita Harbour - Old Olympic Marina, Excellent location by marina and beach. Bus to Tallinn, Very basic facilities. ACSI Software

Parnu – Kone Motel and Caravan park - Small campsite by river, very basic facilities. ACSI Software

Latvia

Riga – City camping – Ideal for walk or bus into Riga. Good clean facilities. ACSI Software

Lithuania

Vilnius – City camping – Conv. bus into Vilnius – small site – clean facilities. ACSI Software.

Poland

Mikolajki - Camping Wagabunda – Very modern, good clean facilities. CC

Sopot – Camping Kamienny Potok – Small campsite, clean facilities, convenient for walk into Sopot and train to Gdansk. CC

Torun – Camping Tramp – Very nicely located campsite for walk into Torun. Very clean facilities. CC

Warsaw – Majawa camping – Small site, basic clean facilities. Conv. Bus into Warsaw. CC

Suchedniow – Suchedniow Campsite in between Warsaw and Krakow. – Small stop-over site, excellent facilities by a lake. ACSI software

Krakow – Camping Clepardia – Excellent well-kept campsite, excellent clean facilities. Convenient bus into Krakow. CC

Oswiecim (1.5km from Auschwitz) – Campsite located at the Centre for Dialogue and Prayer. CC

Wroclaw – Stadion Olimpijski – Large campsite. Very basic facilities, whole site in need of update. Conv. for tram into Wroclaw. CC

Germany 2

Moritzburg – Camping Bad Sonnenland. Excellent clean facilities. Conv. for bus into Dresden. ACSI

Lubbenhau – Spreewald Caravan and Camping – Excellent facilities. Nice campsite recommended by others. ACSI

Mahlow Campsite – Small friendly campsite. Excellent facilities. Convenient for Shonefield airport and metro into Berlin. ACSI

Weringerode – Stellplatz – Excellent location, water and chemical disposal only. Short walk into the centre. Reise Mobil, Bord Atlas.

Hannover – Camping Birkensee – Good facilities but not location for visiting Hannover (an hours walk to tram stop). CC

Fritzlar – Stellplatz. Excellent location. Minutes from the centre. Limited toilet facilities only. Reise Mobil, Bord Atlas.

Rudesheim – After Fankfurt on the Rhine – In a layby off the main road. Not in books.

Bacherach – Stellplatz. Riverside on the Rhine. Water and Chemical disposal. Excellent clean public toilets close by. Reise Mobil, Bord Atlas.

Winningen – Campingplatz Ziehfurt - By the river Mosel. Good facilities but difficult for disabled as toilets up steps. Reise Mobil Bord Atlas

Cochem – Wohnmobilstellplatz - On the Mozel – very basic next to proper campsite. Reise Mobil Bord Atlas

Mehring – Weingut Zelleuhof – On the Mosel – good facilities. Reise Mobil Bord Atlas.

Trier – Stellplatz. Large car park. Limited clean facilities. Reise Mobil. Bord Atlas.

France 2

Stenay – Aire de Camping Port Plaisance – Good clean facilities, nice location. Reise Mobil, Bord Atlas.

Beaugency – Stadt Beaugency – Parking area with limited facilities. Excellent location next to the Loire and a short walk into Beaugency. Reise Mobil, Bord Atlas.

Fontainebleau – Camping Les Pres - Facilities in need of update. ACSI.

Amboise – L'Ile d'Or – Excellent campsite, good clean facilities. Short walk into Amboise. ACSI.

Champtoceaux – Aire on car park at the back of Tourist Information. Good location for stop over on the Loire. Reise Mobil, Bord Atlas.

Reading Matter

This is a list of the books we used and how helpful we found them.

Rough Guides	Very good for information including prices. We used two, one which was called 'Europe on a Budget' and the other 'France'. The former proved very helpful in planning our visits to cities and which museums and gardens were free to enter.
Michelin Guides	We used the one volume 'Europe' which we found of limited use and very brief.
DK Eye Witness	We found these very inspirational, we had one for just about every country we visited. While they are a bit limited on entry price information, they are excellent for illustrations of buildings, places and scenic routes to see. Also a good read for a potted history of each country. Excellent for what they are.
Caravan Club	Camping Sites in Europe Part 2. Full of useful information on each countries customs and requirements. The campsites are a good backup but there are no discounts. We relied on this for information and campsites.
ACSI	We used both books which were included in the price and the software version on our lap top. We rate this as our number one resource for reasonably priced campsites and ease of finding

locations. The software version is excellent and contains sites not in the books such as Estonia, Latvia and Lithuania. The off season discounts were brilliant. (Available from Vicarious Books) These paid for themselves in four stop-overs.

Vicarious Books	All the Aires and LPG sites in Benelux and Scandinavia. This proved an excellent resource not only for the free or low priced campsites, but also for locating LPG stations for filling up our Gaslow tanks. The pictures proved of great help in deciding whether to use a site or not. Paid for itself in one stop-over.
Bord Atlas	Reise Mobil – There are two books, one which gives German Reisemobil-Stellplatz and one giving the rest of Europe. It's in German, but once you get your head around the way to use it, it is excellent. We used it extensively for Germany and our later trip through the Loire. (Available from Vicarious Books) Paid for themselves in two stop-overs.
Planet Earth	We had one book only and while it contained good information it was little used being outplayed by the "rough guide".
MMMagazine	Excellent Motorhome Magazine resource for all sorts of things, including the on-line forums which cover most topics we needed to plan our trip.

Appendix iii

Playlist

Played on random setting

Temptations	Aint too proud to beg
Prince Buster	Al Capone
Sonny & Cher	Baby Please Don't Go
Jace Everett	Bad Things
Charles Trenet	C'est si bon
Cheryl Crow	Can't Cry Anymore
Perry Como	Catch a Falling Star
Atomic Rooster	The Devil's Answer
Jonathan Richmond	Egyptian Reggae
Marvin Gaye	I Heard It Through The Grapevine
Four Tops	If I Were a Carpenter
Diana Ross & the Supremes	My World Is Empty Without You
Diana Ross & the Supremes	Reflections
Rod Stewart	Da Ya Think I'm Sexy?
Elvis Presley	Suspicious Minds
Temptations	Just My Imagination
Sugababes	Too Lost in You
Amy Winehouse	Valerie
The Kinks	Victoria
Gene Pitney	24 Hours from Tulsa
Razorlight	Hey Ya
Sophie Ellis Bextor	Murder On The Dance Floor
Kasabian	Fast Fuse
Kaiser Chiefs	Ruby
Paulo Nutini	Jenny Don't Be Hasty
Charles Trenet	La Mer
Paulo Nutini	Last Request
Kings Of Leon	Use Somebody

Johnny Cash	One
Johnny Cash	Hurt
Marc Almond	Say Hello Wave Goodbye
Marc Almond	The Days Of Pearly Spencer
Marc Almond	Jacky
Marc Almond & Soft Cell	Bedsitter
Paulo Nutini	Rewind
Whitney Houston	My Love Is Your Love
Jackie Wilson	Higher And Higher
The Love Affair	Everlasting Love
Baz Luhrman	Everybody's Free to Wear Sunscreen
Kings of Leon	Sex On Fire
Mel Tormé	Comin' Home Baby

41 songs 2.4 hours

BUDGET

Exchange rate 2011 £1 = 1.1 euro or $1.55

It would be fair to say that analysing our budget has proved very difficult and has relied on recollection rather than actuals for the small detail. The headline spend is good as we kept records of totals rather than every last detail on each spend. The other difficulty is in true *"Rigg"* style when we were in the countries that where expensive for us to live in, we lived down to our budget and when we were in countries that were cheap to live in we lived up to our budget. For example in Norway we did not buy any booze from the supermarkets and just bought food. The other side of the coin was Estonia where we went mad for everything because it was so cheap by comparison and we also ate out a lot. This meant the mix between food and spending money was always a grouped item of mainly food or eating out and bus/train fares to places we wanted to visit.

I have split the analysis into two parts, "The Budget" and "The Countries" for ease of reconciliation.

The Budget

£150/$232.5/165 euro per week for food
£75/$116.25/82.5 euro per week spending money (mainly for eating out)
£150/$232.5/165 euro a week for campsites
15,000 miles worth of petrol (which subsequently was revised to 20000 miles)
£1000 van insurance
£1000 contingency plus some other ancillary costs

FOOD

We managed to stay in budget throughout all the countries and if we had set our minds to it could have lived on far less in most of the countries we passed through. But then this was never about living frugally, more about enjoying ourselves. There was some cross over into eating out.

SPEND
This was mainly used for bus/train/ferry fares into the places we wanted to visit and eating out. In the more expensive countries we ate out less and so some of this spend would then go on food.

SITES
This was an area of big saving for us with most campsites costing 16 euro (using ACSI discount sites) low season and 30 euro high season. Plus, as we became more confident we started to use the Aires (France) and Stellplatz (Germany) which cost us little or nothing to stay on. Our average weekly spend on campsites would be £109 overall, a saving of £41 per week

PETROL
We had allowed for 15000 miles worth of diesel at £5 gallon or £1.10 litre (1 imperial gallon = 4.546 litres) which we soon altered to 20000 miles at £1.40 litre by the time we set off at the then UK pump price. Most countries were cheaper for diesel than the UK and by managing our fill ups, we filled to the max in the lower priced countries. The most expensive diesel was £1.50/1.65eu in Norway and the lowest was £1.13/1.25eu in Luxemburg.

INSURANCE/CONTINGENCY
The van insurance cost just under £500 so we were on course here for our two years. We had allowed for £1000 of contingency costs for emergencies and the like. This got eaten into when Jackie had to fly back to the UK. Other than this there was a service cost on the motorhome when we returned to the UK, so we were still on course here also.

The Countries

I have split the countries we travelled through into three categories, the cash neutral, the more expensive and the less expensive.

The Cash Neutral
These were similar in costs for us to the UK, France, Belgium, Germany, Luxemburg and The Netherlands. The biggest difference in budget here was the cost of campsites in France and Germany, where we stayed mainly on Aires or Stellplatz which were either free are very low cost, saving on average £100/110eu a week. The cost of food was very similar, although the variety did differ greatly. For instance, we ate a lot of sausage while in Germany, because this was the most popular meat item in the supermarkets.

The More Expensive
These by varying degrees were more expensive for most items, Denmark, Sweden, Norway and Finland. In these countries the cost of just about everything food and drink wise, was more expensive. Norway being the most expensive by far, with a pint of beer costing 11 euros (2.6euro in UK) in Bergen, a loaf of bread over 2 euros (1 euro in UK) and a litre of diesel 1.65 euros (1.40 euro in UK). Eating out wasn't too bad, although the cost of a bottle of wine would be at least 25 euros and not that good. The biggest surprise in these countries (which we assumed were fishing nations), was the cost of fish. Which in Denmark was expensive, compared to Norway, where the price per kilo was astronomical, and so for us unaffordable.

The Less Expensive
In most cases these were cheaper than the UK, Estonia, Latvia, Lithuania and Poland. Here we had the life, eating out on far more occasions, as food and drink costs a lot less. In Poland we had Chateaubriand (the best end of steak) for 25

euros for two people (cooked to perfection) and a decent bottle of wine for 10 euros, all in a top class restaurant. In some of the tourist spots prices were similar to the UK, but mainly the cost of living was much lower.

Summary

Without going into every detail, we were about £1000 under budget at the end of part one of our adventure. It had been a great relief to know we were in budget, as this was an important aspect of remaining relaxed during our travels. We did know that it was possible to be spending far less, as we witnessed others we met along the way, who were doing it on a shoestring. Then there were those who were spending far more and for whom money appeared to be no object. The most important thing is that we are all enjoying our own route to happiness.